Sovereignty Conflicts and International Law and Politics

Many conflicts throughout the world can be characterized as sovereignty conflicts in which two states claim exclusive sovereign rights for different reasons over the same piece of land. It is increasingly clear that the available remedies have been less than successful in many of these cases, and that a peaceful and definitive solution is needed. This book proposes a fair and just way of dealing with certain sovereignty conflicts. Drawing on the work of John Rawls in *A Theory of Justice*, this book considers how distributive justice theories can be in tune with the concept of sovereignty and explores the possibility of a solution for sovereignty conflicts based on Rawlsian methodology. Jorge E. Núñez explores a solution of egalitarian shared sovereignty, evaluating what sorts of institutions and arrangements could, and would, best realize shared sovereignty, and how it might be applied to territory, population, government, and law.

Jorge E. Núñez is Senior Lecturer at Manchester Law School, UK and Visiting Professor at Facultad de Ciencias Jurídicas y Sociales, UNLP, Argentina.

Table of Contents

relations, and philosophy. I hope the scholars, students, and public in general see my point and main motivation: to offer a platform for discussion in order finally to be able to put all the parties in a sovereignty conflict together regardless of language, background, personal or group history, pride, and prejudices. Indeed, we may agree to disagree. That is the parties in a sovereignty conflict might agree to disagree, but they would at least finally be considering mutually as what they are: human beings able peacefully and respectfully to listen to each other, even to the point of disagreement.

In writing this book I have been graced with the help and comments of many. In a form, this book has already fulfilled its original aim since I have witnessed discussions around the world and I am forever indebted to the participants. Without any individual name, since it would be unfair to forget even one, I want to express my gratitude to staff, members, and students of the Universidad Nacional de La Plata and Colegio de Abogados de La Plata, both from Argentina; the many universities in the United Kingdom in which I delivered presentations and participated in discussions: Manchester, Liverpool, London School of Economics, Edinburgh, Durham; the State University of Saint Petersburg and the State University of Ivanovo, in Russia; the China University of Political Science and Law in Beijing; Bilkent University in Turkey; ATINER in Athens, Greece; Georgetown University in the United States of America; Universidad Nacional de México; and many others that escape my memory at the time I write these lines.

Many thanks as well to the many reviewers the original had and the many discussion groups for their insightful comments in Cambridge, Oxford, and Edinburgh. My special thanks to the participants in Juris North discussion group, of which I am one of the proud founding members and chairs.

Valuable criticism came from both legal scientists and philosophers and political scientists and philosophers thanks to IVR, IVR Argentina, IVR UK, and IPSA/AISP.

Many persons from the non-scientific community participated too; that is, society at large. My deepest gratitude goes to them. Thanks to the comments received through emails, Twitter, my blog, face-to-face, formally or informally in Argentina, the United Kingdom, the Malvinas/Falkland Islands, Spain, México, Perú, China, Turkey, Russia, the United States of America, Brazil, Nigeria, Gibraltar, Kashmir, and Israel. These pages would have been meaningless without their input. For science and philosophy with any relevance to a positive impact on people and their lives are, for this writer, what make these pages meaningful.

Jorge E. Núñez
La Plata, Argentina
Manchester, United Kingdom
October 2016

Part I

1 Sovereignty conflicts as a distributive justice dilemma

> A wheel within a wheel . . . is considered . . . as an absurdity in politics: But what must we say to two equal wheels, which govern the same political machine . . .
>
> David Hume, *Essays: Moral, Political and Literary* (Liberty Fund, 1985), p. 370.

Introduction

It is arguably a truism in international law and politics that an ultimate sovereign, with a common legal bond or system of norms, will govern one territory with population. What would happen if that one territory and population had two ultimate and hierarchically equal sovereigns (legally speaking) and, at the same time, two valid sets of norms?[1] Would it be possible, for instance, that Israel and Palestine had sovereign authority at the same time over Jerusalem? Would it be possible that Argentina and the United Kingdom were at one time sovereign over the territory and population of the Falkland/Malvinas Islands? If the answer were positive, what would the consequences be—in terms of territory, population, government, and law?

There are many cases that can be characterized as sovereignty conflicts in which international agents (namely, two sovereign states and the population of the third territory under dispute) claim sovereign rights for different reasons over the same piece of land. Besides, these conflicts have a particular feature: Their solution seems to require a mutually exclusive relation among the agents because it is thought that the sovereignty over the third territory can be granted to only one of them. Indeed, sovereignty is often regarded as an absolute concept—*i.e.* exclusive, and not shareable.[2]

1 The possibilities in the case of a joint enterprise in terms of law can be numerous (*e.g.* it could be an independent valid set of norms for that territory or a third system, it could be a combination of the two systems or anchored to both or just to one of the sovereign states, it could be the system of one of the claimants but jointly administered).

2 The concept of state sovereignty has raised and is still linked to fervent debate. For an insight into the discussion, *see* Robert Jackson (ed.), *Sovereignty at the Millennium* (Oxford: Blackwell

authority but yet accepts limitations it becomes clearer how limitations can work in another supposedly supreme concept such as sovereignty. Chapter 5 highlights the main remedies applied at international level to sovereignty conflicts and will explore each in order to determine whether any of them could be a reasonable solution to the sovereignty conflicts object of this project. What this chapter will argue is that there is a need for a reasonable solution that the reviewed international remedies cannot offer.

Part III—*i.e.* Chapters 6, 7, and 8—will explore the use of Rawlsian methodology in order to put a solution to certain sovereign conflicts, and discuss if the outcome is a reasonable remedy for them. Chapter 6 will introduce and explore: (a) the conditions for achieving justice—toleration, peace, etc.; (b) why the "just acquisition" principle[9] may not work; and (c) why the Rawlsian method of conceiving of the respective claimants as behind a "veil of ignorance"[10] just might. The latter is of utmost importance as the analysis will be conducted under these circumstances; that is, in an original position in which the three representatives will be in a particular situation, both in regard to their particular circumstances and that of the original position itself.

Chapter 7 will test the proposed model by working out what sorts of institutions and arrangements could, and would best, realize it. In order to do that this chapter will make use of some sovereign conflicts to show that the model can be extended from the general principles to workable institutions that realize those principles in: (a) population; (b) territory; (c) government and law; and (d) all that they imply (*e.g.* defense, natural resources, financial system). Finally, Chapter 8 will conclude by assessing the model's potential and highlighting any possible limitations and implications.

Simplifying assumptions: Sovereignty conflicts of various natures

At first glance, the international scene presents several sovereignty conflicts of very different types; to name a few: Falkland/Malvinas Islands (Argentina and the United Kingdom), Jerusalem and other surrounding areas (Israel and Palestine), Gibraltar (Spain and the United Kingdom), Kashmir (India and Pakistan), Cyprus (Greek Cyprus and Turkish Republic of North Cyprus), Transnistria (Trans-Dniester or Transdniestria and Moldova), Quebec (Quebec and Canada), Kuril Islands (Japan and Russia), Tibet (and China), Hong Kong (and China), Northern Ireland (the Republic of Ireland and the United Kingdom), South Ossetia (and Georgia), Abkhazia (and Georgia), Nagorno-Karabakh (and Azerbaijan).

9 Robert Nozick's notion, developed in *Anarchy, State and Utopia*, which will be clarified and applied in subsequent sections.

10 John Rawls's idea of the original position, mainly developed in *A Theory of Justice* (also, to some extent, in *Justice as Fairness* and *Political Liberalism*). Details of its application will be discussed in subsequent sections.

Although all the above international disputes are interesting in their own way, in order to be sure the outcome of this project will generalize, some simplifying assumptions are introduced. The main reason is to leave aside conflicts in which not only the sovereignty over a third territory is disputed but also basic notions such as statehood are still discussed. That is to say, if statehood is feasible that is what may happen. But this project assumes that statehood (for whatever reason) is not possible. Consequently, because of the scope of this monograph, it is more useful to analyze in depth international differences in which the basic elements that form state sovereignty are settled rather than to make a comprehensive study of cases in very different stages, which would have only an outline. Besides, the conclusions may be applied to a wide range of conflicts by method of analogy. With these reasons in mind, two clarifications should be made at this point in order to define the object of this project.

In the first instance, it is true that although these cases have in common a sovereignty issue they have their own peculiarities:

(a) Some states are fully sovereign both *de jure* and *de facto* (*e.g.* Argentina, the United Kingdom, China, etc.).
(b) Some states are only *de facto* sovereign (*e.g.* Palestine—which in fact still has only partial local autonomy, Turkish Republic of North Cyprus, etc.).
(c) Others have already solved the conflicts or are approaching an integration process into a larger legal order (*e.g.* Hong Kong, Northern Ireland, etc.).
(d) A few cases are difficult to define as belonging to any of the previous categories. They possess most of the elements that could potentially grant their statehood but there is no foreseeable evidence this will happen (*e.g.* Tibet).

Following the previous categorization the focus will be only on disputes concerning two fully sovereign states (both *de jure* and *de facto*) over a third populated territory.

Furthermore, two groups can be identified, using another classification criterion:

(a) One in which there are two sovereign states (*de jure* and *de facto*) disputing their rights over a third territory and its population;
(b) One in which there are two states, one sovereign *de jure* and *de facto*, and the other one having only *de facto* sovereignty over the territory under dispute.

For the purpose of this analysis, only the first set of cases will be of interest.

So this book will deal with disputes between two sovereign states (*de jure* and *de facto*) over the sovereignty of a populated nonsovereign third territory (*e.g.* Falkland/Malvinas Islands, Gibraltar, Kashmir, and the Kuril Islands). That is not to say the analysis will not generalize to other disputes. In other words, although practical reasons make it impossible to include every single sovereignty conflict in the analysis—even if they were only seen theoretically, the principles that will be reached may be generalized in order to be applicable to cases left aside or simply not considered here.

Rawlsian methodology

The model proposed in this monograph is constructed using many theoretical elements. However, the core proposal will be based on Rawlsian methodology—*i.e.* not his theory. Therein, two main issues must be addressed before advancing this project, mainly in order to avoid tangential criticism that may have to do with elements foreign to this work. First, the tension between ideal and nonideal or realist theory in the conception of distributive justice insofar applied in this project as the obligations and duties associated with sovereignty are now interwoven with moral issues. Second, the arguably problematic application of Rawlsian methodology, in particular the original position and the veil of ignorance, in a critical enough manner, and its extension to the international level.

In what has to do with the existent and evolving tension between ideal and nonideal theory, this monograph is circumscribed to claims about ideal moral theorising only, and therefore, does not include claims about practical application. It uses the Rawlsian method to determine how states should conceive the issue as a matter of first principle, and does not claim to do more than this. To be more precise, this monograph is in effect an exercise in ideal theory, and does not claim it has applicability as a nonideal theory or really explores the relevant nonideal issues—*e.g.* lack of compliance. It follows that to discuss the practical usefulness of this project or whether this theorization of a problem in international law and politics may bring actual results and create rights and obligations for the agents[11] is irrelevant—*i.e. contra negantem principia non est disputandum.*

It is Rawlsian methodology that will be applied in order to explore a reasonable remedy to some sovereignty conflicts. That is to say that these pages and the outcome may agree with Rawls's theory as a whole and its outcome but does not need to. Nevertheless, even though this monograph will only make use of Rawlsian methodology—*i.e.* not Rawls's theory—it must be acknowledged that it will not be exempt from controversy and criticism. Because of the arguably very problematic application of Rawls methodology, it is necessary to consider the challenges to this idealism via this already existent criticism in scholarly literature. Thus, not only may the criticism refer to Rawlsian methodology but also to its application at international level. Indeed, there has been much critical discussion of these issues—*e.g.* Beitz, Pogge, Kuper, Caney, Buchanan, Reidy, Martin, and Reidy. Therein, in order to develop the model proposed in this monograph and devise its own angle or justification for applying Rawlsian methodology and extending it to a particular

11 Ronald Dworkin, "Justice and Rights," in: *Taking Rights Seriously* (Cambridge MA: Harvard University Press, 1977).

issue at international level such as sovereignty conflicts, there are some critical points to be noted by working through a hefty literature for that matter.

On the one hand, with regard to Rawlsian methodology, as in *A Theory of Justice* the model here is based on a hypothetical situation.[12] Hence, this original position in which the negotiations take place assumes certain features. Indeed, the content of the original position is something constructed to reflect what is thought to be morally relevant. Similar to what Rawls does at the individual level, the characteristics of the original position will be determined in order to avoid any possible interference from factors that can cause bias and that may lead to a partly unjust or unfair outcome. A redefined "veil of ignorance"[13] will be applied at international level in order to address sovereignty conflicts. Many criticisms have been presented against Rawls's original position and veil of ignorance:

(a) The moral point of view.
(b) The social contract doctrine.
(c) The choice in the original position is indeterminate.

The moral point of view is not of Rawlsian exclusive or original application. Hume's "judicious spectator," Smith's "impartial spectator," Kant's categorical imperative, Rousseau's general will, Sidgwick's "point of view of the universe" are among several examples in which the moral point of view is taken into account in order to assess a given situation.[14] It is indeed a mistake to confuse moral justification with democratic political legitimacy, the latter not claimed by or argued for in this project.[15] The main reason behind this choice has previously been—and it is in this project too—to secure impartial judgment once agents leave aside their interests and evaluate a given situation from what is assumed to be an impartial point of view.[16] Hence, this monograph will explore if it is possible

12 For complete details about the hypothetical agreement, original position, veil of ignorance, and the negotiations, see Chapter 6.

13 Rawls mainly develops the veil of ignorance in his *A Theory of Justice* but it is also present in his *Justice as Fairness, A Restatement* and *Political Liberalism.*

14 Samuel Freeman (ed.), *The Cambridge Companion to Rawls* (Cambridge: Cambridge University Press, 2003); Samuel Freeman, "Reason and Agreement in Social Contract Views," *Philosophy and Public Affairs* 19 (1990): 122–57; Samuel Freeman, *Justice and the Social Contract: Essays on Rawlsian Political Philosophy* (Oxford: Oxford University Press, 2009); Samuel Freeman, *Rawls* (London: Routledge, 2007); Simon Caney, *Justice Beyond Borders* (Oxford: Oxford University Press, 2006), *esp.* p. 54.

15 Andrew Kuper, "Why Deliberation Cannot Tame Globalization: The Impossibility of a Deliberative Democrat," *Analyse and Kritik* 25 (2003): 176–98, *esp.* p. 192, fn. 35.

16 For a better understanding on Rawls's methodology, see Thomas Pogge, *John Rawls: His Life and His Theory of Justice* (Oxford: Oxford University Press, 2007), *esp.* pp. 42–59, 63–64, and 66; Jon Mandle and David A. Reidy (eds.), *The Cambridge Rawls Lexicon* (Cambridge: Cambridge University Press, 2015), pp. 579–85; Jon Mandle and David A. Reidy (eds), *A Companion to Rawls* (Chichester: Wiley Blackwell, 2014), Part II; Samuel Freeman (ed.), *The Cambridge Companion to Rawls* (Cambridge: Cambridge University Press, 2003), *esp.* pp. 139–67.

The Law of Peoples. This monograph does not claim that its outcome is the one Rawls would necessarily come up with. It is using his methodology to arrive at its own solution in order to explore a way in which sovereignty conflicts may be solved. Therein, neither this project is a development of *A Theory of Justice* nor *Political Liberalism.*

By way of example, Rawls makes clear in *The Law of Peoples* that it is "peoples" that take the place of persons.[27] He makes it explicit that not persons but peoples are the units of representation.[28] From there, *The Law of Peoples* introduces not one but two original positions.[29] Rawls goes further and leaves no doubts that sovereignty is not central for his proposal.[30] This monograph, on the contrary, follows the traditional view that states are constituted by a population ("peoples") and also recognizes territory, government, and law as constitutive elements, and sovereignty as an attribute. That is because this monograph is centered on sovereignty disputes, issues that Rawls himself does not address.

There are many other points that have been raised directly or indirectly related to Rawls's work: The general conflict between cosmopolitan ideals and national sentiment,[31] whether there is a need for a conception of international distributive justice,[32] social versus cosmopolitan liberalism,[33] the moral standing of states,[34]

27 Charles R. Beitz, "International Liberalism and Distributive Justice: A Survey of Recent Thought," *World Politics* 51 (1999): 269–96, *esp.* pp. 273–76; Thomas W. Pogge, "An Egalitarian Law of Peoples," *Philosophy and Public Affairs* 23 (1994): 195–224, *esp.* pp. 197–98.

28 Charles R. Beitz, "Rawls's Law of Peoples," *Ethics* 110 (2000): 669–96; Thomas W. Pogge, "Do Rawls's Two Theories of Justice Fit Together," in: Rex Martin and David A. Reidy (eds.), *Rawls's Law of Peoples: A Realistic Utopia?* (Oxford: Blackwell Publishing, 2006).

29 Charles R. Beitz, "Rawls's Law of Peoples," *Ethics* 110 (2000): 669–96, *esp.* p. 674.

30 Rawls specifically uses in *The Law of Peoples* (1999) the term "peoples" and maintains that "peoples" lack traditional sovereignty. This monograph, on the contrary, uses the terms "state" and "sovereignty" as generally accepted in legal and political sciences. *See* Chapter 2 for more details about sovereignty and state sovereignty and Chapter 6 for further discussion and analysis of *The Law of Peoples. See also* Andrew Kuper, *Democracy Beyond Borders: Justice and Representation in Global Institutions* (Oxford: Oxford University Press, 2006), *esp.* p. 13.

31 Charles R. Beitz, "Cosmopolitan Ideals and National Sentiment," *The Journal of Philosophy* 80 (1983): 591–600.

32 Charles R. Beitz, "International Liberalism and Distributive Justice: A Survey of Recent Thought," *World Politics* 51 (1999): 269–96; Charles R. Beitz, "Recent International Thought," *International Journal* (1988): 183–204; Thomas W. Pogge (ed.), *Global Justice* (Oxford: Blackwell Publishing, 2004), for example pp. 15, 59, 62; Simon Caney, "Global Interdependence and Distributive Justice," *Review of International Studies* 31 (2005): 389–99.

33 Charles R. Beitz, "Social and Cosmopolitan Liberalism," *International Affairs* 75 (1999): 515–29.

34 Charles R. Beitz, "The Moral Standing of States Revisited," *Ethics and International Affairs* (2010): 325–47.

international justice and self-sufficiency of "nation-states",[35] problems about natural resources,[36] the empirical foundation of national self-sufficiency,[37] cosmopolitanism and sovereignty,[38] global distributive justice and the normative significance of the state,[39] theories of justice and representation for global institutions,[40] distinct approaches to international distributive justice,[41] and whether a global principle of equality of opportunity is defendable.[42] Arguably directly or indirectly pertinent to Rawls's theory and its application, the previously mentioned points have little to do with the present project and to include them either in the analysis or its criticism is a misinterpretation of this work. For distributive justice principles by application of Rawlsian methodology are brought into this project only to offer a solution to sovereignty conflicts, and not to put an end to inequalities among the claiming agents' comparative situations or to bring about a solution of global distributive justice nature. This book, although seeking for a just and fair outcome, is not about global justice or morality but about particular sovereignty conflicts—*i.e.* those with two sovereign states claiming sovereignty over a populated third territory. That is to say, the model here will make use of distributive justice principles by application of Rawlsian methodology in order to explore a potential remedy to some sovereignty conflicts. Ergo, the model does not intend to use sovereignty conflicts as an example of global distributive justice.

Conclusion

The present chapter had a Janus-faced intertwined aim. First, to introduce the core idea behind the project: To explore how distributive justice principles by application of Rawlsian methodology may help in finding a remedy to at least some sovereignty conflicts—*i.e.* the ones with two sovereign states claiming sovereignty over a populated third territory. Second, to acknowledge some potential preliminary criticisms that may have to do more with the Rawlsian theory than with the present work in order to avoid possible misunderstandings with regard to the methodology used here and the nature of this project.

35 Charles R. Beitz, "Justice and International Relations," *Philosophy and Public Affairs* 4 (1975): 360–89.

36 *Ibid.*

37 *Ibid.*

38 Thomas W. Pogge, "Cosmopolitanism and Sovereignty," *Ethics* 103 (1992): 48–75.

39 Simon Caney, "Global Distributive Justice and the State," *Political Studies* 56 (2008): 487–518.

40 Andrew Kuper, *Democracy Beyond Borders: Justice and Representation in Global Institutions* (Oxford: Oxford University Press, 2006).

41 Simon Caney, *Justice Beyond Borders* (Oxford: Oxford University Press, 2006), *esp.* pp. 3–15; Simon Caney, "International Distributive Justice," *Political Studies* 49 (2001): 974–97.

42 Simon Caney, "Cosmopolitan Justice and Equalizing Opportunities," *Metaphilosophy* 32 (2001): 113–34.

The following chapters will introduce and assess many conceptual elements and theories pertinent to law, political sciences, and international relations in the context of certain kinds of sovereignty conflicts and defend the conclusion that principles of just distribution provide a reasonable remedy to at least some of them. This reasonable remedy lies in viewing sovereignty conflicts as a problem of distributive justice. The first steps of this path start with the next chapter by considering the first of these issues that is limited sovereignty.

Bibliography

Beitz, Charles R. "Cosmopolitan Ideals and National Sentiment." *The Journal of Philosophy* 80 (1983): 591–600.
Beitz, Charles R. "International Liberalism and Distributive Justice: A Survey of Recent Thought." *World Politics* 51 (1999): 269–96.
Beitz, Charles R. "Justice and International Relations." *Philosophy and Public Affairs* 4 (1975): 360–89.
Beitz, Charles R. "Rawls's Law of Peoples." *Ethics* 110 (2000): 669–96.
Beitz, Charles R. "Recent International Thought." *International Journal* (1988): 183–204.
Beitz, Charles R. "Social and Cosmopolitan Liberalism." *International Affairs* 75 (1999): 515–29.
Beitz, Charles R. "The Moral Standing of States Revisited." *Ethics and International Affairs* (2010): 325–47.
Beitz, Charles R. *Political Theory and International Relations.* Princeton NJ: Princeton University Press, 1999.
Buchanan, Alex. "Rawls's Law of Peoples: Rules for a Vanished Westphalian World." *Ethics* 110 (2000): 697–721.
Caney, Simon. "Cosmopolitan Justice and Equalizing Opportunities." *Metaphilosophy* 32 (2001): 113–34.
Caney, Simon. "Cosmopolitanism and the Law of Peoples." *The Journal of Political Philosophy* 10 (2002): 95–123.
Caney, Simon. "Global Distributive Justice and the State." *Political Studies* 56 (2008): 487–518.
Caney, Simon. "Global Interdependence and Distributive Justice." *Review of International Studies* 31 (2005): 389–99.
Caney, Simon. "International Distributive Justice." *Political Studies* 49 (2001): 974–97.
Caney, Simon. *Justice Beyond Borders.* Oxford: Oxford University Press, 2006.
Cohen, Gerald Allan. *Self-Ownership, Freedom and Equality.* Cambridge: Cambridge University Press, 1995.
Dworkin, Ronald. *Taking Rights Seriously.* Cambridge MA: Harvard University Press, 1977.
Fleischacker, Samuel. *A Short History of Distributive Justice.* Cambridge MA: Harvard University Press, 2004.
Freeman, Samuel, ed. *The Cambridge Companion to Rawls.* Cambridge: Cambridge University Press, 2003.
Freeman, Samuel. "Reason and Agreement in Social Contract Views." *Philosophy and Public Affairs* 19 (1990): 122–57.

Freeman, Samuel. *Justice and the Social Contract: Essays on Rawlsian Political Philosophy*. Oxford: Oxford University Press, 2009.

Freeman, Samuel. *Rawls*. London: Routledge, 2007.

Hoffman, John. *Sovereignty*. Buckingham: Open University Press, 1998.

Jackson, Robert, ed. *Sovereignty at the Millennium*. Oxford: Blackwell Publishers, 1999.

Kuper, Andrew. "Rawlsian Global Justice: Beyond the Law of Peoples to a Cosmopolitan Law of Persons." *Political Theory* 28 (2000): 640–74.

Kuper, Andrew. "Why Deliberation Cannot Tame Globalization: The Impossibility of a Deliberative Democrat." *Analyse and Kritik* 25 (2003): 176–98.

Kuper, Andrew. *Democracy Beyond Borders: Justice and Representation in Global Institutions*. Oxford: Oxford University Press, 2006.

Laski, Harold J. *The Foundations of Sovereignty and Other Essays*. London: George Allen & Unwin Ltd., 1921.

MacCormick, Neil. "Beyond the Sovereign State." *The Modern Law Review* 56 (1993): 1–18.

MacCormick, Neil. *Questioning Sovereignty: Law, State, and Nation in the European Commonwealth*. Oxford: Oxford University Press, 1999.

MacIntyre, Alaistair. *After Virtue*. Notre Dame IN: Notre Dame Press, 1981.

Mandle, Jon and Reidy, David A., eds. *The Cambridge Rawls Lexicon*. Cambridge: Cambridge University Press, 2015.

Mandle, Jon and Reidy, David A., eds. *A Companion to Rawls*. Chichester: Wiley Blackwell, 2014.

Martin, Rex and Reidy, David A., eds. *Rawls's Law of Peoples: A Realistic Utopia?* Oxford: Blackwell Publishing, 2006.

Nozick, Robert. *Anarchy, State and Utopia*. New York: Basic Books, 1974.

Pogge, Thomas W. "An Egalitarian Law of Peoples." *Philosophy and Public Affairs* 23 (1994): 195–224.

Pogge, Thomas W. "Cosmopolitanism and Sovereignty." *Ethics* 103 (1992): 48–75.

Pogge, Thomas W. "Rawls on International Justice." *The Philosophical Quarterly* 51 (2001): 246–53.

Pogge, Thomas W. "The Incoherence Between Rawls's Theories of Justice." *Fordham Law Review* 72 (2004): 1739–59.

Pogge, Thomas W. *Realizing Rawls*. Ithaca and London: Cornell University Press, 1989.

Pogge, Thomas W., ed. *Global Justice*. Oxford: Blackwell Publishing, 2004.

Pogge, Thomas. *John Rawls: His Life and His Theory of Justice*. Oxford: Oxford University Press, 2007.

Rawls, John. *A Theory of Justice*, Revised Edition. Oxford: Oxford University Press, 1999.

Rawls, John. *Justice as Fairness, A Restatement*. Cambridge, MA: Harvard University Press, 2003.

Rawls, John. *Political Liberalism*. New York: Columbia University Press, 2005.

Rawls, John. *The Law of Peoples*. Cambridge MA: Harvard University Press, 1999.

Reidy, David A. "Rawls on International Justice." *Political Theory* 32 (2004): 291–319.

Roemer, John E. *Theories of Distributive Justice*. Cambridge MA: Harvard University Press, 1996.

Sandel, Michael. *Liberalism and the Limits of Justice*. Cambridge: Cambridge University Press, 1982.

Sen, Amartya. *The Idea of Justice*. Cambridge MA: Harvard University Press, 2009.

- Whether sovereignty is something possessed within a limited jurisdiction (*e.g.* "I have authority over matter X but not over matters Y and Z, but my authority over X is final and complete, so I am sovereign over X") or whether sovereignty must entail a notion of unlimited jurisdiction.

Before starting with the conceptual clarifications it is important to highlight that the concept of sovereignty—hence its conceptual implications—is used here as it already exists in legal and political sciences scholarly literature and hence this monograph does not propose a new definition. From there sovereignty has one meaning: Supreme authority. But that is different from defining sovereignty as absolute authority. So, the first conceptual clarification is to differentiate between absolute sovereignty and supreme authority.[5] There are some terms that need clarification first in order to have a better understanding: (a) supreme versus subordinate; (b) absolute versus limited; and (c) undivided versus divided.

Supreme authority means the highest power to rule—to create and apply law—in a certain territory and for a certain group of people—as opposed to inferior or subordinate authority. Therefore, while absolute sovereignty is not possible—hence sovereignty is always limited—supreme authority is the way in which power is understood within a state. To be more precise, the difference between supreme and subordinate refers as Hart says "to a relative place on a scale."[6] In relation to sovereignty, it has to do with a vertical view—*i.e.* that one that has a superior cannot be a sovereign since sovereignty means supreme, the highest authority on a scale. In that sense, when dealing with international agents, a state is sovereign as long as it has supreme authority over its territory and population. If it does not, it may be something else—*e.g.* a colony, a member of a federal state, etc., but not a sovereign state.

Undivided sovereignty means a power or authority that is not apportioned in segments whereas divided sovereignty has to do with segmenting that power or authority in different parts. It is indeed a notion that sees sovereignty in a horizontal manner. In that respect, there are sovereign states that divide internally their power between different institutions—*e.g.* legislature and executive. But, in the international scenario, the sovereign state is mostly seen as an indivisible power no matter how it is internally organized.

These classifications are indeed interlinked. From there, absolute sovereignty must always be supreme and undivided. That is because if sovereignty was either subordinated to any other authority or power or it was divided among different agents or institutions it would be somehow limited—*i.e.* it would either have vertical or horizontal constraints or limitations given by the superior or the other institution or authority, respectively.

5 For a further analysis about the distinction between supreme and absolute *see* Hart (n. 4), pp. 105–06. Hart uses the word "unlimited," whereas this monograph uses the term "absolute."

6 *Ibid.*

It is important to make clear that to limit sovereignty does not necessarily mean to divide it. There are indeed two different criteria here. For instance, there can be supreme authority that can be limited and undivided. Consider a sovereign state with a unipersonal supreme authority. There are many historical cases in which the sum of the three powers is in "one hand"—*e.g.* Juan Manuel de Rosas in Argentina. However, even if this authority was supreme and undivided both internally and externally, it would still have a series of limitations—*e.g.* internally, the national legal order, factual circumstances such as the local economy, and so on; and externally, the mere presence of other sovereign states and the international context.

This book faces a problem: To show how to share sovereignty is possible. That is not how to divide sovereignty but how, by acknowledging its limits, sovereignty can be shared. Sovereignty is not absolute—*i.e.* it accepts limitations. However, it may remain supreme and undivided. The problem stems from equating limits with divisions. Indeed, to divide sovereignty is a way in which sovereignty can be limited. However, it is not the only one. And it is not enough for this project either. That is because to divide may imply to share but it does not need to. Indeed, "to divide" and "to share" sovereignty mean somehow to limit it. But these expressions mean something slightly different—*i.e.* for one thing is "to divide" sovereignty, yet another thing is "to share" it.[7]

For hermeneutic reasons the vocabulary here requires more precision: "to divide" and "to share" imply more than one entity involved. However, to divide sovereignty implies to separate it into "sections," "areas," parts. But, it does not necessarily mean that the division has to be reciprocal, multilateral and, in a certain way, fair. To share, on the contrary, assumes a relationship of some kind; to share something presupposes a certain division, appropriation, participation, accord with others. In other words, while "to divide" only means the existence of more than one entity and a partition, "to share" implies all this and that these entities have a certain relationship. The extent of this way of understanding sovereignty—*i.e.* shared sovereignty—will be discussed in the following chapters.

A second conceptual issue is whether sovereignty is a form of authority or power or both. Indeed, it is a form of exercise—*i.e.* a form of authority. For instance, the governor of a colony in the British scheme of the 19th and 20th centuries could make certain decisions, but they were revocable by a body outside and higher in the scale—*i.e.* a form of authority, metropolitan, and part of the imperial government. But it is also a form of power, for example, in the exercise of maritime jurisdiction. The following quotation illustrates clearly this point:

> Is sovereignty independence? Is it autonomy? The first is a notion of authority and right, but the second is a notion of power and capability. Historians,

7 Specificities in relation to different conceptions of "shared sovereignty" will be discussed in Chapter 3.

> international lawyers and political theorists tend to operate with the first concept. Political economists and political sociologists tend to employ the second concept.[8]

They are indeed intertwined ideas. For the historical reasons detailed in the next section, nowadays power is territorially organized into states that are members of the international society. However, these territorially organized powers so-called states have to possess the quality of sovereignty to be members of that international society. Sovereignty is in fact one of the faces of authority—*i.e.* the one that defines who are the states in a given international society.[9]

In relation to this point, language may also play an important part. In English political theory, there is a difference between power and authority. Power is the ability to have one's commands obeyed; authority is the existence of a sense that it is (or is usually) right to obey these commands. They go together, politically (although on the personal level an agent can have power without authority, as with the gunman, or authority without power, as with the aged and infirm father, or the small and slight mother)—loss of power means loss of authority, and loss of authority with the army and police means loss of power. But they are different, although not all languages mark the difference—*e.g. macht* in German means both.

Intrinsically linked to the way in which sovereignty is understood either as authority or power or both is the distinction between the case of *de jure* and *de facto* sovereignty, the third conceptual issue—*i.e.* it all depends on the legitimacy. Consider the case in which the occupying power in a war exercises sovereign functions dictating military orders. At a later stage, territorial transfer (*debellatio bellica*) through a peace agreement, all that remains, then, becomes legitimized, *ab initio* in exercise of sovereign rights (the state is *de jure* sovereign of the formerly occupied territory). But if a body such as the United Nations—*e.g.* its Security Council—declared the occupying power was an aggressor state, the issue remains only as a *de facto* sovereign exercise.

Another key point, the fourth conceptual issue, is whether sovereignty is possessed only by a state or it may be also possessed by an institution within a state. There are particular cases in which there seems to be sovereignty without a state. However, these peculiarities have to do with very specific elements. For instance, the birth of the Order of Malta[10] was attributable to the influence

8 Jackson (n. 3), p. 2.

9 *See* Philpott's view in Jackson (n. 3), pp. 144–67. In what is important here, Philpott understands that authority at the international level appears in three faces that answer three different questions respectively: "The first face answers: Who are the polities in a given international society? The second face answers: Who may belong to the society: And, who may become one of these legitimate polities? The third face answers: What are the essential prerogatives of these polities?"

10 *See Scarfo v Sovereign Order of Malta* (1957) 24 ILR 1, Tribunal of Rome, Italy. In what matters here: "The limitations on the sovereignty of the Order of Malta which undoubtedly

of the Catholic Church. Leaving aside exceptional cases, sovereignty is understood in principle as possessed only by states. For example, Argentine provinces, constituent of the federal state after the national dissolution in 1820, and then, with the demise of President Rivadavia, introduced in the Constitution of 1826, demonstrate how sovereign entities delegate a portion of their sovereignty in the federal state (Federal Pact of 1831), and then do it in a text encompassing the organization of the new state in 1853. In Germany, the process is reversed. Arguably, the federal state transferred sovereignty to the Länder with the Bonn Constitution of 1949.

It is common use to say that there are sovereign institutions within a state. Once again this is an issue related to the use of the vocabulary. To be more precise, what varies—and may be argued—is whether any institution, person, or body has this authority (or, for the political theorists, ought to).

The word "sovereignty" means supreme authority; the word "authority" means power, command; the words "power" and "command" imply that there are individuals, group of individuals—even for some, institutions such as a constitution—who have the power to dictate certain commands and individuals who must obey them. There are three levels of sovereignty depending on how an individual is understood in relation to any authority: In his individuality, in his relationship with other individuals (a community), and as a member of a community as a whole in relation with other communities. It is for this reason that political, legal and philosophical literatures distinguish: (a) a sovereign individual; (b) a sovereign authority/representative; (c) a sovereign society/nation/state.

Indeed, in all three cases the word "sovereignty" is used. In the first case, "sovereign individual" refers to a particular human being and the power he has over himself—and all that this implies. This particular person might be sovereign either due to his individuality—per se—or because he somehow relates to others—reflective sovereignty. Chaucer's thoughts on women's sovereignty and Nietzsche's idea of the sovereign individual are examples of this first use of the word "sovereignty."[11] In the other two cases, the term "sovereignty" can be applied either to: (a) the highest authority in a political community in a given territory (the sovereign);[12] (b) the political community as a whole in its relation with other political communities (the sovereign state).[13] Bodin's and Hobbes's modern notions exemplify this line of interpretation.[14] As this monograph deals with state sovereignty, the focus will be on these latter two ways of understanding sovereignty.

exist result mainly from the absence of State territory and citizens [. . .]. These limitations, however, are not such as to be able to negative its sovereignty. Its sovereignty exists in law and is determined by its own legal order [. . .]."

11 Refer to *The Canterbury Tales (The Tale of the Wife of Bath)* by Geoffrey Chaucer and *The Genealogy of Morals* by Friedrich Nietzsche.

12 F. H. Hinsley, *Sovereignty* (Cambridge: Cambridge University Press, 1986), p. 1.

13 *Ibid.*, p. 158.

14 Refer to *The Six Books of the Republic* by Jean Bodin and *Leviathan* by Thomas Hobbes.

The fifth conceptual issue has to do with seeing the same phenomenon and its two sides. Every state has two faces of sovereignty: (a) internal or inward looking sovereignty; (b) external or outward looking sovereignty. Internal sovereignty refers to the right every state has to determine its type (monarchy, democracy, etc.), governmental structure (prime minister, president, congress, etc.), and rules for its citizens or whoever inhabits its territory. That is to say, it refers to the exercise of a monopoly of power by one or a series of public institutions within a territory in order to create and apply law for its population. By international or external sovereignty is meant the capability each state has to deal on an equal basis with other states. This view assumes the legal personality of the state and implies, among others, the principle of inviolability of state borders. Indeed, both spheres of sovereignty may share the same "space." For example, a bilateral treaty of dual nationality between two sovereign states is signed within an international context and will have legal effects in the two sovereign states in relation to their respective populations.

It is important to mention at this point that this monograph will be largely located in the second domain as sovereignty conflicts mainly concern questions of international nature. However, it will also draw extensively on material located in the first domain or internal sovereignty. That is because, as the next section will show, the beliefs, assumptions, and justifications in order mistakenly to see sovereignty as absolute—hence, nonshareable—have to do with societal evolution. Therein, the use of examples of limited sovereignty in the domestic context (internal sovereignty) so as to show more clearly that current misconceptions in international relations (external sovereignty) stem from ancient ideas that have been anthropomorphized in a larger context, that of the international scenario.

Notions such as "popular" sovereignty, the sixth conceptual issue, are political in nature. Primarily aimed for the reform or creation of the law that gives shape to fundamental institutions, it focuses on people's power to give themselves a constitution, or to elect a new government by the will objectified in the suffrage. The idea that sovereignty is an attribute that people as a collective have and that by delegation rests on their representatives is key in social contract theories. Some of them will be reviewed in the historical section of this chapter.

The seventh conceptual issue is whether sovereignty is something possessed within a limited jurisdiction or whether sovereignty must entail a notion of unlimited jurisdiction. The way in which a state exercises its sovereignty through its executive, legislative, and judicial authorities is what is called jurisdictional sovereignty. In principle, a state extends its jurisdiction within the boundaries it is sovereign of. While a sovereign state may have exclusive power to prescribe what is law within its boundaries, the same cannot be said about its enforcement. Either understood as prescriptive or as enforcement, jurisdictional sovereignty is far from being absolute. In the former case, a sovereign state indeed has supreme authority to create and apply the law for its population within its boundaries. However, there are many cases in which limitations apply—*e.g.* immunities from legal process by states and international organizations in the courts of a peer state—in which diplomatic immunities are but one of many cases; certain crimes such as genocide which foreign bodies may enter a sovereign state to punish or prevent; cases of concurrent jurisdiction; to mention only a few. In the latter case—*i.e.* enforcement—jurisdictional sovereignty is limited by the nature of international relations itself. In other words, the limitation of the enforcement has to do with states and their sovereign equality recognized in international public law as the noninterference principle. This notion is so important for international relations that it is expressly included in the text of the United Nations Charter (art. 2.7).

So far this section introduced the concept of "sovereignty" and discussed some conceptual limitations. It is time now to identify specific theorists or bodies of literature that take sovereignty to be absolute. The following section will introduce a brief historical overview of a few major thinkers and explore their ideas about sovereignty and its limitations.

Aim of the historical account

Substantive limitations have to do with the inability to perform or certain restrictions in the performance or functioning of a given activity. While conceptual limitations are crucial to understanding sovereignty in subsequent chapters, substantive limitations complete the picture. It is time then to give some attention to the arguments of sovereign theorists on why they have thought that authority must take the form of sovereignty. Indeed, not only is this a conceptual issue but also a substantive one about the form that authority must take if it is to function satisfactorily.

The following paragraphs show that the main reason for authority to take the form of sovereignty has to do with beliefs, assumptions, and justifications that respond to societal evolution. The concept of "sovereignty" is a modern one but the elements that give it flesh have been always present in society (at least in the Western world). And that is the purpose of the historical account below, to show how the ideas developed by modern and contemporary scholars depart from beliefs, assumptions, and justifications that had been already used before when referring to authority. Furthermore, this form of viewing authority has always had in one way or another certain limitations. To put it in other terms, the so-called sovereign authorities from the Ancient and Middle Ages and their characteristics find a parallel in the modern and contemporary idea of sovereign states. The notions once applicable to the individual (and hence the limitations to those notions) have been anthropomorphized in that of the state.

In relation specifically to the state and as a juridical idea, the concept of sovereignty was brought to life between the 15th and 16th centuries, and had originally to do with monistic conceptions of sovereign power.[15] Nevertheless, in order to avoid unnecessary confusion, it is imperative to be aware that the term

15 Dora Kostakopoulou, "Floating Sovereignty: a Pathology or a Necessary Means of a State Evolution?," *Oxford Journal of Legal Studies* 22 (2002): 135–56.

has had different uses during its history (from a mere notion or idea to a more clearly defined concept). With this in mind, the historical review will focus on the notion and concept of sovereignty in relation to the specific ages in which it was used.[16]

Arguably, the selection of philosophers and scholars could have been either narrower or broader—why these specific authors and not others? It is important to highlight once again that this monograph is not about sovereignty but a particular kind of sovereignty conflicts and how these conflicts may be resolved; hence, it is imperative for the success of this theoretical enterprise to show how a concept that is thought to be absolute can be (in fact, is) limited. The main point is to bring evidence that there have been authors throughout history who have shown that the notion or concept of sovereignty can be limited. To quote and analyze every single author and school of ideas related to sovereignty is empirically impossible and theoretically unnecessary. At the same time, at least a glimpse of the idea of limited sovereignty is a "must" in order to develop the shared sovereignty paradigm.

Two last clarifications must be made before starting with the historical account. First, the limitations to sovereignty may be actual, theoretical, or both. That is to say, (a) the powers of the ruler were always in some way limited; and/or (b) theories always introduce some limitations to sovereignty, even though some theorists did not admit it. Second, these actual and/or theoretical limitations have to do with internal sovereignty, external sovereignty or both. However, as stated in the previous section, to refer to external and internal sovereignty is to refer to two facets of the same phenomenon. Therefore, the limitations to one facet always affect in some way sovereignty as a whole.

The ancient world

It is a fact that sovereignty as a theoretical concept was coined by Bodin in the early modern age. However, sovereignty as a notion has been always present in human interrelations.[17] There is arguably a strong case for thinking sovereignty

16 Francis Charles Milsom Stroud, *A Natural History of the Common Law* (New York: Columbia University Press, 2003), p. xvi.

17 For a more detailed account on sovereignty and the ancient world, *see* Jorge E. Núñez, "About the Impossibility of Absolute State Sovereignty: The Early Years," *International Journal for the Semiotics of Law* 27 (2014): 645–64. *See also* Nicholas Greenwood Onuf, "Sovereignty: Outline of a Conceptual History," *Sage Publications Inc., Alternatives: Global, Local, Political* 16 (1991): 425–46; Jorge Emilio Núñez, "The Origins of Sovereignty in the Hellenic World," in: David A. Frenkel (ed.), *International Law, Conventions and Justice* (Athens: ATINER, 2011); Heinrich A. Rommen, *The State in Catholic Thought: A Treatise in Political Philosophy* (London: B. Herder Book Co., 1950), *esp.* Chapter XVII; Martin Van Creveld, *The Rise and Decline of the State* (Cambridge: Cambridge University Press, 2004); Hinsley (n. 12); Ernst H. Kantorowicz, *The King's Two Bodies: A Study of Mediaeval Political Theology* (Princeton NJ: Princeton University Press, 1997); Mark Munn, *The Mother of the Gods, Athens, and the Tyranny of Asia: A Study of Sovereignty in Ancient Religion* (Berkley:

may have been limited even in early days. Indeed, most of these limitations were actual and had to do with factual circumstances. But there are even in these early stages some theoretical ones too. There are several reasons that support this idea: (a) the available information about a few big empires and some particular tribal societies; the numerous other societies may have been different; (b) in a polytheistic system divine authority does not mean unfettered authority—even a supreme God, let alone a "mortal god" like the Pharaohs, has to respect the various spheres of influence of other gods; (c) the Code of Hammurabi's reference to the succeeding rulers in case they annulled his law—requesting Anu, the father of the gods, to withdraw the new ruler from his throne;[18] (d) if the *Book of Esther*[19] is reliable in that respect, even the Persian king (who seems to have been particularly powerful) may have been able to pass any law, but having passed it had no authority to repeal it.

In ancient ages, the Pharaoh, the chief of the tribe, the king or the emperor was the highest and only authority (moral, religious, and legal). The monarch was at the same time the positive and natural source of norms. His commandments and decisions were irrevocable and perpetual. There is one characteristic the conception of sovereignty loses later on in history: Perpetuity. As an authority whose power came directly from the gods (in some cultures, the ruler was a god himself) the sovereign essentially represented permanence in time, and inalterability. Moreover, any action or omission that was legally wrong was also incorrect morally and religiously.

At this point, the three normative systems had the same contents, the same creator, and the same interpreter. Although there was no state,[20] technically speaking (at least as defined nowadays), the sovereign was already present (maybe the terminology was nonexistent but the populations had in fact an ultimate and supreme authority or group of them). Tribes without one ruler, tribes with one ruler, city-states, and empires, all shared a few similar characteristics: The state was not present, the communities were small, but they all had an authority, however diffuse and however appointed. And in many of these civilizations (if not all) the ruler seemed to be almost unrestricted, with unlimited power. However, they all had by default at least one constriction: Although they were in most cases

University of California Press, 2006); C. E. Merriam, *History of the Theory of Sovereignty since Rousseau* (Kitchener: Batoche Books, 2001); Jaques Maritain, "The Concept of Sovereignty," *The American Political Science Review* 44 (1950): 343–57; Walter C. Opello and Stephen J. Rosow, *The Nation-State and Global Order, a Historical Introduction to Contemporary Politics* (Boulder CO: Lynne Rienner Publishers, 1999); James J. Sheehan, "The Problem of Sovereignty in European History," *The American Historical Review* 111 (2006): 1–15; and many others.

18 Charles F. Horne, *The Code of Hammurabi* (Charleston SC: Forgotten Books, 2007), Epilogue.

19 R. C. Morgan, *The Book of Esther: Typical of the Kingdom of God* (London: Binns and Goodwin, 1854).

20 See Van Creveld (n. 17), *esp.* Chapter 1.

representative of the gods (if not the God themselves), their powers were constricted by religion.[21]

Whether the sovereign was a representative of a god or the God himself, in both cases religion was above them. Even the immortal God might have had limitations.[22] It seems a holdover of mankind's past hyper-religious fervour that sovereignty is assumed to be as a unitary, unlimited concept. Without entering into a debate, such a high, unitary, and unlimited hierarchy has never been repeated in human history. Thus, such an absolute sovereign above all three normative systems has never existed again (at least in practice) as the rest of this historical account will show.

The Middle Ages

"Sovereignty" in the Middle Ages can be interpreted in two ways: Either there was not a proper sovereign and the concept of sovereignty loses its shape[23] or the Medieval peoples did have a notion of sovereignty that, in effect, was dual (natural and positive law, holy and human secular sovereignty).[24] It is also in the Middle Ages that the word "sovereignty" is introduced but in a different context: Literature. In *The Tale of the Wife of Bath* (*The Canterbury Tales*, 1380) Geoffrey Chaucer mentions sovereignty as a desire every woman has in relation to men. At this early stage the word "sovereignty" already implied a kind of supreme authority but at individual level.

In actual terms, with the decline of the Roman Empire, the social and political spheres fragmented into smaller societal organizations.[25] Since it had many different societal groups in different conditions, it is not strange that this period[26] is characterized by constant tension among them in terms of power, each trying to be the highest one.[27] However, throughout the period there were two well-differentiated higher sovereigns: The church (the Pope) and the king (emperor,

21 *Ibid.*, *esp.* p. 54.

22 *See* Genesis 18:25, when Abraham asks the Lord: "Shall not the Judge of all the earth do what is just?" *See also* Genesis 47:22 and Genesis 47:26, when during the famine in Egypt the land of the priests is the only one that did not become Pharaoh's property. *See also* Hebrews 6:13–20: God's promise to Abraham. In the latter example, God gave his promise and his oath (Hebrews 6:18). The oath is binding (Hebrews 6:16). So, God is bound and this will never change (Hebrews 6:17). Therefore, God limits himself his absolute sovereignty.

23 *See* Maritain (n. 17).

24 For a more detailed account on sovereignty and the Middle Ages, *see* Jorge E. Núñez, "About the Impossibility of Absolute State Sovereignty: The Middle Ages," *International Journal for the Semiotics of Law* 28 (2015): 235–50.

25 See Van Creveld (n. 17), Chapter 2.

26 I refer here to the medieval times in Europe only. For further details with regard to other empires and civilizations, *see* Van Creveld (n. 17), Chapter 2.

27 Noemí García Gestoso, "Sobre los Orígenes Históricos y Teóricos del Concepto de Soberanía: Especial Referencia a los Seis Libros de la República de J. Bodino," *Revista de Estudios Políticos, Nueva Epoca* (2003): 301–27; Opello and Rosows (n. 17), *esp.* Pt I, Chapters 2 and 3.

feudal lord). For some scholars the sovereignty of the Pope was above the sovereignties of any emperor or king as it was delegated by God himself (this was the reason why as a ritual solemnity the Pope had to crown the new monarch validating his secular sovereignty). Others considered them equal. Others still, depending on the circumstances, rejected that authority (*e.g.* Henry VIII and the creation of the Anglican Church).[28] At first, even the emperor owed his position to the church as the eternal and natural law was held to be above human law.[29] However, later on both of them claim absolute power over the totality (ideal and real).

Actual limitations were accompanied by theoretical ones in this period. From the idea of the "two swords" (the church and the king) to the one of "two kings, two bodies," the medieval times show how sovereignty was limited (there was no shared sovereignty but—at best—dual sovereignty). In regard to the king, the idea of *gemina persona* (human by nature and divine by God's will and hence the doctrine of "two kings, two bodies") was coherent with the duality between the sensible world and the world of God.[30] He represented both the contingencies of time and the perpetuity of power. However, that did not mean his powers were absolute: He was not allowed to do wrong (*lex solutus*[31]—unlimited, absolute law—*against rex infra et supra legem*—the king was the highest authority and hence above the law, but at the same time he remained below the law of God).[32]

It is in fact a constant in mediaeval times that any kind of positive law was limited by natural law, even in the event that the sovereign was considered to be above the positive law.[33] The mutual influences between the church and the kings were continuous too, so it is unsurprising that some concepts are shared (perpetuity, holiness, symbols, etc.).[34] Between both church and king the links were multiple (hence, the similarities in many aspects) and also the tensions (disputes in relation to wealth obtained through taxation and revenues for instance are a recurring issue in this period).[35] What happens after the mediaeval period is crucial, because that is when the kings try to get all the power into their hands, and theories of total sovereignty are presented, like those of Bodin and Hobbes.

28 Gerald B. Phelan (trans.), *On the Governance of Rulers (de regimine principum) of Saint Thomas Aquinas* (Toronto, Canada: St. Michael's College, 1935); A. P. D'Entreves (ed.) and J. G. Dawson (trans.), *Selected Political Writings of Aquinas* (Oxford: Basil Blackwell, 1948).
29 *See* Hinsley (n. 12), *esp.* Chapter 3.
30 *See* Kantorowicz (n. 17), *esp.* Chapter 3, pp. 78 ff.
31 *See* Rommen (n. 17), p. 397.
32 *See* Kantorowicz (n. 17), *esp.* Chapter 3, pp. 95 ff.
33 Otto Gierke, *Political Theories of the Middle Age* (Cambridge: Cambridge University Press, 1913), *esp.* pp. 87–100.
34 *See* Kantorowicz (n. 17), *esp.* Chapter 5.
35 *See* Opello (n. 17), *esp.* Part I, Chapters 2 and 3.

The modern age

The medieval age saw sovereignty linked to moral and religious elements; modernity is mainly characterized by a secular power trying to separate itself from the church and at the same time to obtain total control over its affairs in response to social disorder.[36] Classical Greek and Roman authors give the modern age the basis for supporting this enterprise.[37]

The word "sovereignty" had been used before, but it is Bodin in France who mainly defines its characteristics as known nowadays. There are indeed limitations to power that have to do with actual circumstances. Western Europe had a struggle between church and state; principalities and other societal organizations were fighting for power.[38] In response to this situation, Bodin offers his theory of unlimited sovereignty. However, even at the theoretical level he introduces some limitations on sovereignty. At first glance, Bodin's definition seems to grant unlimited sovereignty in order to stop and control that chaos: "*Aieltie* or Sovereignty is the most high, absolute, and perpetual power over the citizens and subjects in a Commonwealth . . .".[39]

Literally interpreted, the above definition clearly states sovereignty's main elements: Highest, absolute, and perpetual power. However, Bodin includes in his work two kinds of limitations: First, those related to natural law; second, those related to customary law and property rights.[40] Particular examples of these limitations are the law of succession, required in order to have a perpetual sovereignty, and the prescriptions to respect private property, keep one's promises and (specifically related to private property), the sovereign's obligation to ask the consent of his citizens before imposing taxes.[41]

Similarly to continental Europe, fights for power were also present in England, arguably limiting sovereignty in actual terms. As a theoretical reaction, Hobbes gives shape to what is labeled as absolute sovereignty.[42] Nevertheless, his work also includes limitations on that supposed absoluteness. Like his predecessors he followed the Greek tradition. Like the ancient philosophers, he uses the metaphor of the human body as a representation of the city (or state for the purpose of this research).[43] He gives the idea or notion of sovereignty a key role to play.[44] Sovereignty is no longer just another element for him. He clearly thinks it is a

36 *See* Hinsley (n. 12), *esp*. pp. 69 ff. and 126 ff.; Opello (n. 17), *esp*. Part II, Chapter 4; Van Creveld (n. 17), Chapter 3; D'Entreves and Dawson (n. 28), Part II, Chapters 4–6.

37 See Hinsley (n. 12), *esp*. pp. 72 ff.

38 *Ibid*., *esp*. pp. 120 ff.

39 Jean Bodin, *The Six Bookes of Commonweale* (London: Impenfis G. Bishop, 1903), p. 84.

40 *See* Hinsley (n. 12), *esp*. pp. 122–23; García Gestoso (n. 27), pp. 318–19.

41 *See* Bodin (n. 39), Bk I, Chapter 8.

42 *See* Hinsley (n. 12), *esp*. pp. 141 ff.

43 Thomas Hobbes, *Man and Citizen* (New York: Humanities Press; Brighton: Harvester Press, 1972), p. 188.

44 Thomas Hobbes, *Leviathan or the Matter, Form and Power of Commonwealth, Ecclesiastical and Civil* (Oxford: Basil Blackwell, 1955), p. 5.

necessary one in order to have a real state or city. Hobbes together with Locke and Rousseau are contractualists. However, he implies something further than a contract: A merge of wills[45]—*i.e.* the Leviathan.[46]

Despite the fact that Hobbes's idea of sovereignty appears to be completely absolute, unlimited,[47] he makes a deep distinction that arguably goes against that theory: "[f]or it is one thing if I say, I give you the right to command what you will; another, if I say, I will do whatsoever you command."[48] Although it may seem that Hobbes supported the idea of an absolute sovereign he is particularly keen on securing the citizens' wellbeing by limiting what he characterized before as absolute sovereignty.[49] Further evidence supporting the argument that Hobbes's sovereign was limited is present in the Leviathan when he makes clear the subordination of human law in respect to divine natural law. Moreover, he places the immortal God above the mortal god or the Leviathan (or the sovereign).[50]

It is at least questionable how absolute sovereignty is in Hobbes's theory. First, for Hobbes the power of the Leviathan is restricted, at least practically, if not absolutely, by rules of natural law. In tune with this, the fact that he recognizes a super-empirical authority such as God over the Leviathan adds a constraint that is not part of the concept of sovereignty itself. Second, people have contracted to obey the sovereign, the Leviathan, who can be one person, a few or many. There are limitations in two ways here: Related to the Leviathan and related to the Leviathan and the citizens. Clearly, the Leviathan can be a parliamentary assembly, an artificial personality, so there would be reciprocal limitations among the assembly members, at least of practical nature. More importantly, and in what has to do with citizens' wellbeing, it has been maintained that Hobbes's theory "seems incompatible with his defense of absolute sovereignty."[51] Expressions such as "safety of the people" make questionable how absolute sovereignty is for Hobbes. Debates in relation to this point have existed since Hobbes's time[52] and are contemporarily seen as the Achilles' heel of his theory.[53]

There are others that develop theories of sovereignty. But in different ways from Hobbes, these theorists acknowledge limitations. In due turn, it is Locke who

45 *Ibid.*, p. 112.
46 *Ibid.*
47 *See* Hobbes (1972) (n. 43), pp. 180–81.
48 *Ibid.*, p. 182.
49 *Ibid.*, p. 258.
50 Hobbes (1955) (n. 44), p. 112.
51 Sharon A. Lloyd and Susanne Sreedhar, "Hobbes's Moral and Political Philosophy", *The Stanford Encyclopedia of Philosophy* (2008) http://plato.stanford.edu/entries/hobbes-moral/(last accessed December 30, 2016)
52 *Ibid.*
53 *Ibid. See also* Eleanor Curran, "Can Rights Curb the Hobbesian Sovereign? The Full Right to Self-Preservation, Duties of Sovereignty and the Limitations of Hohfeld," *Law and Philosophy* 25 (2006): 243–65; and Eleanor Curran, *Reclaiming the Rights of Hobbesian Subjects* (Hampshire: Palgrave Macmillan, 2007).

introduces a clearer notion of limited sovereignty.[54] For Rousseau, the particular wills that once existed independently give way to a common will and the state is born. He understands sovereignty as the active result of the union of the persons' wills.[55] In other words, the collective subject is the real sovereign, but each and every individual subject who is integrated into that collective has a proportional part of sovereignty; so their sovereignty is mutually limited.[56]

The three previously mentioned thinkers, namely Hobbes, Locke, and Rousseau, understand state sovereignty as focused on the relationship between represented and representative.[57] The interesting fact is that for different reasons, they all limit sovereignty within this mutual relationship.[58] In that same historical period, Kant seems to concede unlimited power to the representatives once they become chosen authorities.[59] At first glance, Kant's conception of internal sovereignty appears to offer an absolute notion.[60] In some passages of his works he even identifies the notion of sovereign with head of state.[61] And that position cannot be shared since if that happened, it would imply a contradiction in itself.[62] But what at first glance may seem absolute in Kant's theory, in fact is not. He includes limits both at national and international level to sovereignty. At national level, his first definitive article in *Perpetual Peace* clearly highlights the necessity of a republican constitution within a representative system.[63]

At the international level, it is essential to create an interstate system and hence, mutual limitations among states appear.[64] One extremely interesting point he makes is that he integrates the economic factor as key in the maintenance of a state's sovereignty,[65] introducing another limitation to the ones the sovereign power already should have (*e.g.* noninterference in ecclesiastical organization, the sovereign being forbidden to do what people are not able to do, prohibition of

54 *See* Merriam (n. 17), pp. 16–17.

55 G. F. H. Cole (trans.), *The Social Contract and Discourses of Jean-Jacques Rousseau* (London: Everyman's Library, J. M. Dent & Sons Ltd., 1988), pp. 192–94, 201; Opello (n. 17), *esp.* Part II, Chapter 5.

56 *See* Cole (n. 55), p. 231.

57 E. J. Lowe, *Locke* (London and New York: Routledge, Taylor & Francis Group, 2005), pp. 161–63.

58 For an extensive analysis of essential differences in the arguments of Hobbes, Locke, and Rousseau, *see* Hinsley (n. 12), pp. 153–54; and Van Creveld (n. 17), Chapter 3, pp. 177 ff.

59 M. Gregor (trans.), *The Metaphysics of Morals of Immanuel Kant* (Cambridge: Cambridge University Press, 1998), pp. 95–96.

60 Merriam (n. 17), *esp.* p. 25.

61 *Ibid.*, pp. 110–11.

62 H. Reiss (ed.) and H. B. Nisbet (trans.), *Political Writings of Immanuel Kant* (Cambridge: Cambridge University Press, 2000), pp. 74–75.

63 *Ibid.*, pp. 99–102.

64 *See* Gregor (n. 59), p. 114.

65 Reiss (n. 62), p. 95. Kant expressly forbids the contracting of national debts if they may cause friction among states.

hereditary nobility).[66] However, and unlike other writers after Hobbes (who think the people have a right to remove the sovereign), for Kant it may be a right only to tell the sovereign to go and not to use force.

For Hegel the state is a rational idea with ethical content.[67] Therefore, he maintains that individuals have the duty to be members of it.[68] Within this theoretical construction, sovereignty appears as an aspect of the state.[69] He then analyzes the meaning of the phrase "sovereignty of the people" and maintains that they (alone) are not the sovereign.[70] From there, he supports the notion that the monarch is the one who gives the "formless mass" of people the status of a state and sovereignty is presented as "the personality of the whole."[71] In other words, and at least in relation to internal affairs, sovereignty for Hegel is an attribute that characterizes a state and the relationship between the population and the monarch. The two parties are mutually necessary in order for the state to exist, and so, they are reciprocally limited. In what matters to external sovereignty (or international affairs), each state's sovereignty is limited by that of its peers.[72]

The theories previously mentioned are applied between the 17th and 19th centuries with the creation of new national legal orders worldwide with the same result: Sovereignty is limited at national level. The era of the empires gives way to that of the constitutional republics with the characteristic of including the idea of separation of powers. For example, the United States of America, Argentina, and most of the American countries that achieved their independence adopted a republican constitution with separate executive, legislative, and judicial powers. There is no longer only one supreme authority; or better, there is one supreme authority divided into three different areas with representatives for each office limiting reciprocally their spheres of influence, without necessarily reciprocally checking their activities. That is to say, it may appear to be one way of limiting sovereignty but in fact there are here two limitations that may work together but do not need to, namely (a) the "separation of powers"; and (b) the "checks and balances system." As a result, "separation of power" implies that the sovereign power of a state is divided in different branches and "checks and balances system" that these different branches can reciprocally check the activities of the other branches in order to keep a balance of power. However, "division of power" does not necessarily imply the "checks and balances system"—*i.e.* the "checks and balances system" may or may not be part of the legal order of a state even though that state has "division of power."

66 Merriam (n. 17), *esp*. p. 25.
67 T. M. Knox (trans.), *Philosophy of Right of Georg Wilhelm Friedrich Hegel* (Oxford: Clarendon Press, 1967), p. 155.
68 *Ibid*., p. 156.
69 *Ibid*., p. 181.
70 *Ibid*., p. 182.
71 *Ibid*., pp. 182–83.
72 *Ibid*., pp. 212–13.

Contemporary age

The transition between the modern and contemporary ages sees a change, with the population being the origin of sovereignty. People choose their representatives in elections (a democratic type of government)[73] and these representatives hold the sovereignty of the respective state. It is a reflective sovereignty since it is not a personal attribute of the representatives as individuals. The population grants that privilege to certain people, delegating their sovereignty. Then the church comes back into the game with theories more in tune with that period and as a reaction to—mainly—contractualist visions followed by patrimonial theories, rational explanation, historical analysis, and even utilitarian interpretations.[74]

Among new theories of sovereignty in the contemporary age, Schmitt offers a very particular insight. He accepts (as his predecessors) sovereignty as the highest power.[75] After reviewing historical conceptions of sovereignty, he concludes that it can be characterized as the power to make a certain kind of exception,[76] and the sovereign is that one able to decide upon it.[77] In brief, the legal order is valid under conditions of normal circumstances in a society. But, if for whatever reason the situation turns out to be abnormal, the legal order may be suspended (hence the suspension of the legal order is exceptional). So, the one who is able to suspend the legal order—to decide upon the exception—is the sovereign, for Schmitt.

The basis on which to define the state, for Schmitt, is a certain homogeneity, which is given by dividing people into friends and enemy.[78] This idea characterizes the relations of exclusion and, in the extreme case (war) the sovereign is the one deciding who the enemy is. In contrast, a population that decides not to defend itself, surrendering to another power, loses its sovereignty. Therefore, it is fundamental for Schmitt that a population maintains any power that is given to the sovereign. The concord between people and sovereign—or their obedience—is a must for a sovereign to remain as such. Hence, and in what is specific to this historical review, sovereignty is both defined and limited in Schmitt by: (a) internally, the relationship between the population and the sovereign; (b) externally, the determination of friends and enemies.

Kelsen mentions on several occasions the term "absolute sovereignty"[79] referring to the highest law within a territory. In that sense Kelsen is a clear

73 Technically, it is "partial democracy" because universal adult voting is not the rule in early contemporary age.

74 Merriam (n. 17), Chapters 3–8.

75 Carl Schmitt, *Political Theology: Four Chapters on the Concept of Sovereignty* (Cambridge MA: The MIT Press, 1985), *esp.* pp. 6 and 17.

76 *Ibid.*, p. 5.

77 Hidemi Suganami, "Understanding Sovereignty Through Kelsen/Schmitt," *Review of International Studies* 33 (2007): 511–30.

78 *See* Schmitt (n. 75), Introduction.

79 Hans Kelsen, *Introduction to the Problems of Legal Theory* (Oxford: Oxford University Press, 1992), *esp.* pp. 100, 116, and 121; Hans Kelsen, *General Theory of Law and State* (New York:

example of how legal scholars often, by defining state through one of its elements (law), maintain that sovereignty is absolute. His works, however, include limitations to sovereignty both at national and international level.

In terms of national order, for Kelsen state and law interdefine each other: The state "is the personification of a legal order"[80] and "the legal order is a system of norms."[81] In other words, the state is the national legal order; hence, the sovereign for Kelsen is not the people or their representatives (since they are not the state) but the law. Law does not limit the sovereign's powers but is the actual sovereign. So, as purely theoretical argument, to say the state creates obligations and duties for the sovereign would mean that the legal order creates obligations and duties for the legal order, and that is a tautology.[82]

The key point, to untangle the role sovereignty plays in relation to law and to see the limitations on sovereign power in Kelsen's theory, is directly linked to the way he perceives the national and international legal orders. The difference between national and international law is the degree of centralization in regard to the application and creation of law.[83] The state is a legal order that is centralized, with designated authorities to create and apply law; in contrast, international law lacks central authorities for the creation and application of law in respect to all international legal subjects. When Kelsen analyzes the relationship between national and international law, he understands that the idea of unlimited sovereignty is incompatible with it.[84]

Current views on legal and political sovereignty

From the previous sections it is unquestionable that sovereignty is complex, both conceptually and in substance. There are indeed two realms intertwined in all these views: Politics and law; that is to say sovereignty as competence or ability to take decisions and sovereignty as lawmaking power. In the following, the focus will be on some contemporary authors that deal with sovereignty. The selection of these scholars follows strict criteria: (a) pre-eminence either in law or politics as sciences; and (b) expertise in what has to do with sovereignty in their respective fields. In other words, they are leading figures in their field, legal and political sciences respectively and, in particular, in what matters to sovereignty. In addition to this, they acknowledge the fact that sovereignty has legal and political facets. And in what is crucial to this monograph, all of them see sovereignty as limited.

Russell & Russell, 1945), pp. 383 ff.; Hans Kelsen, *Principles of International Law* (New York: Rinehart & Company Inc., 1952), pp. 108 ff. and 438–47; Hans Kelsen, *Essays in Legal and Moral Philosophy* (Boston MA: D. Reidel Publishing Company, 1973), Chapter 5, *esp*. pp. 107–9.

80 Kelsen (1945) (n. 79), p. 197.

81 *Ibid*., p. 110.

82 *Ibid*., pp. 197–200.

83 *Ibid*., p. 325.

84 For an extensive view, *see* Kelsen (1992) (n. 79), Chapter IX, *esp*. pp. 112 *in fine* and 113, 121; Kelsen (1945) (n. 79), p. 385; Kelsen (1952) (n. 79), pp. 155–57.

The following quotation is an excellent starting point since it very briefly shows both how sovereignty is currently seen in legal and political sciences and provides an indication of the most recent bodies of scholarly literature in the matter:

> Why are we constantly "questioning sovereignty?" Why are we inclined to accuse sovereignty of "hypocrisy" or to reduce it to a "game?" Why are we concerned to "relocate" sovereignty or to search for its "fragments?" Why do we consider sovereignty to be "in transition", perhaps even "in crisis?"[85]

Indeed, sovereignty has been (is still being) questioned. Although being primarily a legal scholar, MacCormick sees sovereignty as both a legal and political concept.[86] In order to define it from a legal point of view, he borrows Dicey's idea that sovereignty simply refers to the power of lawmaking unrestricted by any legal limit.[87] In what matters to political sovereignty, MacCormick maintains that it "is interpersonal power over the conditions of life in a human community or society."[88] Additionally, he says that: "[political sovereignty] is the ability to take effective decisions on whatever concerns the common well-being of the members, and on whatever affects the distribution of the economic resources . . ."[89] In tune with these two characterizations he maintains that there is a certain relationship between them. He argues that "law is then dependent on political sovereignty"[90] in the sense that whoever holds the power in a given territory is the one that will issue commands to the population.

MacCormick goes some way towards making clear some notions already covered in this chapter—*e.g.* internal and external sovereignty, popular sovereignty, and so on. In what is important to this monograph, and *brevitatis causa* as these points have been reviewed in previous sections, he argues against classical authors who thought the coexistence of rival supreme powers in a single legal or political order a contradiction in terms.[91] Although MacCormick does not develop this point to a great extent, he refers to limitations to both internal and external sovereignty. For instance, he mentions reciprocal checks and controls internally among organs of the state and the existence of other states in international relations.[92]

85 Neil Walker, "Sovereignty Frames and Sovereignty Claims," University of Edinburgh, School of Law, Working Papers (2013), p. 1.

86 Neil MacCormick, *Questioning Sovereignty: Law, State, and Nation in the European Commonwealth* (Oxford: Oxford University Press, 1999), p. 127.

87 *Ibid.* In particular, *see* A. V. Dicey, *Introduction to the Study of the Law of the Constitution*, 8th edn (Indianapolis: Liberty Fund, 1982), p. 27.

88 MacCormick (1999) (n. 86), p. 127.

89 *Ibid.*

90 *Ibid.*, p. 128.

91 *Ibid.*, p. 129.

92 *Ibid.*, pp. 131–32. *See also* Neil MacCormick, "Beyond the Sovereign State," *The Modern Law Review* 56 (1993): 1–18.

A similar view is presented by Krasner in political science. In tune with this he maintains that: "[s]overeignty was never quite as vibrant as many contemporary observers suggest. The conventional norms of sovereignty have always been challenged."[93] The following quotation illustrates how Krasner defines sovereignty through states:

> Sovereign [S]tates are the building blocks, the basic actors, for the modern state system. Sovereign states are territorial units with juridical independence; they are not formally subject to some external authority. Sovereign [S]tates have also *de facto* autonomy. . . . An implication of *de facto* autonomy is the admonition that [S]tates should not intervene in each other's internal affairs. Sovereign [S]tates are also generally assumed to have some reasonable degree of control over both their borders and their territory.[94]

This paragraph shows some of the elements that are familiar to any characterization of sovereignty. From a conceptual point of view, he recognizes four uses[95] of the term "sovereignty:"

(a) Domestic sovereignty: Referring to the organization of public authority within a state and the level of effective control exercised by those holding authority.
(b) Interdependence sovereignty: Referring to the ability of public authorities to control trans-border movements.
(c) International legal sovereignty: Referring to the recognition of states or other entities.
(d) Westphalian sovereignty: Referring to the exclusion of external actors from domestic authority configurations.

Like MacCormick, Krasner also acknowledges sovereignty as both a legal and political phenomenon. And like the legal scholar, he refers as well to some criteria covered in this chapter, which *brevitatis causa* will not be reviewed here again.

In principle, it may seem that Krasner concedes that sovereignty is losing its preeminent place in the legal and political arenas. He specifically says that: "[t]he polities of many weaker [S]tates have been persistently penetrated, and stronger nations have not been immune to external influence."[96] Nevertheless, while this may appear at first to be a concession it is not. That is because he is insightful in noticing that the challenges sovereignty has to cope with nowadays have been

93 Stephen D. Krasner, "Sovereignty, Think Again," *Foreign Policy*, January/February (2001).
94 Stephen D. Krasner, "Abiding Sovereignty," *International Political Science Review* 3 (2001): 229–51.
95 Stephen D. Krasner, *Sovereignty: Organized Hypocrisy* (Princeton NJ: Princeton University Press, 1999).
96 Krasner, "Sovereignty, Think Again" (2001) (n. 93).

somehow always present. And that is indeed what the previous historical account has shown as well to a greater extent.[97] Both weak and strong states' sovereignties are continuously penetrated.[98] Krasner mentions several examples that make this very clear: Capital market integration, international migration rates, international trade increase, AIDS, MTV, human rights norms, etc.[99]

Both MacCormick and Krasner offer their view with regard to sovereignty. They both follow the traditional idea of a form of authority: Supreme authority. Additionally, they recognize sovereignty's two facets. Indeed, they refer to political and legal sovereignty as complex phenomena. And in what is crucial to this monograph, they highlight conceptual limitations and substantive ones too, all of which were covered in the previous sections.

Others have maintained that sovereignty is in fragments.[100] They claim that as a concept, sovereignty is a contested one through history. That is to say, similar to the previous sections, by following conceptual and historical analysis it is possible to argue that sovereignty is limited in many ways—*i.e.* it is constituted by many fragments. In what has to do with the state, even the genealogy of the latter demonstrates the same outcome.[101] Conceptually, the term had to refer to unity of power for historical reasons but which had included limitations of different natures since the outset.[102]

Similarly, in international relations sovereignty has been (and still is) one of the many myths.[103] Because of historical reasons sovereignty as a conceptual construction has fulfilled (and still does) a role in international relations, national and international culture, and ideology. Therein, like any myth, the ideology behind these stories appears to be true.[104] Reconsidering further the concept upon which this particular ideology rests brings about a different reality.[105] Understood as a set of practices, state sovereignty indeed differs across time and space and its limitations are evident.[106] To an extreme, sovereignty seen as a set of practices in

97 Krasner, "Abiding Sovereignty" (2001) (n. 94).
98 Krasner, "Sovereignty, Think Again" (2001) (n. 93).
99 Krasner, "Abiding Sovereigntys" (2001) (n. 94).
100 Hent Kalmo and Quentin Skinner (eds.), *Sovereignty in Fragments: The Past, Present and Future of a Contested Concept* (Cambridge: Cambridge University Press, 2010), *esp.* pp. 1–25.
101 Quentin Skinner, *The Foundations of Modern Political Thought*, Volume 2 (Cambridge: Cambridge University Press, 1978); Quentin Skinner, "A Genealogy of the State," *Rivista di Storia delle Idee* 2:1 (2013): 46–61.
102 Quentin Skinner, "A Genealogy of the State," *Rivista di Storia delle Idee* 2:1 (2013): 46–61, *esp.* p. 60, fn. 115.
103 Cynthia Weber, *International Relations Theory: A Critical Introduction* (Abingdon: Routledge, 2010), *esp.* Introduction. *See also* Luke Glanville, "The Myth of 'Traditional' Sovereignty," *International Studies Quarterly* 57 (2013): 79–90.
104 *Ibid.*, pp. 6–8.
105 Cynthia Weber, "Reconsidering Statehood: Examining the Sovereignty/Intervention Boundary," *Review of International Studies* 18 (1992): 199–216, *esp.* p. 199, fns 1 and 2.
106 *Ibid.*, 199–216, *esp.* p. 200, fn. 7.

international relation may appear paradoxical.[107] Whether considered as a myth or a set of practices, sovereignty is a product of social construct.[108] Realists' accounts of sovereignty (Morgenthau, Carr, Waltz), interdependence and dependence writers, recent conceptual analyzes (Hinsley, Jackson), and even social constructions theories highlight different characteristics of the same concept. All these accounts recognize conceptual, historical, domestic, and international limitations.[109]

Domestically, sovereignty may be seen as indivisible or concentrated in the hands of one man, and as dispersed in the social body.[110] Indeed, indivisibility has been a characteristic assumed to define sovereignty since Bodin.[111] However, even assumed as correct, this way of characterizing sovereignty implies that in the international system there is an absence of unit and hence limitations are reciprocal among states.[112] The concept of sovereignty has been revisited time and time again.[113] But, there is an agreement in that sovereignty confers indivisibility on the state—and not the other way around.[114]

Sovereignty may be in fact a machine behind the *Empire*.[115] It may be transcendental and representational.[116] It is clear by now that sovereignty as a concept was born within an historical context and because of that historical context. *Les Six Livres de la République* are not a coincidence.[117] Analyzed in the context of the nation, the crisis of modernity, colonialism, as part of a passage, or a common characteristic between the "old empire" and the "new empire", sovereignty has

107 Dominik Zaum, *The Sovereignty Paradox: The Norms and Politics of International Statebuilding* (Oxford: Oxford University Press, 2007), *see esp.* Pt I, Chapter 1. Zaum argues that sovereignty as practices has been (still is) influenced by democracy, human rights, the rule of law, a free market economy, and effective administration. Zaum goes further and compares the way in which international agents compromise sovereignty in order to have a sovereign state with Rousseau's idea of "forcing a man to be free."

108 Thomas J. Biersteker and Cynthia Weber (eds.), *State Sovereignty as Social Construct* (Cambridge: Cambridge University Press, 1996), pp. 1–21.

109 *Ibid. See also* Cynthia Weber, "Writing Sovereign Identities: Wilson Administration Intervention in the Mexican Revolution," *Alternatives: Global, Local, Political* 17 (1992): 313–37, *esp.* p. 334, fns. 1 and 2.

110 Jens Bartelson, *A Genealogy of Sovereignty* (Cambridge: Cambridge University Press, 1995), p. 26.

111 *Ibid.*, p. 28.

112 *Ibid.*

113 Jens Bartelson, "The Concept of Sovereignty Revisited," *The European Journal of International Law* 17 (2006): 463–74.

114 Jens Bartelson, "Second Natures: Is the State Identical with Itself?" *European Journal of International Relations* 4 (1998): 295–326. For a better understanding on how sovereignty "became indivisible," *see* Jens Bartelson, "On the Indivisibility of Sovereignty," *Republic of Letters: A Journal for the Study of Knowledge, Politics, and the Arts* 2 (2011): 85–94. For a more thorough analysis, *see* Jens Bartelson, *The Critique of the State* (Cambridge: Cambridge University Press, 2001).

115 Michael Hardt and Antonio Negri, *Empire* (Cambridge MA. Harvard University Press, 2000), p. 87.

116 *Ibid.*, p. 84.

117 *Ibid.*, p. 97.

been playing a central role in both domestic and international arenas for a long time. Arguably, the "empire" based on this myth may be in decline and free fall.[118] The crucial point for this chapter, and in large part for this monograph, is that conceptually and historically sovereignty is limited. It has always been limited.[119]

Finally, whether the end of history is approaching, the era of conflicts has finished and sovereign power expands globally,[120] the evolution of human society is not open-ended and the final destination has been reached,[121] international relations are characterized by a world made up of liberal democracies,[122] or the world is still "in transition" both with regard to domestic and international realities, the myth, the notion, the practices that have to do with sovereignty still play a central role. Even taking Fukuyama's central thesis to the extreme and assuming Kojève's "universal homogeneous state"[123] was not nominal expectation but current in realpolitik, the limitations to sovereignty would still be the many covered in this chapter—*e.g. brevitatis causa* domestically, each individual's freedom against his peers and represented and representatives limiting reciprocally; internationally, national interests, principle of recognition, principle of effectiveness at conceptual level and in international relations, level of development, financial position, market, among many factual circumstances.

A new "empire" may come, the "end of history" has yet to arrive, or the end of evolution in terms of historical and conceptual paradigms has long ago taken place, sovereignty, and in particular state sovereignty is still present in legal and political sciences. And, from the above account it is clear that even if it was in transition fragmented, questioned, or in crisis, and whether a preeminent concept or a peripheral one, in decay, in all cases it is a limited one.

Conclusion

This chapter examined the concept of "sovereignty" and has shown that it is a limited one. In order to show the limitations in sovereignty, the chapter followed mainly two lines of analysis: (a) conceptual; and (b) historical. First, it considered the concept of "sovereignty" and some of its conceptual issues—*i.e.* in particular, the ones that have to do with the nature of this monograph. Second,

118 *Ibid.*, pp. 351 ff.

119 *Ibid.*, *see esp.* pp. 89–92 and the references to Weber and Foucault. *See also* Jean L. Cohen, "Whose Sovereignty: Empire Versus International Law," *Ethics and International Affairs* 18 (2004): 1–24.

120 Cf. Francis Fukuyama, *The End of History and the Last Man* (London: Penguin Books, 1992). *See also* Michael Hardt and Antonio Negri, *Empire* (Cambridge MA: Harvard University Press, 2000), p. 189.

121 Francis Fukuyama, *The End of History and the Last Man* (London: Penguin Books, 1992), p. xii.

122 *Ibid.*, p. xx.

123 Francis Fukuyama, "The End of History?" *The National Interest* (1989).

it identified some theories or bodies of literature throughout history that showed how sovereignty has always had in one way or another limitations.

God, the church, the king, the nobles, an emperor, the people, the law, the state itself have all been considered sovereign at some point in history. Although most (if not all) of the theories that supported the idea of sovereignty have tried to show an unrestricted, unlimited, absolute concept, both in practice and theory sovereignty has always been restricted. And that is the main point of this review: To illustrate how a notion or a concept that has been regarded as absolute has always had theoretical and empirical limitations (at least for Western thinkers and societies). On the one hand, the limitations in practice appear at all times, either to avoid rebellion or by the actual acceptance or moral and legal limitations. On the other hand, all theories either present sovereignty as limited (Locke, Kant, Kelsen), or although they intend to introduce an unlimited sovereignty, they fail because they in fact accept limitations (Bodin, Hobbes). Current accounts of the notion only recognize and repeat in what appear to be more elaborated theories what classical thinkers already said.

In political and legal sciences there are few concepts more basic and at the same time more important than state sovereignty. This monograph does not intend to reinvent the concept of sovereignty. On the contrary, it aims to make use of the concept as it has been always regarded: Supreme authority. Nevertheless, this chapter has shown that in all reviewed ages and places sovereignty supposedly understood as an absolute concept has been limited in practice and even in the concept—and it has been held that it should be limited. Moreover, for most theories it has been seen as limited *de jure* as well as *de facto*. Therefore, sovereignty has three kinds of restrictions: Conceptual; *de facto* constraints on power; and legal limitations—both by internal and international law, which in the latter although they seem to be modern realities and have increased in importance were already recognized by the Romans with their *ius gentium* coexistent with *ius civile* and *ius naturale*.

Bibliography

Bartelson, Jens. "On the Indivisibility of Sovereignty." *Republic of Letters: A Journal for the Study of Knowledge, Politics, and the Arts* 2 (2011): 85–94.

Bartelson, Jens. "Second Natures: Is the State Identical with Itself?" *European Journal of International Relations* 4 (1998): 295–326.

Bartelson, Jens. "The Concept of Sovereignty Revisited." *The European Journal of International Law* 17 (2006): 463–74.

Bartelson, Jens. *A Genealogy of Sovereignty*. Cambridge: Cambridge University Press, 1995.

Bartelson, Jens. *The Critique of the State*. Cambridge: Cambridge University Press, 2001.

Biersteker, Thomas J. and Weber, Cynthia, eds. *State Sovereignty as Social Construct*. Cambridge: Cambridge University Press, 1996.

Bodin, Jean. *The Six Bookes of Commonweale*. London: Impenfis G. Bishop, 1903.

Carrio, Genaro. *Notas Sobre Derecho y Lenguaje*. Argentina: Abeledo Perrot, 1965.

Cohen, Jean L. "Whose Sovereignty: Empire Versus International Law." *Ethics and International Affairs* 18 (2004): 1–24.

Cole, G. F. H., trans. *The Social Contract and Discourses of Jean-Jacques Rousseau.* London: Everyman's Library, J. M. Dent & Sons Ltd., 1988.

Curran, Eleanor. "Can Rights Curb the Hobbesian Sovereign? The Full Right to Self-Preservation, Duties of Sovereignty and the Limitations of Hohfeld." *Law and Philosophy* 25 (2006): 243–65.

Curran, Eleanor. *Reclaiming the Rights of Hobbesian Subjects.* Hampshire: Palgrave Macmillan, 2007.

D'Entreves, A. P., ed., and Dawson, J. G., trans. *Selected Political Writings of Aquinas.* Oxford: Basil Blackwell, 1948.

Dicey, A. V. *Introduction to the Study of the Law of the Constitution.* Indianapolis: Liberty Fund, 1982.

Fukuyama, Francis. "The End of History?" *The National Interest*, 1989.

Fukuyama, Francis. *The End of History and the Last Man.* London: Penguin Books, 1992.

García Gestoso, Noemí. "Sobre los Orígenes Históricos y Teóricos del Concepto de Soberanía: Especial Referencia a los Seis Libros de la República de J. Bodino." *Revista de Estudios Políticos, Nueva Epoca* (2003): 301–27.

Gierke, Otto. *Political Theories of the Middle Age.* Cambridge: Cambridge University Press, 1913.

Glanville, Luke. "The Myth of 'Traditional' Sovereignty." *International Studies Quarterly* 57 (2013): 79–90.

Gregor, M., trans. *The Metaphysics of Morals of Immanuel Kant.* Cambridge: Cambridge University Press, 1998.

Hardt, Michael and Negri, Antonio. *Empire.* Cambridge MA: Harvard University Press, 2000.

Hart, H. L. A. *The Concept of Law.* Oxford: Oxford University Press, 1994.

Hinsley, F. H. *Sovereignty.* Cambridge: Cambridge University Press, 1986.

Hobbes, Thomas. *Leviathan or the Matter, Form and Power of Commonwealth, Ecclesiastical and Civil.* Oxford: Basil Blackwell, 1955.

Hobbes, Thomas. *Man and Citizen.* New York: Humanities Press; Brighton: Harvester Press, 1972.

Horne, Charles F. *The Code of Hammurabi.* Charleston SC: Forgotten Books, 2007.

Jackson, Robert, ed. *Sovereignty at the Millennium.* Oxford: Blackwell Publishers, 1999.

Kalmo, Hent and Skinner, Quentin, eds. *Sovereignty in Fragments: The Past, Present and Future of a Contested Concept.* Cambridge: Cambridge University Press, 2010.

Kantorowicz, Ernst H. *The King's Two Bodies: A Study of Mediaeval Political Theology.* Princeton NJ: Princeton University Press, 1997.

Kelsen, Hans. *Essays in Legal and Moral Philosophy.* Boston MA: D. Reidel Publishing Company, 1973.

Kelsen, Hans. *General Theory of Law and State.* New York: Russell & Russell, 1945.

Kelsen, Hans. *Introduction to the Problems of Legal Theory.* Oxford: Oxford University Press, 1992.

Kelsen, Hans. *Principles of International Law.* New York: Rinehart & Company Inc., 1952.

Knox, T. M., trans. *Philosophy of Right of Georg Wilhelm Friedrich Hegel.* Oxford: Clarendon Press, 1967.

Kostakopoulou, Dora. "Floating Sovereignty: A Pathology or a Necessary Means of a State Evolution?" *Oxford Journal of Legal Studies* 22 (2002): 135–56.

Krasner, Stephen D. "Abiding Sovereignty." *International Political Science Review* 3 (2001): 229–51.

Krasner, Stephen D. "Sovereignty, Think Again." *Foreign Policy* (2001).

Krasner, Stephen D. *Sovereignty: Organized Hypocrisy.* Princeton NJ: Princeton University Press, 1999.

Lowe, E. J. *Locke.* London and New York: Routledge, Taylor & Francis Group, 2005.

MacCormick, Neil. "Beyond the Sovereign State." *The Modern Law Review* 56 (1993): 1–18.

MacCormick, Neil. *Questioning Sovereignty: Law, State, and Nation in the European Commonwealth.* Oxford: Oxford University Press, 1999.

Maritain, Jaques. "The Concept of Sovereignty." *The American Political Science Review* 44 (1950): 343–57.

Martin, Elizabeth A. and Law, Jonathan, eds. *A Dictionary of Law.* Oxford: Oxford University Press, 2006.

Merriam, C. E. *History of the Theory of Sovereignty since Rousseau.* Kitchener: Batoche Books, 2001.

Morgan, R. C. *The Book of Esther: Typical of the Kingdom of God.* London: Binns and Goodwin, 1854.

Munn, Mark. *The Mother of the Gods, Athens, and the Tyranny of Asia: A Study of Sovereignty in Ancient Religion.* Berkley: University of California Press, 2006.

Núñez, Jorge E. "About the Impossibility of Absolute State Sovereignty: The Early Years." *International Journal for the Semiotics of Law* 27 (2014): 645–64.

Núñez, Jorge E. "About the Impossibility of Absolute State Sovereignty: The Middle Ages." *International Journal for the Semiotics of Law* 28 (2015): 235–50.

Núñez, Jorge E. "The Origins of Sovereignty in the Hellenic World," in: David A. Frenkel, ed., *International Law, Conventions and Justice.* Athens: ATINER, 2011.

Onuf, Nicholas Greenwood. "Sovereignty: Outline of a Conceptual History." *Sage Publications Inc., Alternatives: Global, Local, Political* 16 (1991): 425–46.

Opello, Walter C. and Rosow, Stephen J. *The Nation-State and Global Order: A Historical Introduction to Contemporary Politics.* Boulder CO: Lynne Rienner Publishers, 1999.

Phelan, Gerald B., trans. *On the Governance of Rulers (de regimine principum) of Saint Thomas Aquinas.* Toronto: St. Michael's College, 1935.

Reiss, H., ed., and Nisbet, H. B., trans. *Political Writings of Immanuel Kant.* Cambridge: Cambridge University Press, 2000.

Rommen, Heinrich A. *The State in Catholic Thought: A Treatise in Political Philosophy.* London: B. Herder Book Co., 1950.

Schmitt, Carl. *Political Theology: Four Chapters on the Concept of Sovereignty.* Cambridge MA: The MIT Press, 1985.

Sheehan, James J. "The Problem of Sovereignty in European History." *The American Historical Review* 111 (2006): 1–15.

Skinner, Quentin. "A Genealogy of the State." *Rivista di Storia delle Idee* 2:1 (2013): 46–61.

Skinner, Quentin. *The Foundations of Modern Political Thought.* Cambridge: Cambridge University Press, 1978.

Stroud, Francis Charles Milsom. *A Natural History of the Common Law.* New York: Columbia University Press, 2003.

Suganami, Hidemi. “Understanding Sovereignty Through Kelsen/Schmitt.” *Review of International Studies* 33 (2007): 511–30.

Van Creveld, Martin. *The Rise and Decline of the State*. Cambridge: Cambridge University Press, 2004.

Walker, Neil. “Sovereignty Frames and Sovereignty Claims.” University of Edinburgh, School of Law, Working Papers, 2013.

Weber, Cynthia. “Reconsidering Statehood: Examining the Sovereignty/Intervention Boundary.” *Review of International Studies* 18 (1992): 199–216.

Weber, Cynthia. “Writing Sovereign Identities: Wilson Administration Intervention in the Mexican Revolution.” *Alternatives: Global, Local, Political* 17 (1992): 313–37.

Weber, Cynthia. *International Relations Theory: A Critical Introduction*. Abingdon: Routledge, 2010.

Zaum, Dominik. *The Sovereignty Paradox: The Norms and Politics of International Statebuilding*. Oxford: Oxford University Press, 2007.

Part II

3 What should "shared sovereignty" mean?

Introduction

If no sovereignty is absolute, all sovereignty is limited to an extent. Chapter 2 showed that one of the ways in which sovereignty is limited is the fact that it can be shared (*e.g.* representatives and represented, the king and the church, etc.). However, how can sovereignty be shared when dealing with states? Unfortunately, there is no single answer but there are various ways in which sovereignty can be shared. That is to say, there are various conceptions of "shared sovereignty." Among all the conceptions of "shared sovereignty," there is one that may be used to solve sovereignty conflicts—that is not out there, this book intends to propose. This chapter discusses a possible way of characterizing "shared sovereignty" in order to address some sovereignty conflicts.

Many scholars in legal and political theory and international relations use the expression "shared sovereignty" and similar terminology to refer to various different realities. It is mainly for this reason, and in order to avoid unnecessary confusion, that these different conceptions will be given a specific name. The list may not be exhaustive and it does not need to be. This is because the aim is solely to illustrate the actual vast use of terms that at first glance appear appropriate in discussing international conflicts. By arguing against these previous views it will be possible to define negatively the features that should denote "shared sovereignty." As a result, this will lead to characterizing the problems that a reconceived conception should address in order to offer a just and fair solution for sovereignty conflicts.

Previous uses of the terminology

The first conception is "neocolonial shared sovereignty." Advocates of this position apply the label "shared sovereignty" to situations in which there is one sovereign state (usually a weak one)[1] and an international organization or another

1 For a view of weak, collapsed, or pseudo-states, *see* Tanja E. Aalberts, "The Sovereignty Game States Play: (Quasi-)States in the International Order," *International Journal for the Semiotics*

state "helping" it in one way or another. In this case, they define it as follows: "[s]hared-sovereignty entities are created by a voluntary agreement between recognized national political authorities and an external actor such as another state or a regional or international organization. Moreover, "[s]uch arrangements can be limited to specific issues areas like monetary policy or the management of oil revenues."[2]

A few characteristics are immediately obvious in the above quotation: Firstly, it is a voluntary actual agreement; second, not all the parties need to be sovereign states (they can be recognized national political authorities, regional, or international organizations); third, it can be limited to specific areas (the examples given are related to economy and finance).[3] Some authors assert that weak states could observe this proposal as a solution to their problems since—they maintain—"[l]eft to their own devices, collapsed and badly governed states will not fix themselves because they have limited administrative capacity, not least with regard to maintaining internal security."[4] Therefore, international organizations or strong states would be supporting the development in certain areas of states that for whatever cause were considered weak.

There are two main reasons why "neocolonial shared sovereignty" is not of use. The first concerns its constitutive elements, since it is applicable to realities that assume two agents: A weak one (a state) and a strong one (another state or an international organization). This book, however, deals with a conflict between two already sovereign states in relation to a populated third territory—*i.e.* it assumes three agents. Second, the implications of defining in such a fashion "shared sovereignty" do not agree with a just and fair way of dealing with sovereignty conflicts. While this account of "shared sovereignty" is theoretically intended to assist weak states and hence may be considered useful—even fair—at first glance, it is both too narrow and too ample: Too narrow in the sense that the

of Law 17 (2004): 245–57; Stephen D. Krasner and Carlos Pascual, "Addressing State Failure," *Foreign Affairs* 84 (2005): 153–63; Paul Collier, "The Political Economy of State Failure," *Oxford Review of Economic Policy* 25 (2009): 219–40; and many others.

2 Stephen D. Krasner, "The Case of Shared Sovereignty," *Journal of Democracy* 16 (2005): 69–83. In particular, incorporating the idea of "shared sovereignty" as characterized by Krasner, *see* Richard Caplan, "From Collapsing States to Neo-Trusteeship: The Limits to Solving the Problem of 'Precarious Statehood' in the 21st Century," *Third World Quarterly* 28 (2007): 231–44; Brennan M. Kraxberger, "Failed States: Temporary Obstacles to Democratic Diffusion or Fundamental Holes in the World Political Map?" *Third World Quarterly* 28 (2007): 1055–71.

3 Analysis regarding applications of this way of interpreting shared sovereignty can be seen in: Hadii Mamudu and Donley T. Studlar, "Multilevel Governance and Shared Sovereignty: European Union, Member States, and the FCTC," *Governance: An International Journal of Policy, Administration, and Institutions* 22 (2009): 73–97; Kari A. Hartwig and others, "AIDS and 'Shared Sovereignty' in Tanzania from 1987 to 2000: A Case Study," *Social Science and Medicine* 60 (2005): 1613–24.

4 Stephen D. Krasner, "Sharing Sovereignty, New Institutions for Collapsed and Failing States," *International Security* 29 (2004): 85–120.

weak state sees its policies being dictated by external authorities without much internal input; too ample since the strong agent has the prerogative to be involved in affairs of the weak one without control other than its own goodwill. For although this model involves already "recognised national political authorities," these scholars presuppose that collapsed or badly governed communities (weak states) cannot dictate for themselves proper policies and create efficient institutions to achieve a sustainable development. So the way to fix these realities—they propose—is to let the strong states be involved in the internal affairs of the weak ones. Yet, instead of presenting shared sovereignty this appears to be a means to dictate to another supposedly sovereign state how to proceed under certain circumstances.

Furthermore, what is clear is the fact that both sovereign states—the weak and the strong one—would not have the same level of authority: The strong sovereign state would be determining the advisable policies to be followed by the weak "sovereign" state. In other words, the "neocolonial shared sovereignty" is unidirectional and unequal (only one of the involved states is the real sovereign, maybe not *de jure* but, at least, *de facto*), resulting in one agent dictating the other's internal policies.

Those who are in favor of "shared sovereignty"—so defined—maintain that humanitarian reasons support this form of international aid. Violation of human rights, natural disasters, and weak economies are only examples of many actual circumstances that make the internal situation of some sovereign states highly volatile. Nevertheless, behind this aura of humanitarian aid strong states would be interfering in the internal affairs of their weak peers. In that sense, other scholars have claimed that: "[t]he idea of 'shared sovereignty' is a novel attempt to formulate a foreign policy of creative intervention by strong states in weak target states."[5] By applying the 'shared sovereignty' label in this way, both states seem to be equally sovereign with one of them—the strong one—assisting the other one by being involved in its internal affairs. But although it may seem at first glance that they are equal sovereign powers, they are only equal in terms of their *de jure* sovereignty; *de facto*, one of the states is determining, or advising, or forcing, or instructing, the other state's way of addressing its internal issues. From that angle, these states are not sharing sovereignty; in fact, only one of them is the ultimate authority in regard to certain issues which are actually supposed to be in the sovereign sphere of the other one. Indeed, the "sharing" may be, or become, involuntary.

Other authors also argue against this way of understanding "shared sovereignty" when it is applied to particular actual cases. When referring to this approach they maintain that "[s]hared sovereignty represents a softer version of (neocolonial)

5 Tod Moore, "Violations of Sovereignty and Regime Engineering: A Critique of the State Theory of Stephen Krasner," *Australian Journal of Political Science* 44 (2009): 497–511.

international and transitional administration . . ."[6] Leaving aside the discussion about the specificities related to particular cases, the common thread is that in all instances the local governments follow policies created by authorities not part of their legal system (other sovereign states and/or regional and international organizations). Consequently, to understand "shared sovereignty" as a way in which a strong state "assists" a weak peer does not seem to agree with the nature of the concept itself. The whole theory has been developed so as to justify what may result in a violation of state sovereignty. In fact, to give the strong states a new legal and political device such as this way of understanding "shared sovereignty" means simply to justify their international neocolonial policies in relation to weaker states. Moreover, it is incompatible even with recent modified classifications of types of sovereignty.[7]

This project—on the contrary—aims to offer all the involved agents an equal footing[8] at the outset, so as to reach a final agreement just and fair in its contents as well as in its application. For this reason, the model proposed here is based on a voluntary hypothetical agreement among the agents who take part in a sovereignty conflict and therefore it would be unreasonable for any party to reject its outcome. Thus, the agreement is only among already sovereign states with the inclusion of a nonsovereign agent such as the population of the third territory (no international organization has any participation). Additionally, there will not be any distinction between strong and weak agents in the decisionmaking process—*i.e.* no criterion will be used in order to differentiate in any way the participant agents in that respect as it is assumed their representatives will be free and equal, following Rawls's methodology in Chapter 6. Finally, the arrangements are not limited to certain areas but they include all activities related to the third territory (not only territory, but also population and government and all that each of them involves).

A particularly interesting application of the term "shared sovereignty" is the case of divided societies or "cultural shared sovereignty" (*e.g.* Northern Ireland

6 Oliver P. Richmond, "Shared Sovereignty and the Politics of Peace: Evaluating the EU's 'Catalytic' Framework in the Eastern Mediterranean," *International Affairs* 82 (2005): 149–76. For another critic of Krasner's notion of shared sovereignty, *see* Moore (n. 5).

7 Stephen D. Krasner, *Power, the State and Sovereignty: Essays on International Relations* (Abingdon: Routledge, 2009). Originally, Krasner sees four different conceptions of sovereignty: (a) Domestic sovereignty: referring to the organization of public authority within a state and the level of effective control exercised by those holding authority; (b) Interdependence sovereignty: referring to the ability of public authorities to control transborder movements; (c) International legal sovereignty: referring to the mutual recognition by states; (d) Westphalian sovereignty: referring to the exclusion of external agents from domestic authority. *See* Stephen D. Krasner, *Sovereignty: Organized Hypocrisy* (Princeton NJ: Princeton University Press, 1999).

8 By "equal footing" is meant that all the participants in the model either will have equal rights and obligations before reaching the final agreement and once the agreement is in place; or that they may have different rights and obligations to which they equally agree and which are equally respected. The characterization of the equal rights and obligations will be analyzed in due course—in particular in Chapters 6 and 7.

with two clearly defined sectors, that of the nationalists, mainly Roman Catholics, and that of the unionists, mainly Protestants). This model applies to two ethnic or nationality groups living in the same territory neither of which wants to belong to a state dominated by the other.[9] Thus, it contemplates the existence of two communities within a single state (or in the case of Northern Ireland, in a single sub-state) who deal with their divisions by sharing in the exercise of political authority. Additionally, it gives a hint of how to deal with power-sharing institutions by including sharing groups and differentiating them between compulsory and voluntary.

On the positive side, the institutional scheme of the "cultural shared sovereignty" offers all the claimants certain degrees of participation. It is not easy to imagine how the institutions would work in practice but, in principle, and at least in theory, it seems a potentially just and fair solution. In spite of this, the model is constructed on the basis of a particular context that, although seemingly ideal as a whole, assumes a divided society that takes into account two populations with different ethnic or national elements that result in mutual exclusion. So, despite initial amplitude, "cultural shared sovereignty" leaves aside cases of contested sovereignty over territories with other realities—*e.g.* a homogeneous population living in a geographically separated territory that does not want to integrate into a certain sovereign state.

The model developed in this book differs in actual and ideal terms. In actual terms, there are not two but three groups of people living in different territories. More specifically, there is a "third party" at issue: The population of the third territory. In that sense, there may be not just two interests in conflict but three, that of each of the two sovereign states and that of the population of the third territory, which may be opposed to each other—*e.g.* the population of the third territory aiming for independence, whereas the two sovereign states aim for incorporation. In ideal terms, this book leaves aside factual circumstances so as to offer a really equal starting point since it assumes diversity in each of the competing populations—*e.g.* ethnic background, religion, language. Even more, it leaves aside the historical arguments in relation to sovereignty the claimants often introduce in sovereignty conflicts so as to avoid endless discussion—*i.e.* how to agree what historical account is accurate or what principle of distribution is fair, depending on considering the territory in question *res nullius* or *res communis.* Then, the conditions in which the characteristics of shared sovereignty will be agreed are guaranteed to be fair and just, with no reference to special features of any kind.

A further conception is more related to human rights and it is labeled here as "moral shared sovereignty." Some scholars maintain that human rights, in particular those concerned with minorities, affect the concept of sovereignty. From there, they try to apply the notion of shared sovereignty in order to

9 Anthony Oberschall, "Preventing Genocide," *Contemporary Sociology* 29 (2000): 1–13.

secure the respect for an individual as a unique human being—and all that this implies. The following quotation illustrates the point:

> [m]inority demands have become driving forces in the process of the changing of the international framework of relations and law, because the concept of sovereignty and the notions of minorities are . . . interrelated and intertwined. . . . Minority demands for a change of their status, therefore, automatically means an infringement of the notion of sovereignty.[10]

This statement contains a strong claim: Minorities must have right against the majority, and therefore there are some principles that the majority cannot override. Nonetheless, even if that postulate is accepted, this does not necessarily mean that the state as a whole is not still sovereign. That is because, although this position highlights the importance of minorities within the state, it does not add anything new. Societies are all constituted by minorities. In fact, from an extreme point of view, every single individual belongs to different minorities. Communities are formed by the aggregation, for different reasons, of smaller societal groups, such as families. These small societal cells must have a certain level of concord among them and respect for the established authorities in order for a society to be achieved and developed (in legal theory, to have effectiveness or efficacy).[11] The normative system is only one of the elements that is added to the whole picture as a frame of rules to determine ways of behaving as a member of a social organization. However, the key in this kind of interpretation is not the legal system but the population itself: The individuals that form the population of a given sovereign state owe each other reciprocal respect, no matter whether they are part of the majority or a minority; from there, individuals of different sovereign states and sovereign states themselves also owe each other reciprocal respect.

It is at this point in the argument that this line of thinking includes the notion of "shared sovereignty" when affirming that: "[t]he overarching idea of respect for human dignity, and its practical implications of ensuring security, identity, and a continuous and sustainable development of the individual human being in relation to the new social function of the State, forms the basis for a notion of shared sovereignty."[12] Once again, another well known set of principles that could be labeled as "human rights" are included in the legal theory. The only divergence is that in this case the author identifies "shared sovereignty" with the attitude the global community should have in order to live in a peaceful environment.

10 Wolf Mannens, "Minority Claims and State Authority," in: Gerard Kreijen (ed.), *State, Sovereignty, and International Governance* (Oxford: Oxford University Press, 2002), p. 157.

11 The concepts "validity" and "effectiveness" are used in the present piece of writing with a Kelsenian meaning. *See* Hans Kelsen's *General Theory of Law and State* and *Introduction to the Problems of Legal Theory*.

12 *See* Mannens (n. 10), p. 159.

Despite the fact that the final intention of this interpretation is worthy, the term "shared sovereignty" defined in this manner has a meaning not suitable for the kind of conflicts approached here. This concept implies a form of shared responsibility between individuals, a state as a societal organization, and mankind as component of a global community, which requires everyone to respect and defend human rights (in particular the rights of the people belonging to minorities—without giving a clear definition). In plain terms this conceptualization means a universally shared moral responsibility that involves respect for diversity and aims at a global concord under the protection of human rights (similar indeed to Kantian principles). Although this is a desirable way to see international relations, it is not broad enough to offer a solution to sovereignty conflicts for two reasons: (a) sovereignty conflicts are not only a question of human rights; (b) some sovereignty conflicts may in fact leave aside the question about human rights—*e.g.* when the competing parties are dictatorships.

"Shared sovereignty" in the model proposed in this book also includes protecting the claimed rights of the competing populations, and in particular those of a minority—*i.e.* the population of the third territory. But it is not limited to human rights. It aims to take into consideration the interests of all the involved agents and to offer a way of acknowledging their claimed rights. To be more precise, it is taken for granted that all of them have a right to claim sovereignty over the third territory. That is different, however, from saying that they have sovereign rights. As the evaluation of their claims and the extent of their respective sovereign rights—if granted—over the third territory will be discussed among the agents in the negotiations held to that effect under particular circumstances—their representatives will be free and equal, and the agreement reached will have a more robust permanent feature since it would be unreasonable to reject it.[13]

Another concept that appears to be similar at first glance to "shared sovereignty" is "dual sovereignty."[14] This concept is present in the literature of the United States of America. It refers to the phenomenon of having both local and national authorities and legal orders and to the way they interact with each other. But this concept is not appropriate for this book. Despite the fact the states (or provinces in other countries) reserve certain prerogatives in some instances (*e.g.* natural resources, local administration, regional services) the ultimate authority remains in the central government (President, Congress and Supreme Court) for some other issues (*e.g.* to declare war, to hear extraordinary appeals). Consequently,

13 For the difference between principles "which no one could reasonably reject" and principles "which everyone could reasonably accept," *see* T. M. Scanlon, "Contractualism and Utilitarianism," in: Amartya Sen and Bernard Williams (eds.), *Utilitarianism and Beyond* (Cambridge: Cambridge University Press; Paris: Editions de la Maison des Sciences de l'Homme, 1982).

14 Richard E. Levy, *The Power to Legislate. A Reference Guide to the United States Constitution* (Westport CT: Greenwood Press, 2006), pp. 35–38; John J. Parker, "Dual Sovereignty and the Federal Courts," *Northwestern University Law Review* 51 (1956): 407–23; and many others.

there are not two equal sovereigns but always one real ultimate authority, although which it is depends on the issue. For instance, the state or province may have ultimate authority over its natural resources and the central government may have ultimate authority over citizenship.

In both cases, if another sovereign state wanted to achieve an international agreement about natural resources it would have to deal with the representatives of the states or provinces; if only citizenship issues were involved, the state's central government would be playing the main role. In neither of the cases would the decision be a joint one. It may be objected that the state or province could use its power over natural resources to force the federal government to do what it wants on immigration—or vice versa; however, if that happened it would only prove that there is one and only one sovereign in regard to the issues in federal organizations—either the states or the central government. So, if any of them wanted something to be done in relation to an issue out of the scope of their sovereign powers, they would need the actual sovereign in regard to that specific issue to act upon it.

This seems only a semantic issue related to the meaning of concepts rather than what the legal institutions imply. Thus, even if it was accepted that this type of sovereignty was dual, it would only be dual internally—at national or municipal law level. The duality might be between two parts of the same national legal system: State or province law and federal law. In contrast, this monograph focuses on the relation between two national and independent legal systems as a whole in what matters specifically to law. Thus, it contemplates many other elements that characterize the sovereign states involved and the populated third territory.

A different combination of terms that could also mislead the reader is the expression "bi-polar sovereignty."[15] Although it does refer to sovereignty it is in relation to the division of powers, the sovereignty a state has between its legislative and judicial powers. For this book, such analysis is not relevant, because it is only concerned with the sovereignty of only one given state—internal sovereignty. There is no sovereignty conflict in the sense of an international issue but only in adjudication of domestic or national law. This monograph, on the contrary, has to deal also with the external facet in the sense that outside parties are always involved.

The meaning of "shared sovereignty" in this book

Having explained what "shared sovereignty" is not, it is now time to focus on what a reconceived conception should learn from the previous section. It is clear now that "shared sovereignty" does not mean the decision of only one of the

15 C. J. S. Knight, "Striking Down Legislation Under Bi-Polar Sovereignty," *Public Law* (2011): 90–114; C. J. S. Knight, "Bi-Polar Sovereignty Restated," *Cambridge Law Journal* 68 (2009): 361–87; Richard Mullender, "A State of Distress? The Judiciary, the Executive, and the Constitution," *Bracton Law Journal* 28 (1996): 7–26.

agents—unilateral—or imply an unbalanced situation between them or unequal sharing—only one agent is *de jure* and *de facto* sovereign.

It is the center of the model under analysis that provides the answer: The third territory. Contrary to what is required in other sovereignty conflicts, the model of shared sovereignty proposed here has to deal with a territory that does not have sovereignty over itself, but with two already sovereign states arguing over their claimed rights. So, their sovereignty over their respective spheres of influence is not discussed in any way; only their claimed rights over the nonsovereign territory. Ergo, the agents will have to take one of two options: Exclusive or shared rights over the territory. And following the latter option, if they decide to share their claimed rights over the third territory, then all of the agents will have a portion or share of its sovereignty.

The remainder of this chapter will highlight the criteria that the conception of "shared sovereignty" should fulfill in order to provide a plausible solution to sovereignty conflicts. These criteria are based on the weak points that other conceptions of "shared sovereignty" present, and are to be used to solve them. The content of the model will be discussed later in this book when it is introduced in particular how the agents would operate should they go into negotiations.[16]

First, the model should guarantee that both claiming sovereign states do genuinely share their rights and obligations over the third territory, and that they do so on an equal footing. This postulate can either mean that all the agents will have both at the onset and once the agreement is reached equal rights and obligations—in relation to the third territory—or that although they may have different rights and obligations in either or both cases—the starting point and the reached agreement—they equally and freely agree upon them and are willing to respect the final decision. This indicates that the agreement must not be merely actually but hypothetically voluntary too so that all the parties not only do agree but also they would agree if they were free and equal agents, even if in fact they are not.

Second, the model should respect the classical nonintervention[17] approach related to sovereignty. In fact, the notion of sovereignty as supreme authority remains unfettered—although sovereignty is not absolute, according to Chapter 2.

16 The hypothetical negotiations the agents would have are developed in Chapter 6.

17 It refers to the nonintervention principle in international public law. In brief, a state should not interfere in any way in the internal affairs of any other sovereign state. *See* UN Charter, art. 2.7: "Nothing contained in the present Charter shall author the United Nations to intervene in matters which are essentially within the domestic jurisdiction of any state or shall require the Members to submit such matters to settlement under the present Charter; but this principle shall not prejudice the application of enforcement measures under Chapter VII." Also stated in the UN General Assembly Resolution 2625 (XXV): "(a) The principle that States shall refrain in their international relations from the threat or use of force against the territorial integrity or political independence of any State, or in any other manner inconsistent with the purposes of the United Nations" and "(c) The duty not to intervene in matters within the domestic jurisdiction of any State . . ."

Yet, the sovereign states will accept limitations in respect to their sovereignty over the third territory so as to let the other agents also secure their interests. That is to say, no state would be interfering with the internal affairs of its peers in the conflict or of the population of the third territory—unless expressly agreed in the hypothetical negotiations that will define the content of the shared sovereignty model. In order to attain that goal, the aim is to develop the idea that through a convention states could agree to share their authority and control over a territory and its population on equal terms,[18] without this involving any kind of interference in their respective spheres of sovereignty.

Third, it should be assumed that sovereign states are internationally equal.[19] Without going into detail about the meaning of this expression, scholarly legal and political literature commonly understands that sovereign states have the same rights and obligations at international level. There are a few exceptions such as the ones created by bi- or multilateral agreements and states' particular factual circumstances (*e.g.* littoral versus inland states).[20]

For the purpose of this book equality has a double meaning: First, what is defined as "equal footing," in the sense that the third territory, as the "object" to be distributed, grants to the sovereign states involved equal rights to claim a share of the sovereignty over that piece of land (and all that this entails in terms of population and government). However, that does not mean that they will be granted a share of the sovereignty by default or, in the case the sovereign states were granted a share of sovereignty that the shares will be exactly equal—the meaning of this equality and the content of the shares is analyzed elsewhere in this book. Second, the sovereign states will be considered as equal in their mutual relations both because of international customary law and international public law and because of the way they will be characterized in the negotiations and how these are conducted in a frame of peaceful international relations—*e.g.* the claimants will have equal bargaining power in the negotiations, they will not use force, economic threat, or any other form of coercion in their mutual relations, and the decisions will be taken by consensus rather than by majority, etc.

Fourth, the distribution and allocation of the shares of sovereignty will be decided following Rawls's methodology concerning principles of justice and fairness. But, there will be no distinction between weak and strong states in what is referred to as the decisionmaking process since their representatives are considered to be free and equal agents. The reason to proceed in this way is twofold: (1) to grant the involved agents real equal footing in the negotiations in

18 This line of argument has influence from Rawls's works, mainly inspired in his *A Theory of Justice*.

19 UN Charter, art. 2.1: "The Organization is based on the principle of the sovereign equality of all its Members." United Nations General Assembly Resolution 2625 (XXV): "(f) The principle of sovereign equality of States."

20 Hans Kelsen, "The Principle of Sovereign Equality of States as a Basis for International Organization," *Yale Law Journal* 53 (1944): 207–20.

which they decide the extent and contents of the shares of sovereignty—*i.e.* the agents will have the same bargaining power; and (2) also to secure a permanent feature in the agreement reached since it would be unreasonable to reject its outcome. That is because the agreement will be just and fair in the sense that the interests of all the agents will be secured, so that all of them will be willing to respect its content—or at least, it would be unreasonable not do so.

Fifth, the population of the third territory will have representation in the hypothetical negotiations in which the principles governing the shared sovereignty paradigm will be agreed. Their participation must be granted through their representatives. This is not because they are a minority or because they are human beings and as such they have human rights.[21] This is not a question of human rights or whether they will have the same status as the sovereign states. They will have representation in the negotiations because whatever decision is made will have nontrivial impact on their way of life and therefore gives them moral standing to object. In the first place, the model this book intends to develop may be used even in situations in which human rights are blurred or nonexistent—*e.g.* if the two competing sovereign states are dictatorships. In the second place, to grant participation to the inhabitants of the third territory in the negotiations does not mean that they are recognized as a sovereign political organization. In contrast, they must be accepted as a community of human beings without any actual sovereign status but with a potential one. This only means that their right to claim acknowledges either the fact that they actually live in the territory under dispute or they have a relevant title to claim, what this monograph refers later as a "colorable claim." Consequently, the inhabitants of the third territory would have a right to participate in the decisionmaking involving their interests either directly or through their representatives.[22] The consequences of this will be spelt out when the negotiations are introduced in detail later on in this book.

From the above notes, the term "shared sovereignty"—in the context of this work—can be characterized as a fair international remedy to be used in sovereignty conflicts when two sovereign states agree to share in just terms the sovereign rights and obligations over a populated third territory—*i.e.* the sharing may not be exactly equal, but that sharing is such that reasonable parties could not reasonably object to it. This particular conception is called "egalitarian shared sovereignty." Yet, the actual content of this model has to be determined.

21 The Universal Declaration of Human Rights (UDHR) http://www.un.org/en/documents/udhr/index.shtml (last accessed December 30, 2016).

22 The International Covenant on Civil and Political Rights (ICCPR) http://www.ohchr.org/EN/ProfessionalInterest/Pages/CCPR.aspx (last accessed December 30, 2016) art. 21.1. The UDHR states that: "Everyone has the right to take part in the government of his country, directly or through freely chosen representatives"; art. 25.a ICCPR declares that: "Every citizen shall have the right and the opportunity . . . To take part in the conduct of public affairs, directly or through freely chosen representatives . . ."

Conclusion

This chapter examined different conceptions of "shared sovereignty" and similar terms. In all cases there are issues that make these conceptions not viable for the kind of sovereignty conflicts reviewed in this book. To be more precise, these conceptions have characteristics that make them fail to embrace what this book aims for: A fair solution for some kind of sovereignty conflicts.

By reviewing these conceptions, however, several positive outcomes resulted. Indeed, by having acknowledged what "shared sovereignty" as this book needs the term is not, some partial conclusions are drawn in order to understand what issues the new conception should address. So, there emerge criteria that enable to identify when shared sovereignty is just.

The remainder of this book will see if it is possible to construct a new conception of "shared sovereignty" that satisfies the aforementioned criteria. However, in order to do that it is crucial first to see if: (a) sovereign states may cooperate together and limit their freedom without sacrificing their sovereignty; and (b) other international remedies for sovereign conflicts may be desirable for the kind of conflicts that are object of this book.

Bibliography

Aalberts, Tanja E. "The Sovereignty Game States Play: (Quasi-)States in the International Order." *International Journal for the Semiotics of Law* 17 (2004): 245–57.

Caplan, Richard. "From Collapsing States to Neo-Trusteeship: The Limits to Solving the Problem of 'Precarious Statehood' in the 21st Century." *Third World Quarterly* 28 (2007): 231–44.

Collier, Paul. "The Political Economy of State Failure." *Oxford Review of Economic Policy* 25 (2009): 219–40.

Hartwig, Kari A. and others. "AIDS and 'Shared Sovereignty' in Tanzania from 1987 to 2000: A Case Study." *Social Science and Medicine* 60 (2005): 1613–24.

Kelsen, Hans. "The Principle of Sovereign Equality of States as a Basis for International Organization." *Yale Law Journal* 53 (1944): 207–20.

Kelsen, Hans. *General Theory of Law and State*. New York: Russell & Russell, 1945.

Kelsen, Hans. *Introduction to the Problems of Legal Theory*. Oxford: Oxford University Press, 1992.

Knight, C. J. S. "Bi-Polar Sovereignty Restated." *Cambridge Law Journal* 68 (2009): 361–87.

Knight, C. J. S. "Striking Down Legislation Under Bi-Polar Sovereignty." *Public Law* (2011): 90–114.

Krasner, Stephen D. *Sovereignty: Organized Hypocrisy*. Princeton NJ: Princeton University Press, 1999.

Krasner, Stephen D. "Sharing Sovereignty, New Institutions for Collapsed and Failing States." *International Security* 29 (2004): 85–120.

Krasner, Stephen D. "The Case of Shared Sovereignty." *Journal of Democracy* 16 (2005): 69–83.

Krasner, Stephen D. and Pascual, Carlos. "Addressing State Failure." *Foreign Affairs* 84 (2005): 153–63.

Krasner, Stephen D. *Power, the State and Sovereignty: Essays on International Relations.* Abingdon: Routledge, 2009.

Kraxberger, Brennan M. "Failed States: Temporary Obstacles to Democratic Diffusion or Fundamental Holes in the World Political Map?" *Third World Quarterly* 28 (2007): 1055–71.

Levy, Richard E. *The Power to Legislate: A Reference Guide to the United States Constitution.* Westport CT: Greenwood Press, 2006.

Mamudu, Hadii and Studlar, Donley T. "Multilevel Governance and Shared Sovereignty: European Union, Member States, and the FCTC." *Governance: An International Journal of Policy, Administration, and Institutions* 22 (2009): 73–97.

Mannens, Wolf. "Minority Claims and State Authority," in: Gerard Kreijen, ed. *State, Sovereignty, and International Governance.* Oxford: Oxford University Press, 2002.

Moore, Tod. "Violations of Sovereignty and Regime Engineering: A Critique of the State Theory of Stephen Krasner." *Australian Journal of Political Science* 44 (2009): 497–511.

Mullender, Richard. "A State of Distress? The Judiciary, the Executive, and the Constitution." *Bracton Law Journal* 28 (1996): 7–26.

Oberschall, Anthony. "Preventing Genocide." *Contemporary Sociology* 29 (2000): 1–13.

Parker, John J. "Dual Sovereignty and the Federal Courts." *Northwestern University Law Review* 51 (1956): 407–23.

Rawls, John. *A Theory of Justice*, Revised Edition. Oxford: Oxford University Press, 1999.

Richmond, Oliver P. "Shared Sovereignty and the Politics of Peace: Evaluating the EU's 'Catalytic' Framework in the Eastern Mediterranean." *International Affairs* 82 (2005): 149–76.

Scanlon, T. M. "Contractualism and Utilitarianism," in: Amartya Sen and Bernard Williams, eds. *Utilitarianism and Beyond.* Cambridge: Cambridge University Press; Paris: Editions de la Maison des Sciences de l'Homme, 1982.

4 How far can sovereign states cooperate together and limit their freedom without sacrificing their sovereignty?

Introduction

Chapter 2 demonstrated that although sovereignty means supreme authority, that authority always accepts limitations—*i.e.* sovereignty is not absolute. Consequently, sovereignty is always—to an extent—shared. However, Chapter 3 showed that the way in which sovereignty may be shared is not always just, fair, or offering the participant agents the same relative situation—*e.g.* if there is unbalanced or unilateral sharing, when only one of the agents is actually dictating how to proceed. So, it is necessary for the success of the "egalitarian shared sovereignty" model to demonstrate how these limitations work, and also, that they do not imply involuntary interference with the sovereignty of any of the participant agents. Therefore, before defining the model of "egalitarian shared sovereignty" in detail, a question must be answered: How multiple agents can cooperate together, limit their freedom without negative consequences either *de jure* or *de facto*, so that none of the agents dictates to the other parties what to do or not to do.

This problem arises because sovereignty is mainly seen as a concept that implies a single agent, limited in one way or another. However, this book assumes the existence of multiple agents that will have an equal relative position in respect of the third territory—*i.e.* a plurality of agents that have equal power, that are simultaneously at the same level—legally speaking, that are sovereign at the same time over the same territory and population.

In order to demonstrate how two sovereign states can share their sovereignty—*i.e.* how far sovereign states can cooperate together and limit their freedom without sacrificing their sovereignty—it is convenient to see: (a) first, what the concept of "sovereignty" means and implies by examining its subatomic or fundamental elements; and (b) second, how a concept with similar features operates and accepts limitations without changing its nature. The former will be achieved by using Wesley N. Hohfeld language for legal analysis.[1] By mastering a

1 Wesley Newcomb Hohfeld, "Some Fundamental Legal Conceptions as Applied in Judicial Reasoning," *Yale Law Journal* (1913): 16–59; and Wesley Newcomb Hohfeld, "Fundamental Legal Conceptions as Applied in Judicial Reasoning," *Yale Law Journal* (1917): 710–70.

number of basic legal concepts it will be possible to analyze a complex one such as "sovereignty," avoid misunderstandings with regards to its meaning and implications, and have a more clearly defined picture of how limitations operate without changing its nature. The latter, by reference to "self-ownership" as a concept.[2]

As in the case of sovereignty, self-ownership establishes a particular relationship between an agent and something: Supreme authority. Unlike sovereignty, this supreme authority is present at the level of the individual. In other words, self-ownership defines the supreme authority an individual has over himself; sovereignty defines the supreme authority a state has over a territory and people. Thus, at first glance both self-ownership and sovereignty appear to be supreme, singular, and hence not shareable. More explicitly, self-ownership has the same kind of relation to an individual that sovereignty has to a state: Both self-ownership and sovereignty are essential characteristics in defining a free individual and a free state, respectively. Then, if limitations in the form of self- or external constraints can be applied to self-ownership, limitations in the form of self- and external obligations can be applied to sovereignty. In consequence, as self- or externally imposed limitations in regard to self-ownership allow any individual to cooperate with any other individual, so self- or externally imposed obligations on sovereignty enable a state to cooperate with other states too without diminishing its sovereignty.

A Hohfeldian take on sovereignty

Hohfeld offered a simplistic yet illuminating way to study "law" by reviewing its terminological framework and reducing the concept to its constituent elements. Therefore, colorful descriptions and value judgments were left aside. To be more precise, Hohfeld did not redefine these constituent elements; he just made them evident by stripping down what was not essential in defining them. Similarly, this section will put aside terminological misunderstandings in relation to "sovereignty" by applying the Hohfeldian methodology and findings.

Hohfeld started by differentiating factual from legal relations. Indeed, he simply made clear the distinction between the world of the rule and the world of the facts. That is to say, on the one hand, any change in the world which may be independent of our will—*i.e.* fact *sensu stricto*—or manifested as a consequence or result of voluntary physical movements or a voluntary abstention—*i.e.* act or omission. On the other hand, the aforementioned facts and acts or omissions considered as legal relations in the sense they are center of imputative rules—*i.e.* in very basic terms, because an individual does or omits to do X a given consequence Y ought to follow. The former are in the world of the senses, while the

2 Self-ownership or property in one's own person, also defined as individual sovereignty. For a thorough analysis, *see* Allan Cohen, *Self-Ownership, Freedom and Equality* (Cambridge: Cambridge University Press, 1995).

latter are purely intellectual creations. For example, a collision in the world of the facts is represented as "tort" in the world of the rule, a piece of paper may be either a contract or a will, and the place an individual lives in could be related to "property" or "possession." Similarly, "sovereignty" may be referred to a populated piece of land or to the rights and obligations that "territory" entails. To be more precise, but without entering into detail at this point, a group of human beings does not "own" the piece of land they occupy—*i.e.* a physical entity—but that "population" *has various rights and obligations*—*i.e.* legal relations—with regard to the "territory"—*i.e.* a legal entity—that relates to the physical space that piece of land occupies.

In due turn, Hohfeld introduces different kinds of facts; that is to say (a) operative facts; (b) facts in issue; and (c) evidential facts. The first group of facts—*i.e.* operative—refers to any fact, specific or particular, that because of its mere existence causes new legal relations. The second group of facts—*i.e.* in issue—is always generic and the facts that are determined by the proof of particular or specific operative facts. Finally, the third group of facts—*i.e.* evidential—refers to any fact that may prove the existence of other facts; these are the ones that appear before a court when dealing with a case.

Combining the factual relations and the legal relations together with the aforementioned classification—*i.e.* operative facts, facts in issue, and evidential facts—the *subatomic particles* can be identified. In other words, when it is said that a certain legal relation exists, it is implied the existence of certain facts too. For example, if A kills B, it is possible to foresee that the police may intervene and start an investigation, that a court may give judgment, and that A may spend the rest of his life behind bars. Similarly, in international relations, if sovereign State A invades sovereign State B's territory, it is possible to foresee that international organizations, State B, or any other state may intervene with international sanctions—*e.g.* war, blockade. Specifically referred to the last example, and to push the things further, because of mainstream understanding in legal and political sciences that "sovereignty" is a concept that implies a single agent, limited in one way or another, it is at least difficult to see how two sovereign states may cooperate, surrender part of their freedom, and still be considered fully sovereign.

It is assumed that, because sovereign State A has exclusive prerogatives over its territory, sovereign State B should not intrude and therefore has the duty to stay out. But what about if sovereign State A had invited sovereign State B to enter? Applied to sovereignty conflicts such as the Falklands/Malvinas, Gibraltar, Kashmir, and many others—*i.e.* those sovereignty conflicts in which two already sovereign states argue over the sovereignty of a populated third territory, what if sovereign State A and sovereign State B agreed upon cooperating, surrendering their freedom over the disputed and populated third territory, and making mutual concessions? This case is perfectly plausible both in the realm of the facts and in that of the law since in Hohfeldian terms each sovereign party would be granting its peers a set of "privileges."

In very basic terms, there are three main deontic modes[3] that may characterize any legal relation, that is (a) permission; (b) prohibition; (c) obligation. Applied to a concept such as "sovereignty," this means:

(a) What sovereign State A *may* do with regards to its populated territory.
(b) What sovereign State A *must not* do with regards to its populated territory.
(c) What sovereign State A *must* do with regards to its populated territory.

This very simplistic analysis including the three main deontic modes is far from a complete picture both in the world of the facts and the world of the rules—*i.e.* what about what other parties such as other sovereign states *may*, *must not*, and *must* do or not to do with regards to sovereign State A's populated territory? Similarly, what *any* party or any sovereign state *may*, *must not*, and *must* do or not to do with regards to a nonsovereign populated third territory such as the Falklands/Malvinas, Gibraltar, Kashmir? Indeed, the three basic deontic modes are not enough to offer a complete conceptual picture.

Hohfeld, however, considered this *gap* in the legal analysis, and offered a more robust and complete way of characterizing these relations with his four pairs of jural opposites and four pairs of jural correlatives. In schematic terms: (Figure 4.1).

Applied to international relations and sovereign states it means that:

(a) If sovereign State A may act in a certain way over its territory, therefore all other sovereign states have no-right over the same piece of land.
(b) In more complete terms, if sovereign State A may act in a certain way over its territory, therefore all other sovereign states have no-right over the same piece of land. That is to say, sovereign State A has a privilege with respect to any other sovereign state, and therefore all other sovereign states have no-right over the same piece of land.
(c) Yet in more complete terms, if sovereign State A may act in a certain way over its territory, therefore all other sovereign states have no-right over the same piece of land. That is to say, sovereign State A has a privilege with respect to any other sovereign state, and therefore all other sovereign states have no-right over the same piece of land. Therein, all other sovereign states have a duty with regards to sovereign State A and its territory.

	(1)	(2)	(3)	(4)
JURAL OPPOSITES	Right No-right	Privilege Duty	Power Disability	Immunity Liability
	(1)	(2)	(3)	(4)
JURAL CORRELATIVES	Right Duty	Privilege No-right	Power Liability	Immunity Disability

Figure 4.1

3 *See* Pablo Navarro and Jorge Rodriguez, *Deontic Logic and Legal Systems* (Cambridge: Cambridge University Press, 2014).

(d) Similarly, if sovereign State A must conduct itself in a certain way, it has a duty to any other sovereign state, and therefore any other sovereign state has a right against sovereign State A.
(e) If by its voluntary conduct sovereign State A can change sovereign State B's legal relations with A, sovereign State A has a legal power and B has a liability.
(f) If sovereign State A cannot by its own voluntary conduct change the legal relations of sovereign State B, then sovereign State A has a disability and B has an immunity.

Although in principle, "sovereignty" appears to imply a single agent, limited in one way or another, that has ultimate power over a given piece of land—*i.e.* one has the right, all others have no-right—the combination of privileges and immunities shows the fully conceptual complexity of this term. That is to say, a given sovereign state may be in principle considered as the exclusive, single agent with regards to a piece of land; but that does not preclude the possibility that the same sovereign state shares that power, cooperates with, or surrenders part of its freedom over a piece of land to other peers, without changing the fact that it is still fully sovereign.

So far, sovereign states may somehow limit their freedom through privileges and immunities. But how far can their freedom be limited? The next sections will show how sovereign states may introduce limitations to their power over a territory, may cooperate, but that does not mean their sovereignty will be blurred or eroded. On the contrary, it is because of these limitations of different nature that a complete understanding of a complex concept such as "sovereignty" in the world of the rules is gained and may be able to offer an answer to sovereignty conflicts in the world of the facts.

From the smallest to the largest societal organization

The previous chapters showed that sovereignty is limited (Chapter 2) and that these limitations may result in different conceptions of shared sovereignty (Chapter 3). The main obstacle for the kind of conception of shared sovereignty needed in sovereignty conflicts is that sovereignty, even conceived as being limited, is mainly assumed to imply a singular supreme authority. But the model proposed here needs a plurality of sovereign agents seen as supreme authority over the third territory that somehow cooperate together, limit their freedom, and still remain sovereign.

At the individual level there is already a similar situation and that situation has been solved by the way in which individual sovereignty is understood. It is for that reason that the following paragraphs will introduce two different kinds of agents: (a) individuals; and (b) states. Although at first glance they may appear different, they are similar in what is important for this book. Both individuals and states have supreme authority over themselves. Furthermore, both individuals and states have relationships of different kinds with their respective peers. Therein, by working out in parallel the way in which individuals may cooperate together with other individuals, limit their freedom, and still be considered to have supreme authority over themselves, in the same manner states may cooperate together with other states, limit their freedom, and still have supreme authority.

An individual and a state are different in many ways, yet similar in some important aspects. In what is specific to the social, legal, political, and moral spheres, an individual offers four different levels of analysis: (a) in their individuality (I); (b) in their relationship with their peers (you and I); (c) in their relationships as part of a community or society (us, from an internal aspect); (d) as a member of a community or society that has relations with other communities or societies (us, from an external aspect). Sovereign states can be analyzed in the same way: (a) in their individuality (internal affairs); (b) in their relationships with their peers (bi- or multilateral agreements); (c) in their relationships as part of the international community (from within their boundaries); (d) as members of the international community (not only related to other states but also to other international agents). A conflict of interest between individuals or states can only happen when more than one agent is involved. Sovereignty disputes are a conflict of interest.

At this point, a hypothetical situation is introduced to show how human interrelation implies shared values and actions in order to fulfill certain goals. The starting point in this hypothetical situation is a world inhabited by three participants named Adam, Eve, and Lilith. They will be defined as sovereign individuals so as to see how their relationships can be developed as pure individuals in solitude or in a joint context and the consequences in each case.

It could be argued that Adam and Eve were the first family. According to the Old Testament, God created Adam as the first man on earth. Following Jewish folklore, Lilith was the first woman created by God and the first wife of Adam. However, as Lilith refused to submit her sovereignty (she was not prepared to become subservient to Adam) she had to leave the Garden of Eden. Thereafter, Eve was created from Adam's spare rib with the consequence that she was more compliant to the will of Adam. Within the aforementioned story it is possible to observe three individual and sovereign figures. There was a conflict of interest among them. One of them did not surrender her sovereignty (or part of it) and, as a consequence, she was cast aside from society. The other two people agreed to share sovereignty (without arguing here to what extent) and they gave birth to a society in their own image.

For the reader, a literal interpretation of the preceding story would be that Eve surrendered her sovereignty, or indeed that she had little sovereignty to surrender having been made from Adam in the first place. It may be also argued against this example that their interrelation is loaded—*i.e.* it has baggage concerning gender relations. But the participants of the story are seen here from a Nietzschean perspective[4] of a sovereign individual, so these characters are free

4 Friedrich Nietzsche, *On the Genealogy of Morality* (Indianapolis/Cambridge: Hackett Publishing Company Inc., 1998), pp. 36–39.

beings. They each have free will and each stand by their word. In consequence, they are autonomous and independent free beings with the free will to decide to remain in solitude without any kind of interrelation, to join in any kind of enterprise or to remain in solitude but being opposed to each other. So, there are three possible options for them to choose:

(a) To become enemies.
(b) To become neither enemies nor allies.
(c) To become allies.

In the first scenario, if Adam and Eve became enemies they would not only compete with each other and each need defense from the other one, but also have no allies against other external dangers. Moreover, as they were the only ones of their species, the whole species would be condemned to extinction—assuming they were from different genders.

The second option would see Adam and Eve in a situation of neutrality. From this standpoint each would not compete or attempt to damage the other one; so they would not be a mutual threat. If it was also assumed there were enough resources for both of them to cover their subsistence necessities, they would not suffer from scarcity or starvation. However, as in the previous scenario, if total neutrality was the background there would not be any mutual advantageous activities—*e.g.* commerce, trade, sexual intercourse, reciprocal protection from outsider threats; hence they would be the object of other species' needs, they would have to endure the environment on their own, and their species would again be condemned to extinction. It is true that they might meet and separate after sexual intercourse like some animals do or choose to do certain other activities for a particular reason and over a period of time. However, the key feature in this situation remains the same: Although they may agree to do certain things together, there will be no constraint on either Adam or Eve to fulfill any obligation in respect of the other.

To be allies is the third option: Two people may decide to be together for several different reasons and possibilities. In an extreme scenario in which there were only two human beings on earth, what is obvious is that—even in the case of conflicts of interest—by having an agreement and staying together they would be able to join forces so as to defend themselves from common threats and attacks, to obtain and mutually provide food and shelter, and finally to propagate the species. It may be argued that in this case—alliance—the agreement could be pursued as a game of chicken, that is, a mixed game of conflict and cooperation. There might be more than one way to cooperate and, these ways might offer differing payoffs, so that one player is better off under one method of cooperation and the other player is better off under the other, even though both are better off under either of the two than if they refused to cooperate.

It may be even the case that, although the participants are both better off if they cooperate, each is better off still if the other cooperates by being subservient. In one case or the other, both sovereign individuals are together in the enterprise. Indeed, the task is to define the extent of the agreement—*e.g.* equal or unequal rights and obligations—and that will be discussed in due turn in this book. However, the point has been shown: It is advisable for them to limit their individual sovereignty—which does not mean to diminish it. In other words, by giving up some autonomy, both Adam and Eve would have a more ample range of possibilities from which to choose. Similarly, individuals can have a situation where they can give themselves more options now by limiting their options in the future.[5]

In an extended picture with more participants, they would basically have the same options open to them; the difference would be given in terms of who their enemy or ally would be. Individuals would group together (for whatever reason) in what may be called aggregations.[6] These groups of people or aggregations would at the same time have interrelations with other peers in three possible ways: As enemies, neutral, or allies. Social contract theories follow this line of reasoning.

Bearing in mind the notion of "sovereign individual" sketched at the beginning of this section (free beings with free will who stand by their word) if an individual decides to have an alliance of any sort with another individual rather than being enemies or remaining neutral to each other, they are both accepting the limit of part of their sovereignty for the achievement of an agreement—they accept limitations so as to live together in concord with other individuals, whether the agreement is for mutual or individual benefit. They still seem to be fully sovereign individuals; they can at any time and in any case withdraw from being part of the agreement; they decide freely to have interrelations with other individual under certain circumstances. Then, to what extent is the individual sovereignty curtailed in joint enterprises?

Mutatis mutandis the same reasoning can be followed at states' level. In the hypothetical situation in which there were only two sovereign states in the world they would have the same options open to them. *Brevitatis causa*, these states as the individuals in the previous example are sovereign in the sense they have supreme authority over themselves—*i.e.* free "beings" with free will to choose to do or not to do. Ergo, the same questions can be asked in regard to the state and its interrelation with its peers and other international agents. Any state has always the option to develop any kind of relationship in the international arena, whether as enemy, neutral or ally. Thus, any state can always exercise its sovereignty in regard to any issue in a joint venture with its peers. Whenever a sovereign state agrees upon a certain matter and frames that agreement in an international accord, it is only exercising its sovereignty. At the same time, and exactly because it is a sovereign international agent, it can withdraw its participation from such an

5 *See* Mark R. Reiff, *Punishment, Compensation, and Law: A Theory of Enforceability* (Cambridge: Cambridge University Press, 2005), pp. 49–50; Thomas C. Schelling, *The Strategy of Conflict* (Cambridge MA: Harvard University Press, 1960), pp. 21–52, *esp.* p. 43; Charles Fried, *Contract as Promise* (Cambridge MA: Harvard University Press, 1981), pp. 13–14; Jon Elster, *The Cement of Society* (Cambridge: Cambridge University Press, 1989), pp. 272–73.

6 *See* Robert Nozick, *Anarchy, State and Utopia* (New York: Basic Books, 1974), *esp.* Part I, Chapter 2.

agreement. In other words, states may find themselves committed because of previous agreements but they may resign unilaterally, make new agreements, or even violate the agreements' original terms. Indeed, these actions may cause consequences for its international prestige, but this is independent from the fact that they still are fully sovereign.

From the previous paragraphs it is clear that individuals—and, on a larger scale, states—are sovereign in the sense they have autonomous free will to choose to act or not to act. However, owing to the fact there are different individuals/ states with different strengths and necessities, it may be convenient for them to associate with other peers. And this implies relationships that somehow limit their sovereignty. The challenge now is to demonstrate how these limitations do not change the nature of sovereignty at individual and state levels.

Self-ownership, sovereignty, and different types of constraints

The hypothetical situations developed in the previous section sketched how individuals—in large part, states—can have relationships of different kinds with their respective peers. So far, a first preliminary conclusion: Both sovereign individuals and sovereign states may cooperate together with their respective peers; they may even enter into commitments and "somehow" limit their freedom. But how far can their freedom be limited?

It is important to show that (a) the limitations on sovereignty are inevitable—*i.e.* it is not just that up to now sovereignty has always been limited, but that for states to operate together it must be; and (b) that there are limitations on sovereignty which do not mean that the state is no longer sovereign.

The following paragraphs will show how different sorts of constraints or limitations operate in relation to sovereign individuals and sovereign states. There are many ways in which these constraints or limitations may be classified. The classification of these constraints or limitations is based here on a very simple and broad criterion: By whom they are imposed. The only goal at this point is to better illustrate with a simple classification how these limitations or constraints operate and differentiate from each other. Only after having a general understanding of this kind of limitations the focus will be more specific to their meaning in legal and political sciences.

In general, sovereign individuals and sovereign states may have two kinds of constraints—*i.e.* their freedom can be limited by: (a) self-imposed constraints; (b) externally imposed constraints.

The first group of constraints can be characterized as those by which a sovereign individual—or a sovereign state—voluntary curtails his/its freedom. For instance, the case in which an agent enters voluntarily into commitments with others—in our examples, to become allies. Indeed, relations between sovereign states would be impossible without these agreements.

The second group of constraints are those imposed either by: (1) other sovereign individuals or sovereign states; (2) the context or the environment they are part of—specifically for this book, the national or international scenario they are members of.

The first sub-group of externally imposed constraints refer to what sovereign individuals or sovereign states can legitimately do in relation to their peers or what others can legitimately do to them. The second sub-group of externally imposed constraints have to do with facts and rules that either sovereign individuals or sovereign states have to deal with only because they are members of a certain national or the international community—*e.g.* states find themselves subject to international public law and newly formed states have to comply with pre-existing international law; an individual is born in a certain country and has to comply with the pre-existing law of that country.

A common feature that the two examples in the previous section have is that the sovereign individuals and sovereign states were part of imaginary situations. From there, it is relatively easy to recognize the first group of constraints—*i.e.* the ones that either sovereign individuals or sovereign states impose on themselves. Indeed, they are voluntary and self-imposed, since sovereign individuals and sovereign states limit their freedom without any external imposition—*i.e.* they freely decide to cooperate with each other.

A different scenario is given when either a sovereign individual or a sovereign state "accepts" a limitation. That is because "accepting" implies external interference, whether from another agent or the context.

Ergo, for the purpose of this project, in the case of self-imposed limitations the freedom of sovereign individuals and sovereign states is limited in their individuality—*i.e.* I. In contrast, in the case of externally imposed limitations the freedom of sovereign individuals and sovereign states is limited in matters relating to their peers—*i.e.* you and I; or in their relationship with the context—*i.e.* I, us, the nation, the international community.

The following paragraphs will review the way these different types of constraints operate in relation to sovereign individuals and sovereign states.

The first kind of limitation that does not destroy sovereignty is one that is self-imposed—*e.g.* by voluntary entering into an agreement. Arguably, relations between sovereign states would be impossible without these agreements. That is, self-imposed limitations do not jeopardize sovereignty. In fact, they may be seen as examples of it.

The second kind of limitation is externally imposed since it either matters the relationships with peers or the context. The first subgroup of externally imposed limitations only exists because there are other agents. Hence, they are imposed by the mere presence of other individuals or states when they somehow limit their freedom. It is true that individuals and states may limit their respective peers in different manners. In order to show more clearly how these kinds of limitations work—*i.e.* externally imposed because of the mere presence of others—the focus will be now on what happens in instances in which either individuals or states have their freedom limited by their respective peers.

One of the ways to understand the relationship between an individual and himself, other people and all that surrounds him is self-ownership (also called property in the person).[7] In self-ownership, each individual owns both morally and legally his person and natural talents and is free to use them and is morally obliged not to invade someone else's sphere of freedom—like a negative liberty.[8] However, even if limitations imposed by others are justified—for whatever reason—how can limitations to negative liberty be tolerated and still be self-owners?[9] In particular, republican liberty that, unlike negative liberty, understands freedom as nondomination.[10] Then, a free man, rather than a slave, may accept a certain level of limitations—negative liberty; and still be a free man. That is because freedom—*i.e.* republican freedom—understood as nondomination means independence from unwanted arbitrary and unreasonable restrictions. Therefore, a state can still be sovereign and be subject to some limitations; it just cannot be subject to domination by another state. To be more precise, it is not that nondomination and freedom are different conceptions. For the purpose of this work, nondomination is the way in which republican freedom will be understood.

Before continuing with the analysis, the meaning of nondomination needs clarification. Without intending to be an exhaustive revision of the concept, and bearing in mind the nature of this book, a preliminary sketch of the idea of nondomination follows. Because the main purpose is to offer a reasonable solution to some sovereignty conflicts through the application of distributive justice principles, it is merely an attempt to conceptualize how nondomination will be understood here, leaving its full assessment for subsequent research. Having made that clear, domination "[r]efers to the relatively unrestrained and systematic (even if unexercised) ability of a group or individuals to exert power over others in

7 The expression "property in the person" is from Carole Pateman, "Self-Ownership and Property in the Person: Democratization and a Tale of Two Concepts," *The Journal of Political Philosophy* 10 (2002): 20–53. For a relation between self-ownership and property, *see* Lloyd P. Gerson, "Who Owns What? Some Reflections on the Foundation of Political Philosophy," *Social Philosophy and Policy* 29 (2012): 81–105; Alan Ryan, "Self-Ownership, Autonomy, and Property Rights," *Social Philosophy and Policy* 11 (1994): 241–58; Eric Mack, "Self-Ownership and the Right of Property," *The Monist* 73 (1990): 519–43.

8 Liberty can be defined—in principle—as the ability to decide upon one's actions and omissions. Negative liberty can be seen as the absence of interferences, freedom of restraints (*e.g.* constraints, barriers, etc.); positive liberty is the freedom to form and make actual a rational and reasonable plan of life. For further analysis, *see* Isaiah Berlin, *Four Essays on Liberty* (Oxford: Oxford University Press, 1969). For interpretations on the topic, *see* Matthew H. Kramer, "On the Unavoidability of Actions: Quentin Skinner, Thomas Hobbes, and the Modern Doctrine of Negative Liberty," *Inquiry* 44 (2001): 315–30; Philip Pettit, "A Definition of Negative Liberty," *Ratio* 2 (2006): 153–68; and many others.

9 *See* Quentin Skinner, "A Third Concept of Liberty," in: *Proceedings of the British Academy 2001 Lectures* (Oxford: Oxford University Press, 2003); Carl K. Y. Shaw, "Quentin Skinner on the Proper Meaning of Republican Liberty," *Politics* 23 (2003): 46–56; and many others.

10 There may be different accounts of republican liberty. *See* Mark R. Reiff, *Exploitation and Economic Justice in the Liberals Capitalist State* (Oxford: Oxford University Press, 2013), pp. 288–89, *esp.* fns 24 and 25. For a view on republican liberty as nondomination, *see* Frank Lovett, *A General Theory of Domination and Justice* (Oxford: Oxford University Press, 2010), pp. 155–56.

pursuit of their own interests at the expense of those subordinate to them."[11] Consequently, nondomination means for this book the capacity for someone's affairs not to be arbitrarily interfered with by someone else.

The previous paragraphs showed that individuals—and, on a larger scale, states—are sovereign in the sense they have autonomous free will to choose to act or not to act. Nevertheless, sovereign individuals and sovereign states have relationships of different kinds with their respective peers that somehow may limit their freedom. So the issue here is whether these limits to their freedom are arbitrary restrictions or not—*i.e.* whether there is domination or nondomination in their interrelation.

In the case of sovereign individuals, to conduct their interactions or interrelations under the idea of nondomination means that no sovereign individual is entitled to limit someone else's freedom in an arbitrary manner. That is to say, interactions among sovereign individuals happen in any society and they may imply restrictions with regards their individual freedom. However, none of these restrictions can be unilaterally and arbitrarily imposed. Therefore, the issue of inequalities among sovereign individuals—*e.g.* poor and rich—that could lead to abuse of power and control is avoided.[12]

Similarly, in the case of sovereign states, to conduct their interactions or interrelations under the idea of nondomination results in no sovereign state being entitled to restrict the freedom of any other sovereign state in an arbitrary manner. In other words, interactions among sovereign states happen as part of global relationships in the international scenario and they may bring about restrictions in relation to states' freedom. However, none of these restrictions can be unilaterally and arbitrarily imposed. So, the potential problem of disparities among sovereign states—*e.g.* resources and power—is neutralized.[13]

The significance of understanding freedom as nondomination in the case of sovereignty is crucial because a state in which freedom was limited would still be considered sovereign since any limitation would have had to be either accepted by such state, or not unreasonably or arbitrarily imposed. A state can still be subject to other kinds of limitations, both internal and external, and still be sovereign within the notion of republican freedom, just as an individual can be subject to some limitation, and still be a self-owner in terms of republican freedom.

For example, in the case of an individual, self-ownership implies that "[e]very person is morally entitled to full private property in his own person and powers."[14]

11 Cécile Laborde, "Republicanism and Global Justice: A Sketch," *European Journal of Political Theory* 9 (2010): 48–69. For a more detailed account about republican freedom and nondomination, *see* Lena Halldenius, "Building Blocks of Cosmopolitanism: The Modality of Being Free," *European Journal of Political Theory* 9 (2010): 12–30; and Philip Pettit, "A Republican Law of Peoples," *European Journal of Political Theory* 9 (2010): 70–94.

12 For more details about individuals and nondomination, *see* Laborde (n. 11), *esp.* pp. 51–52.

13 *Ibid.*, *esp.* pp. 54 ff.

14 Gerald Allan Cohen and Keith Graham, "Self-Ownership, Communism and Equality," *Proceedings of the Aristotelian Society, Supplementary Volume* 64 (1990): 25–61.

From there, the notion can be extended to the environment and things and objects related to it. In other words, an individual owns himself, his actions, and omissions, and the product of his labor—to discuss here how the individual obtains the property of any object is out of the scope of this study. If that same individual were not fully free to decide his way of action in relation to himself or things that belonged to him, his self-ownership would be somehow diminished. By way of example: "[m]y land is not fully mine if someone else has a right of way over it, or a claim to a portion of the income it generates."[15] Similarly, an individual is not fully the owner even of himself if someone has the right to dictate the way he has to proceed—or omit to proceed—or has a certain right over the benefits he generates—*i.e.* his liberty is infringed in a negative form.

The same way of reasoning can be replicated when dealing with states: A state is sovereign—as an individual has self-ownership—if and only if its representatives are free to decide how the state acts or omits to act both internally and internationally. If that same state was not fully free to decide its way of action in relation to its internal or international affairs, its sovereignty—self-ownership—would be somehow affected—as happens to pseudo-states, failed states, etc. But like self-ownership, this does not mean it is not still sovereign. Indeed, while states' sovereignty limits one another's negative freedom, it does not obviously limit their sovereignty at all.

In brief, sovereign individuals or self-owners are not alone. There are other sovereign individuals or self-owners in a community and they have relationships of various kinds. Similarly, sovereign states are not alone in the international community. There are—among other international agents—several sovereign states and they have relationships of various kinds as well. In both cases any interrelation a sovereign individual or a sovereign state have with their peers may imply limiting their freedom, respectively. Indeed, their sphere of freedom is somehow interfered with.

In self-ownership as well as in sovereignty, supreme authority appears to be threatened by other individuals or states. How may constraints be incorporated in self-ownership without blurring its essence? How do constraints operate in relation to supreme authority or sovereignty? Locke, the author behind this theoretical development of self-ownership, gives a hint that can be used to understand limitations in sovereignty. The basis of his theory is, as it was for most of his predecessors, the free will. Locke maintains that:

> [t]o understand political power right, and derive it from its original, we must consider what state all men are naturally in, and that is, a state of perfect freedom to order their actions, and dispose of their possessions, and persons as they think fit, within the bounds of the law of nature, without asking leave, or depending upon the will of any other man.[16]

15 *Ibid.*
16 John Locke, *Two Treatises of Government* (London: Everyman, 1993), p. 6.

It is a prerequisite of his paradigm that men are born free to decide whatever they want to do/not to do. Moreover, he highlights this feature by expressly neutralizing external interference from any other individual. If there is such interference from an external subject in relation to one's free will—in terms of actions or omissions—then freedom is limited. From here it seems—at first glance—that self-ownership must be supreme and singular.

By way of analogy, it would be a prerequisite for a state to be sovereign that it was free to decide whatever it wanted to do or not to do. If there was external interference its freedom would seem to be limited. Indeed, sovereignty is thought and assumed by many to be supreme and singular too.

Van Duffel offers a contemporary view, explaining that in the current legal and political scenario, "[p]roperty is fundamental to libertarianism in that it defines the boundaries that people must not cross."[17] Applied to international relations, it fits perfectly with a classical view in regards to sovereignty: It is the characteristic that defines the boundaries that states must not cross. It defines the ownership any state has over its territory and all that it entails. Van Duffel links later the concept of free will with the idea that every human may be a small-scale sovereign. In what is relevant to this work, he maintains that:

> Small-scale sovereignty is the meaning of "freedom" in libertarian theories of natural rights. People are adjudged free if they are able, within certain confines, to decide what is to be done—that is, to have normative control over a part of the world. Not to have one's freedom violated means not to have anything done in one's domain that goes against one's will.[18]

So far, a sovereign state and a small-scale sovereign (an individual) seem to possess sovereignty and self ownership, respectively. Locke introduces free will and its relationship with self-ownership; Van Duffel labels the individual as a small-scale sovereign. In other words, a free being has the free will to act and refrain from acting in relation to himself, his labor and the things he owns and is thus a small-scale sovereign, able to determine his way of acting and act upon that decision. If a spectrum of options was to be considered in terms of self-ownership, one of the extremes would be given by the fully free being and the other one, by a slave: Anyone bound to limit his actions or omissions upon someone else's volition by way of following his orders, even arbitrary, or prohibitions without being able to disagree—without being able to exercise his free will and hence, there is domination.[19] He who is sovereign has self-ownership of his own acts and omissions, labor, and belongings. He who cannot decide freely upon his own acts

17 Siegfried Van Duffel, "Libertarian Natural Rights," *Critical Review* 16 (2004): 353–75.

18 *Ibid.*

19 For a view on domination, *see* Lovett (n. 10). For a detailed account about positive and negative liberty and domination, *see esp.* pp. 152–54. For a conception of republican liberty defined as "the absence of domination," *see esp.* pp. 155–56.

and omissions, labor, and belongings does not have self-ownership and, hence, is not a small-scale sovereign.

The same can be said about political communities such as sovereign states. Any sovereign state has exclusive prerogatives over the territory it is based on. In consequence, the population of that sovereign state through their representatives has the exclusive prerogative to decide freely what to do or not to do in relation to that territory. If there were a scale of sovereignty grades, one extreme would be given by a fully free state and the other one, by an enslaved one—*e.g.* a colony. But this does not mean that a sovereign state cannot have limitations from others. So, a state may have its freedom limited with and still remain sovereign. That is because, even though there may be limitations, it still has exclusive prerogatives to act (or not) upon its territory and population—*i.e.* there is no imposition, there is no domination. The crucial element seems to be that one state, implicitly or explicitly, gives another the permission to impose limitations or simply accepts them—analogous in some ways to becoming a slave, as opposed to agreeing to serve another individual in specific ways.

The issue at stake here is that if there were a scale, external limitations would represent one extreme and domination the other. In the former case, external limitations only mean—at least here—the existence of several agents—either individuals or states—and the fact that their actions and omissions are voluntary and may have an effect on others. In the latter case, domination has to do with the fact that the limitations are being imposed to one agent by another agent. To be more precise, the imposing or dominating agent limits the freedom of its peer as much and however it wants. Therein, the recipient agent has no other choice but to accept the imposition or go against it by means of confrontation.

Coincidentally, in what has to do with limitations, Van Duffel expressly includes in his characterization of small-scale sovereign the phrase "within certain confines."[20] In tune with these words, it may seem that Locke has something to add to the idea of self-ownership; he refines this conceptualization by distinguishing between freedom and licence:

> [b]ut though this be a state of liberty, yet it is not a state of licence, though man in that state have an uncontrollable liberty, to dispose of his person or possessions, yet he has no liberty to destroy himself, or so much as any creature in his possession . . . no one ought to harm another in his life, health, liberty, or possessions.[21]

In other words, he who has free will to do—or omit to do—whatever he pleases with himself is limited by other individuals' free will, in that he ought not to come into conflict with them or their interests. Human conduct involves inter-subjective

20 *See* Van Duffel (n. 17).
21 *See* Locke (fn. 16), p. 117.

conduct: The acts and omissions of one individual may interfere with the acts and omissions of any other individual, to the extent that both are still free beings able to conduct their actions—and omissions—free from external constraint. This is a cornerstone in Locke's theory that separates it from that of Hobbes. The natural state is not a state of war for Locke; it is a state of freedom limited by mutual respect, and, resembles the international scenario in that states share the same principle.

The same notion applies to sovereign states. As part of the international community sovereign states' conduct implies interrelations: The acts or omissions of one sovereign state may interfere with those of another. So, each other's freedom is limited reciprocally. But in no way can these limitations necessarily imply domination—*i.e.* the principle of non intervention is core in international public law.

In short, sovereign individuals in a community have self-ownership. Being a member in a community implies interrelation with others that can limit (interfere with) their freedom. But that does not imply per se sacrificing it. Similarly, states in the international community have sovereignty. As part of a community, they have interrelations with others that may interfere with (limit) their freedom. But that does not mean that per se they sacrifice their sovereignty.

Thereby, in the case of sovereign individuals as well as sovereign states the interrelation with peers may limit their freedom. These are externally imposed constraints—*i.e.* they exist because both sovereign individuals and sovereign states are part of communities and hence they interrelate with others' freedom. Nevertheless, are these the only constraints they have? In addition to self-imposed limitations and externally imposed limitations in what matters for relationships with peers, there is still a second subgroup of external limitations to consider: External limitations because of the context or environment.

At the individual level, when men live together, Locke maintains that this is a choice made by them by their free will. In his words:

> Men being, as has been said, by nature, all free, equal and independent, no one can be put out of this estate, and subjected to the political power of another, without his own consent. The only way whereby anyone divests himself of his natural liberty, and puts on the bonds of civil society is by agreeing with other men to join and unite into a community, for their comfortable, safe, and peaceable living one amongst another . . .[22]

In any kind of social organization men are part of (families, villages, communities, states), their members have a choice that only depends on their free will to be part—or not—of them. It is true that individuals are all born in certain states or families so they cannot simply choose to join or to leave them and join some

22 *Ibid.*, p. 163.

other group. In that respect, for Locke, it is free will that gives legitimacy to any societal organization: An individual has both the right to be part of a community and to leave it, depending only on his decision. Nevertheless, for an individual even to leave a community is no longer possible (hence certain limitations exist by default). In Locke's days, some people could find uninhabited parts of the world. But now, (a) most people cannot leave the state they find themselves in; and (b) if they can, they have to go to some other state. These are also constraints externally imposed but in virtue of the environment they are in.

To a similar extent, it may be said that states do not have the option of leaving the international scene. So there are some limitations that are now compulsory, because there is no other option. Every sovereign individual in every society is actually affected by the same compulsory constraint. The same can be said about sovereign states: Even if not having the choice to leave the international scene is the case in international relations, it applies to every sovereign state. In other words, all of them have these external constraints because they are members of a community with preexisting facts and rules.

Both sovereign individuals and sovereign states are obliged to accept the constraint of being part of a larger society (national or international), but they are still in the same relative situation to that of their peers. That is to say, the starting point for all of them is the same, a state of things that could not be abandoned. So, the fact that sovereign individuals and sovereign states had an actual possibility to leave their respective societies (national or international) or not does not change the prerogative they have in order to impose self-constraints or accept external ones in regard to their self-ownership or sovereignty, respectively. That is because the basic freedom both individuals and states have is equal freedom, not total freedom. More precisely, they have equal moral and legal freedom but this does not necessarily imply, for example, physical or economic equality.

Sovereignty: Supreme authority and limitations

From the previous section it is clear that a sovereign state may have two kinds of limitations: (a) self-imposed limitations; (b) externally imposed limitations. Thus, the externally imposed limitations may be because of other sovereign states or because of the context or environment.

Undoubtedly, the model in this book will mainly be centered on the second group of limitations, in particular the ones that have to do with other sovereign states. So, as regards "egalitarian shared sovereignty," in order for the model to work, it is a must that sovereignty includes limitations. But these limitations have to be of a special nature, they must not imply domination: They have to allow the two sovereign states to be at the same time sovereign over the same territory to the extent they do not interfere with the interests of the other or that of the population of the third territory. In tune with this, Walker puts all the pieces together when he says: "Jellinek presented a more cautious version of the concept [of sovereignty]. He believed that the State can undertake obligations and limit its freedom without losing sovereignty. For him, sovereignty was the 'ability of exclusive self-determination and thus self-limitation' . . ."[23]

This theory fits within the one proposed here; it follows Locke's idea and, most recently, the ones developed by Van Duffel. However, this theory needs elaborating. Jellinek's theory of self-imposed obligations has received much criticism,[24] mainly concerning the idea that a state as well as having the power to self-limitation can then at any time cancel self-imposed obligations—*i.e.* the final agreement may not offer stability.

Any free state has different kinds of limitations and is still considered sovereign. However, that does not mean that a sovereign state is dominated by any other agent—a sovereign state is a free state, not an enslaved one. In other words, what matters here is not how much a state can limit other states' freedom but the fact that the first state interferes with the freedom of the second state as much and however it wants.

By way of example, consider a sovereign State A and a colony B. Even in the event the sovereign State A had the most benign policies and law towards the colonial population, they would still be a colony. Therefore, the colony would be governed unilaterally by the sovereign State A. Indeed, that would only mean domination—*i.e.* the power State A has over colony B is discretionary and may also be arbitrary.

Consider now that the colonial population exercised their right to self-determination and became independent. In addition to this, their newly elected and independent authorities created a less benign system. At first glance, there is less freedom for the population with the newly acquired independence. Indeed, at first glance it seems counterintuitive. Should not they have gained "more" freedom?

The key in capturing the lesson behind the example is to view it as a whole rather than only the outcome. This example shows that by understanding sovereignty as nondomination the new sovereign state (former colony B) cannot be subject to the arbitrary discretionary power of any other agent. That is because, and at least for the purpose of this work, arbitrary means without a reason, whereas discretionary means there are numerous reasonable choices and one can pick from among these options as one wishes without further reasons. Therefore, while sovereignty in this book is seen as nondomination and hence implies a certain degree of discretionary power, it does not embrace any kind of arbitrariness.

How may arbitrary discretionary power be defined in order to determine when a party is dominating another one? In other words, how much can a state limit its freedom or accept its freedom to be limited and still be sovereign? The answer to this question is given later on in this monograph when it examines whether and

23 Neil Walker, *Sovereignty in Transition* (Oxford: Hart Publishing, 2003), p. 369.

24 Hans Wheberg, "Pacta Sunt Servanda," *The American Journal of International Law* 53 (1959): 775–86; D. M. McRae, "Sovereignty and the International Legal Order," *Western Ontario Law Review* (1971): 56–86.

how the claiming parties may share sovereignty over the disputed third territory. However, it is clear that sovereign states have limitations and, although they restrict their freedom in some ways, not all limitations imply a diminishing of each state's sovereignty. On the contrary, joint ventures may result in bettering every agent's relative position.

These limitations, as well as being a duty to others, greatly increase one's overall freedom of action—*e.g.* by refraining from injuring others, one makes cooperation with others possible, and can then make possible all kinds of things that were previously impossible. This is true of states as well as individuals. In consequence, if limitations are in tune with self-ownership and in fact broaden its sphere of action, self- and externally imposed constraints are in tune with sovereignty, which means that a state is able to achieve results that may be impossible, more complex, or economically disadvantageous if they were done individually. Moreover, domination is a particular kind of limitation that implies arbitrary discretionary power over someone else—in this case, another state. So, although limitations will be part of the model, none of them can be a subterfuge for domination.

Sovereign states are the main agents in the international community, but they are not the only ones, and there are many of them. A state should have the exclusive ability to determine and limit itself in order to be politically and legally sovereign. But, to be part of a wider network, such as the international system, does not mean that sovereignty is eroded or ought to be redefined. Besides, it is in fact a concept that perfectly plays its part in the international arena, also when relating to nonsovereign agents. Even with the assumption that sovereignty means supreme authority, the situation does not change. Each and every state would still be an ultimate lawmaker within its boundaries; but it may use this exclusive prerogative to allow some kinds of limitations.

Certainly at first glance, self-limitations do not offer more guarantee than the goodwill of the involved agents to fulfill what they agreed to do or not to do. But, it is a fact also that there are external obligations that may restrict states both nationally and internationally, as does customary law, and may have a stronger reason to be respected—*e.g.* international sanctions, international prestige when applying for financial aid. Some of these external obligations come in hand with the globalization process and are particularly useful for this project. As a result, there are different types of restrictions in relation to any sovereign state, to name a few: (a) plural jurisdiction; (b) agreements; (c) actions by other equally free states. In consequence, sovereign states can have restrictions that may be either voluntary and able to be canceled or may impose equal restrictions on all. It is the combination of both the self-limitations and the external limitations that will secure the success of "egalitarian shared sovereignty."

Conclusion

To recapitulate, sovereignty is a complex concept. It assumes supreme authority and, for some, that means single nonshareable authority. But this chapter has shown that sovereign states accept internal and external limitations and therefore states may cooperate together, limit their freedom, and still be considered as being sovereign.

In order to show this point, the chapter: (a) first deconstructed the concept of "sovereignty" by examining its subatomic or fundamental elements; and (b) second, reviewed how a concept with similar features operates and accepts limitations without changing its nature. Wesley N. Hohfeld's language for legal analysis helped with the former. The latter had to do with the introduction of "self-ownership," its limitations, and working out in parallel the similarities with sovereignty so as to demonstrate that, even though it may accept limitations of different kinds, it does not affect its nature.

Indeed, sovereign states accept internal and external limitations and therefore states may cooperate together, limit their freedom, and still be considered as being sovereign. Whatever the duration of the limitations, the dependence on the goodwill of the participants in any agreement, and any other elements that may jeopardize the strength of any joint international enterprise, the point has been demonstrated: Limitations do exist and they can be internal (self-imposed) or external (*e.g.* imposed by international custom, exceptional circumstances, other states). In one or the other case, a sovereign state has restrictions that in theory and practice may either limit its choices or enhance them. But, none of these limitations is—or can be—a subterfuge for domination. That is to say, in no case will these limitations entitle or enable a party to do as much as it wants and in whatever way it wants.

From that standpoint it is crucial to determine what limitations each state is willing to—and can—accept. It is for that reason that the question will be examined through lenses of just distribution theory, so as to determine a just and fair way of allocating actual and potential benefits and burdens. The task will be to base the "egalitarian shared sovereignty" paradigm on a revised conception that allows limitations and at the same time applies principles of just distribution in order to allocate the respective portions of sovereignty. The reason is that the final agreement must secure stability for shared sovereignty over time, maintaining a peaceful interrelation between the participants, and avoiding any form of domination.

Bibliography

Berlin, Isaiah. *Four Essays on Liberty*. Oxford: Oxford University Press, 1969.

Cohen, Allan. *Self-Ownership, Freedom and Equality*. Cambridge: Cambridge University Press, 1995.

Cohen, Gerald Allan and Graham, Keith. "Self-Ownership, Communism and Equality." *Proceedings of the Aristotelian Society, Supplementary Volume* 64 (1990): 25–61.

Elster, Jon. *The Cement of Society*. Cambridge: Cambridge University Press, 1989.

Fried, Charles. *Contract as Promise*. Cambridge MA: Harvard University Press, 1981.

Gerson, Lloyd P. "Who Owns What? Some Reflections on the Foundation of Political Philosophy." *Social Philosophy and Policy* 29 (2012): 81–105.

Halldenius, Lena. "Building Blocks of Cosmopolitanism: The Modality of Being Free." *European Journal of Political Theory* 9 (2010): 12–30.

Hohfeld, Wesley Newcomb. "Fundamental Legal Conceptions as Applied in Judicial Reasoning." *Yale Law Journal* (1917): 710–70.

Hohfeld, Wesley Newcomb. "Some Fundamental Legal Conceptions as Applied in Judicial Reasoning." *Yale Law Journal* (1913): 16–59.

Kramer, Matthew H. "On the Unavoidability of Actions: Quentin Skinner, Thomas Hobbes, and the Modern Doctrine of Negative Liberty." *Inquiry* 44 (2001): 315–30.

Laborde, Cécile. "Republicanism and Global Justice: A Sketch." *European Journal of Political Theory* 9 (2010): 48–69.

Locke, John. *Two Treatises of Government.* London: Everyman, 1993.

Lovett, Frank. *A General Theory of Domination and Justice.* Oxford: Oxford University Press, 2010.

Mack, Eric. "Self-Ownership and the Right of Property." *The Monist* 73 (1990): 519–43.

McRae, D. M. "Sovereignty and the International Legal Order." *Western Ontario Law Review* (1971): 56–86.

Navarro, Pablo and Rodriguez, Jorge. *Deontic Logic and Legal Systems.* Cambridge: Cambridge University Press, 2014.

Nietzsche, Friedrich. *On the Genealogy of Morality.* Indianapolis/Cambridge: Hackett Publishing Company Inc., 1998.

Nozick, Robert. *Anarchy, State and Utopia.* New York: Basic Books, 1974.

Pateman, Carole. "Self-Ownership and Property in the Person: Democratization and a Tale of Two Concepts." *The Journal of Political Philosophy* 10 (2002): 20–53.

Pettit, Philip. "A Definition of Negative Liberty." *Ratio* 2 (2006): 153–68.

Pettit, Philip. "A Republican Law of Peoples." *European Journal of Political Theory* 9 (2010): 70–94.

Reiff, Mark R. *Exploitation and Economic Justice in the Liberals Capitalist State.* Oxford: Oxford University Press, 2013.

Reiff, Mark R. *Punishment, Compensation, and Law: A Theory of Enforceability.* Cambridge: Cambridge University Press, 2005.

Ryan, Alan. "Self-Ownership, Autonomy, and Property Rights." *Social Philosophy and Policy* 11 (1994): 241–58.

Schelling, Thomas C. *The Strategy of Conflict.* Cambridge MA: Harvard University Press, 1960.

Shaw, Carl K. Y. "Quentin Skinner on the Proper Meaning of Republican Liberty." *Politics* 23 (2003): 46–56.

Skinner, Quentin. "A Third Concept of Liberty," in: *Proceedings of the British Academy 2001 Lectures.* Oxford: Oxford University Press, 2003.

Van Duffel, Siegfried. "Libertarian Natural Rights." *Critical Review* 16 (2004): 353–75.

Walker, Neil. *Sovereignty in Transition.* Oxford: Hart Publishing, 2003.

Wheberg, Hans. "Pacta Sunt Servanda." *The American Journal of International Law* 53 (1959): 775–86.

5 Why is shared sovereignty desirable?

Introduction

Like any other conflict, sovereignty disputes can be addressed in different ways. The alternatives go from secession (with or without partition) in the form of self-determination and independence to continuing with the *status quo*. The task is now to evaluate when and why shared sovereignty is more desirable than any other international remedy. In other words, there are several ways of dealing with sovereignty conflicts. Some of them have proven to be effective, others are only theoretical solutions, and some are—for whatever reason—not desirable. This chapter will introduce and assess if it is reasonable—at least—to doubt the value of their application. That is because this project assumes the agents want a peaceful solution that acknowledges—to an extent—their claims. So, solutions that imply ignoring claims, unfair policies, use of force or any action that may go against an otherwise peaceful situation will be not viable.

Indeed, shared sovereignty may not be "one way fits all." But this book is not suggesting that shared sovereignty is "the" solution to all sovereignty conflicts. What these pages propose is a reasonable way to approach some of them. Therefore, by addressing the pitfalls of other international remedies that so far have proven to be inadequate in solving these types of sovereignty conflicts, it is possible to identify both the need of a peaceful solution and an opportunity to offer another way of dealing with them.

Possible solutions in sovereignty conflicts

As there are three agents involved in sovereignty disputes of this kind, the possible solutions can be grouped depending on how they interact among themselves: (a) unilateral solutions; (b) international-multilateral solutions; (c) bilateral solutions.[1]

1 This section is inspired by Peter Beck's works. He analyzes the Falkland/Malvinas Islands conflict in detail and offers a clear way of presenting different approaches. In particular, refer to Peter Beck, *The Falkland Islands as an International Problem* (London and New York: Routledge, 1998). *See also* Peter Beck, "The Future of the Falkland Islands: A Solution Made

Unilateral solutions

This group of solutions is centered on one of the agents. The decision regarding sovereignty is taken by one of the agents involved, whatever the consequences to the others. The opposition of the other party or parties is not taken into account, and the rights they claim are either reduced or completely ignored. This could happen in three different ways: (1) the successful party denies that the other party has these rights at all; (2) the successful party admits these rights but claims that other rights overrule them; (3) the successful party admits these rights but chooses as a matter of realpolitik to ignore them.

Fortress

This term was used in particular in relation to the Falkland/Malvinas Islands, which were called "Fortress Falkland."[2] After the 1982 war, the United Kingdom decided to strengthen the defense system of the Falkland/Malvinas Islands. Thus, this policy appears to be an actual reality in the British international agenda. Without entering into specific details in relation to the Falkland/Malvinas Islands case,[3] this approach is characterized by a unilateral decision of one of the sovereign agents to secure the nonsovereign territory against its international rival in the conflict (and any other aggressor). Although the preeminent feature is the defense system, this approach has direct consequences for the economy of both the third territory and the sovereign state providing the means to defend it.

A direct negative result of this solution is that the basic problem related to sovereignty remains unresolved. Sovereignty is not granted either to the third territory or the sovereign state in charge of the defense. Indeed, the *de facto* sovereignty may rest on the agent that defends the third territory; however, no *de jure* sovereignty is recognized by these means. Moreover, the consequent costs of—mainly but not only—defense and diplomacy are substantial and have to be supported only by one of the agents—the one intending to defend the third territory. Finally, although this approach offers a short-term solution, the long term overall situation is uncertain in two ways: First, the sovereignty issue remains unresolved as discussed; secondly, the defense of any territory is a mutable feature (*e.g.* the United Kingdom defense power is a factual variable that depends on many factors, one of them being its economy, currently affected by the international financial crisis). In addition to the previously mentioned practical consequences, there is no reason to think this approach is just.

in Hong Kong?" *International Affairs, Royal Institute of International Affairs* 61 (1985): 643–60; Peter Beck, "Looking at the Falkland Islands from Antarctica: The Broader Regional Perspective," *Polar Record* 30 (1994): 167–80; Peter Beck, "Britain's Falkland Future: The Need to Look Back," *The Round Table* 73 (1984): 139–52; and many others.

2 Cyril Pickard, "Fortress Falkland? The Real Lessons of the Franks Report," *The Round Table* 72 (1983): 233–37.

3 The Falkland/Malvinas Islands case will be reviewed in more detail in Chapter 7.

Integration and free association

Both integration and free association[4] are in essence ways in which individual political organizations join in a larger whole. The difference depends on the degree of sovereignty they are willing to surrender. For instance, integration implies tighter links between the agents: One of the given political communities becomes part of another one. In contrast, free association does not imply full integration but close links in regards to specific areas (*e.g.* economy, security, etc.) usually after independence is achieved from another sovereign state (*e.g.* Cook Islands and New Zealand, Federated states of Micronesia, the United States, etc.).

In these cases, independence is either assumed as a starting point or as an ultimate goal. In what is specific to the kind of sovereignty conflicts that are the object of this book, at least one of the agents is always against this solution (*e.g.* Argentina has been and still is opposed to Falkland/Malvinas Islands' independence). That is because it is common in any sovereignty dispute that the third territory has tighter links with one of the involved sovereign agents in, for example, cultural background, ethnicity, historical links or geographical location. The direct consequence is that the state that is more distant, in whatever way, from the third territory will see its position worsened in comparison to its opponent. When the dispute is still in place none of the sovereign states is in a better position to make use of their intended rights over the third territory (at least in terms of *de jure* sovereignty). However, if the third territory becomes integrated with or associated to the sovereign state with which it had previous tighter links, this state will be in a better position than the more distant one, since now the newly integrated/associated territory will not need to consider the more distant sovereign state.

Indeed, there are cases where this may work. For instance, the proposal for some of Israel's West Bank settlements is integration in Israel with compensation in the form of land to Palestine. But, although integration either in its pure form or as free association may encourage equality between the populations participating in the process, this international institution has been designed bearing in mind situations in which there are only two agents—the one being integrated and the

4 Integration and free association are both defined in the Res. 1541 (XV) of UN General Assembly. In what is of interest here Principle VII declares that: "(a) Free association should be the result of a free and voluntary choice by the peoples of the territory concerned expressed through informed and democratic processes . . . (b) The associated territory should have the right to determine its internal constitution without outside interference . . ." Principle VIII declares that: "Integration with an independent State should be on the basis of complete equality between the peoples of the erstwhile Non-Self-Governing Territory and those of the independent country with which it is integrated. The peoples of both territories should have equal status and rights of citizenship and equal guarantees of fundamental rights and freedoms . . ." And Principle IX states that: "Integration should have come about in the following circumstances: (a) The integrating territory should have attained an advanced stage of self-government with free political institutions . . .; (b) The integration should be the result of the freely expressed wishes of the territory's peoples . . ."

one welcoming party. In the cases contemplated here, the agents are three, so integration would mean leaving one of them out of the equation. Ergo, it would be opposed by that one agent unless they agreed to withdraw, with or without compensation. The consequence is an unbalanced relation among the agents. At least in a *status quo* all of them are in a similar position; with integration, one of the sovereign states might be completely left outside the picture.

Independence

This is the extreme unilateral view, since it entails the absolute separation of the third territory as an autonomous political organization. The third territory would become a new sovereign state. There are several reasons both to support independence and to oppose it.

The main problem is the constant opposition of at least one of the already sovereign states (*e.g.* Argentina in the case of Falkland/Malvinas Islands). Against this position it may be argued that the claims of one of the agents should sometimes be overridden. This could be because of: (a) the legal position (*e.g.* the "New Territories," later part of Hong Kong's territory, had to be returned to China because they were on lease, and the lease came to an end); (b) the desires of the inhabitants in a territory that is viable economically and for defense might be enough to make independence the best option (*e.g.* the wish of the overwhelming majority of the inhabitants of the Falkland/Malvinas Islands to be British).[5]

Undoubtedly, there would be different inhabitants under different circumstances so the question about the legitimacy of which group of inhabitants counts will arise—*e.g.* past, current of future generations. As a result, there is at least an argument for saying that these desires do not count fully or without certain controversy. In addition to this, in one or the other case—the legal issue or desire of the inhabitants—the key point that makes independence neither a useful nor a realistic solution is its viability. Although in most cases the third territory may appear viable on its own to some extent, it cannot be to the extent necessary to be granted the condition of fully independent political organization (*e.g.* both Hong Kong and Falkland/Malvinas Islands do not have a defense system and must depend upon another agent in case of threat or attack, China[6] and the United Kingdom,[7] respectively). In addition to the defense system, sovereignty

5 On March 10–13, 2013, a referendum on the political status of the Falkland/Malvinas Islands resulted in 99.80% cast votes to retain the political status as Overseas Territory of the United Kingdom. For more details *see* Chapter 7; and Chapter I, art. 1 of the Falkland Islands Constitution Order 2008 states that: "[a]ll peoples have the right to self-determination and by virtue of that right they freely determine their political status."

6 The Basic Law of Hong Kong states in its Chapter II, art. 14.1: "The Central People's Government shall be responsible for the defence of the Hong Kong Special Administrative Region."

7 According to Chapter II, art. 25 of the Falkland Islands Constitution Order 2008: "The Governor shall consult with the Commander British Forces before exercising any function which appears to the Governor to relate to defence or internal security . . ."

disputes usually concern a third territory without enough resources, means or development to support their existence in the international arena as a fully autonomous entity (hence, independence is usually replaced by integration or limited by free association).

Against the argument about the viability of the third territory as a fully independent political organization, it is true that there are sovereign states that do not have their own defense system or a strong economy and possess a small territory and population (*e.g.* San Marino, Monaco, Vatican City), but are still respected as sovereign. Nevertheless, the similarities they share with the territories whose sovereignty is disputed are only superficial: They are all small pieces of land with a small population, but strong local authorities and law, and this makes this counterargument irrelevant. Also, although these sovereign states would not be independent political communities without aid from another sovereign state, there are historical, geographical, demographical reasons why this is provided. Moreover, in none of these cases is there a third party (or even a second party) disputing sovereignty. But, in sovereignty conflicts that are the object of this book there are several claimants. Thus, the fact that the third territory has usually tighter links with one of these claimants may imply the consolidation of these bilateral relations if full independence was achieved, leaving aside that sovereign state that was in the first place against it. So independence would be a subterfuge and not a real solution.

One of the ways in which contemporary political literature addresses independence is through the theory of secession. Secession[8] and partition in the context of a sovereignty conflict imply the separation from another sovereign state. The immediate consequence is the birth of an independent political organization that—if recognized by its peers—may be a new sovereign state. It does not imply a revolution as it does not mean the validity of the central authority of the sovereign state is challenged. What is challenged is the fact that the given population that wants to secede understands for whatever reason the necessity of having an independent government.

There is a subtle difference between secession in general and secession in the particular case of sovereignty disputes object of this book. In the first case, secession in general, the ones wishing to secede are actually part of the sovereign state they claim independence from (*e.g.* Croatia and Slovenia seceded from the Socialist Federal Republic of Yugoslavia in 1991). In contrast, the cases analyzed here have a third territory whose sovereignty has been (and still is) under dispute. Hence its respective population is not actually seceding or separating itself from any sovereign (since there is no uncontested sovereign, either *de jure* or *de facto*, for the third territory yet recognized).

8 Although secession as a concept has been treated in Mediaeval and Modern Ages, it has been more developed—at least in legal and political fields—contemporarily. For instance, *see* Beran's "A Liberal Theory of Secession" and Buchanan's "Toward a Theory of Secession."

Is secession justified in sovereignty disputes? Is secession justified at all? If so, under which conditions is secession justified? As in the general case of independence, there are both arguments that justify secession and arguments that oppose it.[9] Some authors consider secession can be a right to be presumed. Some others think it is not permitted unless some requirements are fulfilled. And some others have an eclectic view.[10]

For an extreme interpretation, secession should be applied as a "rule" in the sense "[. . .] any territorially concentrated group within a state should be permitted to secede if it wants to and if it is morally and practically possible . . ."[11] But, even if secession was understood as a "rule," the sovereignty conflicts analyzed in this book make it an unreasonable choice: The populations are not large; as a direct consequence of having a small population, they are not able to allow sub-groups to secede—it would simply be unrealistic for, at the most, a few hundreds of people reach an international status of statehood; there is no population wishing to exploit or oppress the minority (at least in the cases of Falkland/Malvinas Islands, Gibraltar, Kashmir, and the Kuril Islands); the third territories in all disputes are key for the sovereign states at different levels (highly rich in natural resources, geopolitical location, and its relation with strategic defense, cultural, and historical homogeneity).

Although it may be argued that the population of the third territories have continuously refused to be part of—at least—one of the sovereign states, in all these cases at least one of the governments (usually the one with *de facto* sovereignty) protects the population of the third territory against human rights' violations; there is no danger for the population of the third territory in terms of their local authorities; their economic interests are only jeopardized to the extent they cannot be fully exercised due to the *status quo* that characterizes this kind of sovereignty conflicts; none of the national governments ignores the population of the third territory—they do not recognize their right to self-determination but accept a certain degree of autonomy.[12]

In situations in which there is a sovereignty dispute but the agents do not have any other issue between them except that they argue in regards to their claimed

9 Allen Buchanan, "Toward a Theory of Secession," *Chicago University Press* 101 (1991): 322–42.

10 *See* Robert W. McGee, "A Third Liberal Theory of Secession," *The Liverpool Law Review* XIV (1992): 45–66. McGee analyzes Beran's "A Liberal Theory of Secession" and Birch's "Another Liberal Theory of Secession," arguably the first two publications in contemporary times that refer to the idea of secession in detail. In particular, Beran mentions previous ideas on the topic with names like Grotius and Pufendorf. Refer to Harry Beran, "A Liberal Theory of Secession," *Political Studies* XXXII (1984): 21–31; and Anthony H. Birch, "Another Liberal Theory of Secession," *Political Studies* XXXII (1984): 596–602.

11 *See* Beran (n. 10), p. 30.

12 The Falkland/Malvinas Islands are considered in Argentina as one of the autonomous provinces (its official name is Province of Tierra del Fuego, Antarctica, and South Atlantic Islands); in the United Kingdom they are considered a British Overseas Territory.

rights over a given piece of land—and all that it entails—to grant its supreme authority to one of them appears to be a radical decision that guarantees several negative outcomes: The opposition of at least one of the agents; the violation of the principle of territorial integrity; unsettled multilateral relations; unbalanced power given by the fact the third territory—now independent—may give special priority to only one of the sovereign states who took part in the original conflict (*e.g.* in allowing it to exploit natural resources), and many others. Secession is indeed a contested notion with practical and moral reasons both in favor of and against it. Nonetheless, even if it was considered as a positive international solution for certain conflicts, it does not follow that is the desirable one for the kind of cases analyzed here. Otherwise stated, the solution proposed later is designed for situations when secession is either nonviable or not just.

Self-determination

Although it is often thought to be intrinsically linked to independence, self-determination[13] deserves a separate section because: (a) there is a vast quantity and variety of documents related to this international institution;[14] (b) there are many populations around the world at least considering it as an option for their political status; (c) it is important to make clear that it may lead to solutions other than independence. In international relations, self-determination can be understood as a principle that allows a certain group of people who live in a given territory to have the right to decide who will govern them. Although both are legal and political concepts, sovereignty gives priority to the state whereas self-determination gives pre-eminent place to the people.[15] It is not uncommon in sovereignty conflicts that the population of the third territory seeks independence by applying the principle of self-determination. However, the fact that the third territory is granted self-determination—and hence, may become independent—implies

13 *See* Chapter 1, art. 1, part 2 of the UN Charter, which states among its purposes: "To develop friendly relations among nations based on respect for the principle of equal rights and self-determination of peoples, and to take other appropriate measures to strengthen universal peace;" and UN General Assembly Resolution 1514 Article 2: "All peoples have the right to self-determination; by virtue of that right they freely determine their political status and freely pursue their economic, social and cultural development;" UN General Assembly Resolution 2649, Article 1: "*Affirms* the legitimacy of the struggle of peoples under colonial and alien domination recognised as being entitled to the right of self-determination to restore to themselves that right by any means at their disposal;" UN General Assembly Resolution 2625, Article e: "The principle of equal rights and self-determination of peoples;" and others.

14 The list of books and articles referred to self-determination is cumbersome. For an overview about self-determination in the context of the Falkland/Malvinas Islands, *see* H. E. Chehabi, "Self-Determination, Territorial Integrity, and the Falkland Islands," *The Academy of Political Science, Political Science Quarterly* 100 (1985): 215–25; Denzil Dunnett, "Self-Determination and the Falklands," *International Affairs, Royal Institute of International Affairs* 59 (1983): 415–28.

15 P. H. Kooijmans, "Tolerance, Sovereignty and Self-Determination," *Netherlands International Law Review* XLIII (1996): 211–17.

always a negative response from at least one of the agents involved in the original conflict.

More precisely, independence is not the only way in which self-determination may evolve. Indeed, the population may vote to be administered by, or integrated into, one of the states claiming sovereignty (*e.g.* Puerto Rico, where the battle is between statehood and independence). Then self-determination may lead to different results since the population might decide: (a) to be independent; (b) to be administered by or be part of one party—*i.e.* integration or free association; (c) to have shared sovereignty.

If self-determination leads either to independence or to integration/association, there are reasons why to avoid it is—at least—advisable. First, in cases such as the ones which are object of this book, to grant self-determination to the third territory would imply an unbalanced situation among the involved agents as this chapter has just shown. The fact that the third territory was sovereign would mean that its inhabitants had exclusive prerogatives over the third territory including consequent rights and burdens; the rest of the international agents involved in the dispute would not have any actual or future right or obligation to intervene in its internal or international affairs. So, the sovereign state that had closer relations with the third territory before the self-determination would see its position both *de jure* and *de facto* improved as reviewed when independence as a remedy was discussed before in this chapter. The same can be said about integration and free association.

To leave aside self-determination as a solution does not have to do with the international institution itself but with the way it may be applied in the sovereignty conflicts that are object of this project. It might have been useful in historical specific cases due to their own characteristics (*e.g.* Kosovo). But to use the same international institutions in the same manner in cases in which the interrelation among the involved agents is already peaceful—apart from the sovereignty difference—adds an unnecessary element of discord that goes against peaceful international relations.

To recapitulate, self-determination may imply secession from an already sovereign state. In fact, self-determination can be one of the ways to secede but not the only one.[16] However, to obtain independence through self-determination is not a solution that can be taken automatically in sovereignty issues. It is an *ultimum remedium*[17] in situations in which a given sovereign state has a certain tension with a group of people, this group of people is large enough, their human rights are not acknowledged, and they have a common identity and decide to be independent; otherwise, their existence within the sovereign state could be compromised. But secession in the form of self-determination is an extreme remedy that may do more harm than good, in some cases.

16 *See* Beran (n. 10), 22 *in fine* and 23 *supra*.
17 *Ibid.*

To be more precise, this view does not change even with the argument that self-determination is a right, overruling utilitarian considerations. Indeed, these pages are not against this interpretation either. The crucial issue is how self-determination is "weighted"—even considered as a right—against public good, general welfare, a fair and just environment for all (not only the majority or any minority). Then, it is not that self-determination is good or bad as a right or as an international remedy per se. Yet, because of the specific situation in which it is applied and the way in which it is used may be.

Therefore, in the case of sovereignty conflicts like the ones object of this monograph, a solution between *status quo* and complete independence should be reached. Some scholars have tried to re-define the idea of self-determination making it more inclusive but somehow giving shape to an eclectic international institution, and that agrees with shared sovereignty:

> [t]he right to national self-determination must go beyond self-government but to stop short of statehood, and thus I introduce a modified right to self-determination, which states that all national groups have an equal right to self-determination provided that the realization of the right does not require the acquisition of independent statehood as a necessary condition.[18]

Hence, if the relationship between a sovereign state and a large group within its population is already problematic, self-determination leading to independence may in fact be a viable solution. However, in the specific case of sovereignty conflicts in which the involved agents have a peaceful relationship apart from the argument about the sovereignty of the third territory, to apply self-determination in the form of independence or integration/association appears as an inadvisable way of dealing with it. It goes against that relationship and threatens an otherwise peaceful environment. Nevertheless, if self-determination is understood as the collective right a group has to determine their political status,[19] and this group is willing to accept the claims of other agents, it can be an institution that may offer a positive outcome. Besides, it may lead to shared sovereignty.

International–multilateral approaches

This type of solution involves the inclusion of agents other than the ones originally involved in the dispute. Thus, even regional or international organizations may participate in the negotiations. As the aim is usually to produce peaceful relations among the participants in the conflict, they mainly involve a freeze in regard to

18 Anna Moltchanova, *National Self-Determination and Justice in Multinational States* (Dordecht: Springer, 2011), *esp.* p. xvi and Chapter 5.

19 *Ibid.*, *esp.* Chapter 2 and Moltchanova's interpretation of Hart's condition for the existence of moral rights. Refer also to H. L. A. Hart, "Are There Any Natural Rights?" *The Philosophical Review* 64 (1955): 175–91.

the sovereignty dispute (usually a step previous to full independence); so no real ultimate solution is obtained. For these reasons, they are usually opposed by at least one of the claimants.

A NATO-based multilateral security approach

In the hypothetical case of the North Atlantic Treaty Organization (NATO) intervening in the Falkland/Malvinas dispute, this would be opposed not only by Argentina but by all Latin-American sovereign states, as creating an external threat to the region.

The Monroe, Calvo, and Drago doctrines apply here.[20] According to Monroe's doctrine the principle of nonintervention is part of the sovereignty of every state. However, before this policy among sovereign states appeared in the 19th century, intervention or mutual interference in internal and foreign affairs of other states was not uncommon. In that period, and with European states trying to recover their colonies in America, the President of the United States proclaimed in one of his speeches (02/12/1823) what later on would be considered basic principles of international public law: (a) no colonization; (b) nonintervention of European states in the affairs of America; (c) reciprocal nonintervention in European affairs. The Calvo and Drago's doctrines are similar in the sense they forbid the intervention of a sovereign state if the purpose of that intervention is only to oblige that state to fulfill its international financial obligations. In these cases, they are also referred to European intervention in American countries and their internal affairs (specifically, Venezuela and its international public debt in 1901).

The main problem with this approach is that the organization that may be involved is both alien to the sovereignty issue and also to the region in which the disputed territory is located. As a result, it is also usually the case that only one of the involved sovereign states is a member of such an organization which leads to the opposition of its counterpart in the conflict because of the resultant unbalanced situation in terms of bargaining power.

It may happen though that both claimants might be members and the organization might be geographically involved—*e.g.* the European Union. Nonetheless, at the moment, in most places where there are disputes, no such organization exists.

20 *See* Elihu Root, "The Real Monroe Doctrine," *American Society of International Law* 8 (1914): 6–22; Mark T. Gilderhus, "The Monroe Doctrine: Meanings and Implications," *Presidential Studies Quarterly* 36 (2006): 5–16; Amos S. Hershey, "The Calvo and Drago Doctrines," *The American Journal of International Law, American Society of International Law* 1 (1907): 26–45; Luis M. Drago and H. Edward Nettles, "The Drago Doctrine in International Law and Politics," *The Hispanic American Historical Review, Duke University Press* 8 (1928): 204–23; Crammond Kennedy, "The Drago Doctrine," *The North American Review, University of Northern Iowa* 185 (1907): 614–22; and many others.

United Nations trusteeship

According to international law, a trusteeship[21] requires the consent of all the involved agents.[22] Originally conceived for territories under specific circumstances after the First and Second World Wars and under the League of Nations, this model can also be used by voluntary agreement and implies that the United Nations Organization (UN) supervizes the administration. The ultimate goal is the autonomy of the territory in question or its integration with another already sovereign state.

As it implies direct interference from UN in internal affairs of the third territory, the agreement of all the agents involved is difficult to obtain (in particular, that of the already sovereign states) in situations like the ones analyzed here. Two main problems immediately arise. First, as discussed when dealing with unilateral approaches, final independence of the third territory could be contrary to the interests of at least one of the agents. Moreover, although UN aims to grant sovereign equality among the states[23] its own system reveals a contradiction: Veto power in the Security Council is only granted to certain sovereign states. This may be translated—in the perception of at least one of the sovereign states—as an unbalanced and unfair starting point to have negotiations, and with a predictable result: Final independence of the third territory and tighter links only with the one sovereign state that supported the independence process. Not only does the Security Council present these problems but also other UN organizations. Even the UN General Assembly, at first glance a fair environment for sovereign states to participate in, has been regarded as ineffective[24] or irredeemably biased because of the different bargaining powers of its members. Also, in cases of contested sovereignty over populated territories, stateless people are not UN members.

21 For more details about the Trusteeship Council, refer to http://www.un.org/en/mainbodies/trusteeship/ (last accessed December 30, 2016) and http://www.un.org/en/decolonization/its.shtml (last accessed December 30, 2016).

22 UN Charter, art. 79: "The terms of trusteeship for each territory to be placed under the trusteeship system, including any alteration or amendment, shall be agreed upon by the states directly concerned, including the mandatory power in the case of territories held under mandate by a Member of the United Nations, and shall be approved as provided for in Articles 83 and 85."

23 W. Michael Reisman, "The Constitutional Crisis in the United Nations," *The American Journal of International Law* 87 (1993): 83–100.

24 Jack E. Vincent, "Predicting Voting Patterns in the General Assembly," *The American Political Science Review* 65 (1971): 471–98; Axel Dreher, Peter Nunnenkamp, and Rainer Thiele, "Does US Aid Buy UN General Assembly Votes?" *Public Choice* 136 (2008): 139–64; T. Y. Wang, "U.S. Foreign Aid and UN Voting: An Analysis of Important Issues," *International Studies Quarterly* 43 (1999): 199–210; and many others.

Is the Antarctic Treaty a possible model?

The Antarctic Treaty[25] mainly refers to scientific exploration of the Antarctica leaving the recognition of territorial sovereignty undecided.[26] In what is important here, the basic sovereignty conflict remains unresolved.

In addition, one of the main differences this case presents in comparison to the sovereignty disputes is the fact that there is no settled population in Antarctica. Although it may be argued that somehow the rights mankind as a whole has over Antarctica are affected—*e.g.* with regard to exploitation of natural resources and consequent effects in the environment—the fact that there is no settled population means any issue related to human rights is not actual but potential and not related to a particular population. On the contrary, the conflicts contemplated by the model of shared sovereignty assume there is a population living in the third territory, who has certain minimum human rights, so that any decision some or all of the agents take in relation to the third territory will affect them.

Could one appeal to the International Court of Justice?

The International Court of Justice (ICJ) has international jurisdiction and is multi-competent. However, two main problems make sovereignty conflicts of the kind that are object of this monograph difficult to be acknowledged by the ICJ: That there are not only legal but also political issues involved and that the agreement of all the parties in the conflict is needed.[27] Sovereignty entails

25 For a complete version of the Antarctic Treaty, *see* http://www.ats.aq/documents/ats/treaty_original.pdf (last accessed December 30, 2016).

26 Article IV of the Antarctic Treaty refers to territorial claims: "1. Nothing contained in the present Treaty shall be interpreted as: (a) a renunciation by any Contracting Party of previously asserted rights of or claims to territorial sovereignty in Antarctica; (b) a renunciation or diminution by any Contracting Party of any basis of claim to territorial sovereignty in Antarctica which it may have whether as a result of its activities or those of its nationals in Antarctica, or otherwise; (c) prejudicing the position of any Contracting Party as regards its recognition or non recognition of any other State's right of or claim or basis of claim to territorial sovereignty in Antarctica. 2. No acts or activities taking place while the present Treaty is in force shall constitute a basis for asserting, supporting or denying a claim to territorial sovereignty in Antarctica. No new claim, or enlargement of an existing claim, to territorial sovereignty shall be asserted while the present Treaty is in force." *See* J. Peter A. Bernhardt, "Sovereignty in Antarctica," *California Western International Journal* 5 (1975): 297–349.

27 *See* ICJ Statute, in particular art. 36: "1. The jurisdiction of the Court comprises all cases which the parties refer to it and all matters specially provided for in the Charter of the United Nations or in treaties and conventions in force. 2. The states parties to the present Statute may at any time declare that they recognise as compulsory ipso facto and without special agreement, in relation to any other state accepting the same obligation, the jurisdiction of the Court in all legal disputes concerning: a. the interpretation of a treaty; b. any question of international law; c. the existence of any fact which, if established, would constitute a breach of an international obligation; d. the nature or extent of the reparation to be made for the breach of an international obligation . . ."

several different elements that are not only legal (*e.g.* society, economy, etc.). Even though sovereignty claims as a right may be resolved—for example—by granting sovereignty to one, several or all the involved agents, the questions related to specificities in regard to government, population, and territory remain unanswered. The solution, even if it was considered to an extent fair and just, cannot comprehend the whole complexity a sovereignty conflict offers; rather, it deals just with one of its components. Also, to obtain the agreement of all the claimants to its decision—as it has been shown to be the case with other proposed remedies—would be very difficult. Even if was obtained, it would be very limited.

Bilateral approaches

Here, the two sovereign agents involved are included in the negotiations (the population of the third territory is not necessarily represented). Arguably, at the starting point they are equal international agents in relatively equal comparative circumstances in relation to the third territory. Although this may not be translated into real terms (*i.e.* one of the sovereign states may be considerably more powerful, making its bargaining position stronger and giving it an advantage in the negotiations), the main problem with this approach is the fact that the population of the third territory may see their interests being completely overlooked. A bilateral approach of any kind—in its narrow sense—will only bear in mind the interests of the two sovereign states; hence, to acknowledge those of the population of the third territory would be left to the good will of these sovereign states. As a way of example, possible bilateral "solutions" will be considered below.

A condominium

International condominium implies that two or more sovereign states share their respective dominium over a specific territory. There are several examples of this international institution.[28] Although dominium under these circumstances may be understood as equivalent to sovereignty, its real meaning is much narrower. Dominium appears to be similar to sovereignty but is only linked to one of the elements that characterize a state: Its territory. Despite the fact that sovereignty in modern and contemporary legal and political literature is also mainly related to the territorial element, it has a broader content so as to include population, government, and law—and all that each of these elements implies. That is to say, the sovereignty conflicts here all present a populated territory under dispute.

28 Lake Constance (Germany, Austria, and Switzerland; however, there is no agreement in place), Paraná River (Argentina, Brazil, and Paraguay, with many bi-lateral and multilateral projects and agreements in place), Sudan (Egypt and the United Kingdom between 1899 and 1955), and many others. *See The New York Times* (January 23, 2012) http://opinionator.blogs.nytimes.com/2012/01/23/the-worlds-most-exclusive-condominium/ (last accessed December 30, 2016).

Therefore, an international condominium would be a very inadequate way of addressing these conflicts, dealing with the territorial element but leaving aside all the other elements. So, to use an international condominium may be a reasonable solution for those particular cases in which the dispute is only related to a nonpopulated territory or one that although being populated, has certain characteristics that makes the territory the only element actually to be shared—*e.g.* it may be economically advantageous for two states to share the sovereignty over a river that acts as a natural border since they both have inhabitants in either side and there is a strong commercial interchange.

Moreover, some of its particular features make this model either not stable or not feasible specifically for the type of sovereignty conflicts analyzed here. There are several reasons to avoid it: First, sovereignty may not be shared simultaneously but alternately (*e.g.* Pheasant Island, an uninhabited river island condominium between Spain and France, alternating sovereign every six months); second, condominiums are mostly temporary (*e.g.* the Anglo-Egyptian Sudan 1899–1956); third, in most cases, they cover a territory—land or maritime—without a settled population (*e.g.* Paraná River, Lake Constance); fourth, the condominium has to do with special geographical circumstances (*e.g.* Gulf of Fonseca, part of the coastline belonging either to Honduras, Nicaragua, or El Salvador).

In brief, although at first glance international condominiums and shared sovereignty appear to be similar institutions with similar consequences, they are not. International condominiums have further characteristics that make the model an undesirable solution when applied to a populated third territory claimed by two sovereign states. There are many issues that international condominium cannot deal with. First, it is mainly referred to uninhabited territories. Additionally, even though the territory is inhabited, a crucial pitfall is that sovereignty changes every few years. And this variable feature has several negative consequences: It does not offer a solution for many implications (*e.g.* law applicable in case of a crime); it is in fact a temporal way of addressing the problem which translates in avoiding the ultimate discussion about sovereignty; it is a volatile approach because it depends on factual variables (*e.g.* the co-owned river changes its course, the portion of land granted to one claimant becomes useless due to environmental change); it is easy to see how it may work in cases in which the claimants are territorial neighbours but it is hard to see how it could work in those in they were distant—geographically speaking. All these reasons make international condominiums an unstable solution for most—if not all—the involved agents in the conflict and in particular for the inhabitants of the third territory.

Leaseback with guarantees

This model involves a sovereign state that agrees to transfer the sovereignty over a territory to another sovereign state and leases it back for a certain time—*i.e.* the licensor will have the right to "use" the territory until the agreed time finishes. It is often the case that the state that is granted the final sovereignty offers certain guarantees, in particular if the territory in question is populated—*e.g.* language of the inhabitants, applicable law, nationality, etc. Also known as the Hong Kong model of "one country–two systems,"[29] this formula is in between a sovereignty conflict and final full independence or integration as part of another sovereign state. In other words, it does not offer a definitive solution. It is a stage towards a definitive solution—whether final independence or integration, but one which overrides one of the states in dispute (unless, like the United Kingdom, it had accepted this final solution in advance).

Once again, this particular remedy does not guarantee either an equal starting point or result: As detailed, it is the usual case the third territory has tighter links—for whatever reasons—with one of the sovereign states and its final independence or integration would simply be a way to legitimize *de jure* that situation. Besides, to agree upon the length of the leaseback and the way in which the guarantees will be fulfilled is often very controversial.[30] Also, the population of the leased territory rarely gets a say.

A sovereignty freeze

This institution is similar to the one analyzed under the heading "Antarctic Solution" (when discussing international-multilateral approaches before in this chapter). The only difference is that the dispute between the two original sovereign claimants remains. However, the negative consequences are the same. No other international agent has a right to a claim or involvement in the dispute, the original participants are the only ones involved, the third territory is assumed to be populated, but sovereignty is not given to any of the agents, it is not shared among them or distributed in any way.

At first glance it may be argued that a peaceful relationship among the agents is achieved. However, at what cost? First, none of the agents is allowed to put into practice any claimed right over the third territory. Second, even if they intended to put in practice their claimed rights, they would need to agree upon each and every action, since this would imply a break in the sovereignty freeze. Third, the population of the third territory would remain in a legal and political limbo, with both local and international implications (*e.g.* defense, representation in international organizations, etc.).

Abandonment

The two sovereign states would withdraw their claims in regards the sovereignty of the third territory. An immediate consequence for the third territory seems to be either a political and legal limbo or independence. In either of these cases, this

29 Lorenz Langer, "Out of Joint? Hong Kong's International Status from the Sino–British Joint Declaration to the Present," *Archiv des Volkerrechts* 46 (2008): 309–44.

30 For the specific case of the Falkland/Malvinas Islands and the application of the leaseback with guarantees, *see* Guillermo A. Makin, "Argentina 1983: Elections and Items for Negotiations with the United Kingdom," *Bulletin of Latin American Research* 3 (1984): 110–18.

solution offers negative outcomes not only for the third territory but also for the sovereign states. In the case of the third territory, its internal and international position would be precarious (*e.g.* defense, international credit, etc.). For instance, in the best case scenario, the third territory could be fully independent, or associated with or integrated in another sovereign state (several negative consequences have been already analyzed in each case). In the worst case scenario, the third territory could be left in a legal and political limbo, making it an easy target for any other state. In what is of interest to the sovereign states, each would withdraw any actual or potential claim. So, its peer in the conflict, and any other agent, would have a free path to act as they wished in relation to the third territory.

Titular sovereignty and autonomy

The case of the Aland Islands[31] is the leading example: A nonsovereign autonomous territory under the umbrella of an already sovereign state. This self-governing community has a separate and independent administration from that of Finland. This includes having a separate executive power and an autonomous parliament. Yet, they are under the sovereignty of Finland. This solution is possible and desirable for the third territory and for one of the involved sovereign states. However, the other state sees its claimed rights disappear. It is for that reason this type of solution appears to be—at least—not desirable for the kind of conflicts analyzed here. It assumes one sovereign state and one populated territory arguing about sovereignty. Hence, the starting point is different from the one of shared sovereignty.

The *status quo*

As this is both theoretically possible and what often actually happens in sovereignty conflicts, it is advisable and reasonable to consider the possibility of simply maintaining the *status quo*. Obviously, this would mean only postponing the decision; the main question in regard to sovereignty would remain unanswered. A further problem under these circumstances is that none of the involved agents are able to put their rights fully into practice. On the one hand, even in the best possible scenario, if the relations among the agents were peaceful it could only be expected they continue to be that way. On the other hand, reality shows that more often than not the *status quo* is broken by at least one of the agents trying to put their claimed rights into action—*e.g.* by exploitation of natural resources. So, the *status quo*'s main feature is contradictory: Volatility. Since rights and obligations

31 Tore Modeen, "The International Protection of the National Identity of the Aland Islands," *Scandinavian Studies in Law* 17 (1973): 176–210; Holger Rotkirch, "The Demilitarization of the Aland Islands: A Regime 'in European Interests' Withstanding Changing Circumstances," *Journal of Peace Research* 23 (1986): 357–76; Finn Seyersted, "The Aland Autonomy and International Law," *Nordisk Tidsskrift International Ret.* 51 (1982): 23–28; and many more.

are not clearly defined for any of the agents because sovereignty remains undefined, none of them has the actual power to make use of them fully, but at the same time they do not have any more legal restrictions than those of international public law, or any more political ones than those caused by the presence of the other agents.[32]

Conclusion

The first lines of this chapter made clear that the goal was to see if any of the current proposed international remedies for sovereignty conflicts could be a reasonable solution to the ones we are interested in here. In all cases there are reasons that make their application somewhat controversial—if not more problematic by threatening an otherwise peaceful relation between the claimant states.

Precisely, there are various possible solutions for sovereignty conflicts. This revision covered independence, self-determination, the Antarctic solution, and many others. Although they may be the answer for some sovereignty conflicts, they present—for the reasons shown in this chapter—a certain degree of uncertainty that make us doubt about the value of their application.

Indeed, the previous pages did not claim that these other remedies are of no use. In fact, if the parties accept them and they result in a peaceful understanding among them, there is no question about their reasonableness. What this chapter argues and demonstrates is that there is a need for a peaceful solution that the reviewed international remedies cannot offer. A solution that no party may reasonably reject is in need, whereas, all existing solutions may be reasonably rejected by one or more parties. It is time now to see if such a reasonable solution can be offered to these parties. Therefore, the following chapters will attempt to reach a solution that no reasonable party may reject.

Bibliography

Beck, Peter. "Britain's Falkland Future: The Need to Look Back." *The Round Table* 73 (1984): 139–52.

Beck, Peter. "Looking at the Falkland Islands from Antarctica: The Broader Regional Perspective." *Polar Record* 30 (1994): 167–80.

Beck, Peter. "The Future of the Falkland Islands: A Solution Made in Hong Kong?" *International Affairs, Royal Institute of International Affairs* 61 (1985): 643–60.

Beck, Peter. *The Falkland Islands as an International Problem*. London and New York: Routledge, 1998.

Beran, Harry. "A Liberal Theory of Secession." *Political Studies* XXXII (1984): 21–31.

Bernhardt, J. P. A. "Sovereignty in Antarctica." *California Western International Journal* 5 (1975): 297–349.

32 In the case of the Falkland/Malvinas Islands, it is common practice for Argentina to protest in international forums when the United Kingdom acts upon natural resources.

Birch, Anthony H. "Another Liberal Theory of Secession." *Political Studies* XXXII (1984): 596–602.

Buchanan, Allen. "Toward a Theory of Secession." *Chicago University Press* 101 (1991): 322–42.

Chehabi, H. E. "Self-Determination, Territorial Integrity, and the Falkland Islands." *The Academy of Political Science, Political Science Quarterly* 100 (1985): 215–25.

Drago, Luis M. and Nettles, H. Edward. "The Drago Doctrine in International Law and Politics." *The Hispanic American Historical Review, Duke University Press* 8 (1928): 204–23.

Dreher, Axel, Nunnenkamp, Peter, and Thiele, Rainer. "Does US Aid Buy UN General Assembly Votes?" *Public Choice* 136 (2008): 139–64.

Dunnett, Denzil. "Self-Determination and the Falklands." *International Affairs, Royal Institute of International Affairs* 59 (1983): 415–28.

Gilderhus, Mark T. "The Monroe Doctrine: Meanings and Implications." *Presidential Studies Quarterly* 36 (2006): 5–16.

Hart, H. L. A. "Are There Any Natural Rights?" *The Philosophical Review* 64 (1955): 175–91.

Hershey, Amos S. "The Calvo and Drago Doctrines." *The American Journal of International Law, American Society of International Law* 1 (1907): 26–45.

Kennedy, Crammond. "The Drago Doctrine." *The North American Review, University of Northern Iowa* 185 (1907): 614–22.

Kooijmans, P. H. "Tolerance, Sovereignty and Self-Determination." *Netherlands International Law Review* XLIII (1996): 211–17.

Langer, Lorenz. "Out of Joint? Hong Kong's International Status from the Sino–British Joint Declaration to the Present." *Archiv des Volkerrechts* 46 (2008): 309–44.

Makin, Guillermo A. "Argentina 1983: Elections and Items for Negotiations with the United Kingdom." *Bulletin of Latin American Research* 3 (1984): 110–18.

McGee, Robert W. "A Third Liberal Theory of Secession." *The Liverpool Law Review* XIV (1992): 45–66.

Modeen, Tore. "The International Protection of the National Identity of the Aland Islands." *Scandinavian Studies in Law* 17 (1973): 176–210.

Moltchanova, Anna. *National Self-Determination and Justice in Multinational States.* Dordecht: Springer, 2011.

Pickard, Cyril. "Fortress Falkland? The Real Lessons of the Franks Report." *The Round Table* 72 (1983): 233–37.

Reisman, W. Michael. "The Constitutional Crisis in the United Nations." *The American Journal of International Law* 87 (1993): 83–100.

Root, Elihu. "The Real Monroe Doctrine." *American Society of International Law* 8 (1914): 6–22.

Rotkirch, Holger. "The Demilitarization of the Aland Islands: A Regime 'in European Interests' Withstanding Changing Circumstances." *Journal of Peace Research* 23 (1986): 357–76.

Seyersted, Finn. "The Aland Autonomy and International Law." *Nordisk Tidsskrift International Ret.* 51 (1982): 23–28.

Vincent, Jack E. "Predicting Voting Patterns in the General Assembly." *The American Political Science Review* 65 (1971): 471–98.

Wang, T. Y. "U.S. Foreign Aid and UN Voting: An Analysis of Important Issues." *International Studies Quarterly* 43 (1999): 199–210.

Part III

6 How can shared sovereignty be just?

Introduction

The aim now is to present a conception of shared sovereignty that can lead to an abstract model in which the claimants in a sovereignty conflict leave aside reasons that may work against a final and peaceful solution. This chapter will explore if it is possible to adapt the model created by John Rawls in his *A Theory of Justice*[1] to sovereignty conflicts. The idea is to present an argument for hypothetical agreement by coming up with principles that cannot be reasonably refused. Therefore, this is a theoretical exercise to focus on what factors cause bias in sovereignty disputes. Then, the task is to design a procedure which will limit the effect of these factors. As well as highlighting these pitfalls on the way to a peaceful solution, a hypothetical agreement among the claimants will be explored. If such an agreement is reached, it must be one that people could not reasonably reject later on, and so to do this bias must be eliminated.

As in *A Theory of Justice*, the analysis conducted here is based on a hypothetical situation. In consequence, the only thing needed is that all three parties are motivated to obtain a reasonable solution. Therefore, it is assumed that they have appointed free and equal negotiators to achieve this. Hence, this original position in which the negotiations take place assumes certain other features that will be discussed here. Within this environment, the negotiators will examine a series of principles and see if any of them secures their respective ends as representatives of the claimant populations—the two sovereign states and of the third territory.

Indeed, Rawls's thinking on international justice can be found in *The Law of Peoples*. Some of its elements will be explored too. Yet, it is mainly his *A Theory of Justice* and the method he develops there that will be used here. The main reason to proceed this way is that Rawls makes clear in *The Law of Peoples* that it is "peoples" that constitute the relevant moral units of international society leaving aside states per se. In addition to this, he emphasizes that sovereignty is

1 The design of this chapter is mainly inspired by Chapter 3 of John Rawls, *A Theory of Justice*, Revised Edition (Oxford: Oxford University Press, 1999).

not central for his proposal.[2] This monograph, on the contrary, follows the traditional view that states are constituted by a population ("peoples") but also recognizes other constitutive elements. That is because this monograph is centered on sovereignty disputes, issues that Rawls himself does not address.

In other words, Rawls was involved in a different project in *The Law of Peoples*. This book does not argue that the solution is the one Rawls would necessarily come up with or what Rawls would have wanted. It is using his methodology to arrive at its own solution.[3]

Setting the stage for the negotiations

Any community or population consists of individuals who are different in many senses—pluralism, as Rawls says[4]—is a permanent feature that cannot be ignored. The international community does not escape from this, since it includes several agents of very different natures. Therefore, as in the case of civil societies in Rawls's *A Theory of Justice*, it is assumed here that the international society is constituted by several different agents who in their relations recognize some "rules of conduct" and act upon them.[5]

However, only one kind of them, the state, has a specific characteristic: Sovereignty. And even if the international community was only composed of sovereign states, they are different in many ways—*e.g.* strong and weak, developed and nondeveloped, populated and not populated, insular, peninsular, etc. It is for that reason that it is also supposed that their interrelation is for "mutual advantage."[6] That is because it is assumed states are only interested in maximizing their own interest, but they realize they can only do that by taking opportunities for social cooperation available if they act as a well-behaved member of the international community—notion introduced in Chapter 4 when discussing how far sovereign states can cooperate together without sacrificing their sovereignty. But, as in any circumstances in which there are agents of different kinds—so the same is true of a community of states—relations among international agents introduce also identity and conflict of interests[7]—and sovereignty conflicts are one

2 See Chapter 1 for more details on Rawlsian methodology. Rawls specifically uses in John Rawls, *The Law of Peoples* (Cambridge MA: Harvard University Press, 1999) the term "peoples" to distinguish his thinking from that about political States as traditionally conceived. In addition to this, he maintains that "peoples" lack traditional sovereignty. This book, on the contrary, uses the terms "state" and "sovereignty" as generally accepted in legal and political sciences.

3 For a more detailed analysis on the criticism on Rawlsian methodology, *see* Chapter 1 and Rawls's *A Theory of Justice* and *The Law of Peoples*.

4 Referred to Rawls's idea of pluralism as a "permanent feature of a democratic society." See John Rawls, *Justice as Fairness, A Restatement* (Cambridge MA: Harvard University Press, 2003), *esp.* p. 84.

5 Rawls, *A Theory of Justice* (n. 1), p. 4.

6 *Ibid.*

7 *Ibid.* In what matters here Rawls says that: "[t]here is an identity of interests since social cooperation makes possible a better life for all than any would have if each were to live solely

of them. As a result, some criteria are needed for choosing the principles that can put a peaceful end to these conflicts.

Although *A Theory of Justice* offers an insight on how to address conflicts of interest, it is one that deals with them within civil societies and at an individual level and, hence, is not totally appropriate for international issues—at least not to the extent needed in this book. That is because the principles here will be concerned with a special case of conflicts: Sovereignty disputes. Consequently, specific principles are needed in order to determine how to assign sovereign rights and duties over a nonsovereign and populated territory. So, it is essential to adapt Rawls's approach from individual to state level. Thus, it is important to make clear how the elements that Rawls proposes in *A Theory of Justice* at the individual level are also present in sovereignty disputes.

As in any negotiation concerning different agents with a conflict of interest, a particular feature has to be addressed—pluralism—in order to strive for a solution, even more if that solution is intended to be just and fair so as to secure a binding and respected agreement. Addressing this feature at the individual level, Rawls defines the "circumstances of justice" as "the normal conditions under which human cooperation is both possible and necessary."[8] Then, he proceeds to divide them in objective characteristics—*i.e.* characteristics of the environment, physical and mental features of the participant individuals, their capacities and a state of moderate scarcity; and subjective characteristics—*i.e.* even though individuals may have similar needs and interests, each has an individual plan of life.

One of the first points that Rawls makes is that questions of distributive justice arise only under certain "circumstances of justice," that is to say limited resources and limited altruism. In what is crucial for this book, there is also a common interest that is the cause of sovereignty conflicts and there are some "circumstances of justice" that are particular to them. The territory under dispute and all that it implies—is the one element around which the dispute is centered. In other words, what Rawls labels at the individual level as moderate scarcity or limited resources finds its parallel in sovereignty disputes in the nonsovereign third territory—*i.e.* the only "thing" all the agents are claiming exclusive sovereignty over. To be more precise, what is scarce is the rights and obligations that sovereignty entails over the third territory. Thus, what Rawls refers to as an individual's plan of life it is called here a "state plan of life"—each state's interest as a group is also represented by the exclusive rights it claims over the same piece of land.

In order to avoid confusion about what is meant as a "state plan of life," it is important to distinguish between an individual or personal interest—the one that Rawls refers to—and the interest of each claiming party as a whole—the one this book refers to. Each of the claimants—the two sovereign states and

by his own efforts. There is conflict of interests since persons are not indifferent as to how the greater benefits produced by their collaboration are distributed, for in order to pursue their ends they each prefer a larger to a lesser share . . ."

8 *Ibid.*, p. 109.

the population of the third territory—is a community of people who live in a certain territory and have common authorities and law.[9] The individuals in these claiming parties have both common and conflicting interests.[10] But although each claiming party is formed by many different individuals with different interests, each of these claiming parties has as a collective group a common interest for the purpose of this monograph: Sovereignty over the third territory. Thus, this same element—the third territory—is the center of this particular conflict of interest.

In brief, there is a situation in which three populations coexist (two sovereign states and one nonsovereign group of people) and argue about their rights and obligations over the same territory. There are limited resources or there is a moderate scarcity given by the claimed territory that each of them exclusively wants. While these claimants could work together in a mutually advantageous way, they each have, as different groups of people, respectively their own collective "plan of life" that is currently preventing them from doing this: Their respective "plans of life" in relation to the claimed territory are blocked by the other claimants, resulting in a zero sum game.

Formal constraints: A "colorable claim"

Before going into the negotiations to solve the sovereignty conflict it is imperative to decide who will be able to be part of them—*i.e.* who is a legitimate claiming party. This has to do with the "admissibility" steps prior to the negotiations. Therefore, both the claiming agents and the "original position" as a whole are subjected to certain limitations. The agents will be limited in such a way that the right to claim is restricted to those who fulfill certain criteria, while other constraints secure the reasonableness of the procedure.

The agents should have a "colorable claim."[11] That is to say, the represented populations must have a valid reason to claim sovereignty over the third territory—

9 For a notion of society, *see* Rawls, *A Theory of Justice* (n. 1), p. 4.

10 *Ibid.*

11 A "colorable claim" (in American English either a colorable claim or colorable argument) is an expression used in the law of the United States to refer to a claim strong enough to have a reasonable chance of winning—*i.e.* the claim need not actually result in a win. It is a nonfrivolous argument either supported by reference to law or facts that may be proven in Court. The distinction between "colorability" of a claim and a winning claim has to do with two different steps in a judicial procedure. The colorability of the claim is related to admissibility—*i.e.* "X" has a reasonable, nonfrivolous ground to claim. It is only when the right to claim is acknowledged (it is admissible) that the Court will consider facts and law and decide upon the case. There are many cases that can be quoted to illustrate the use of this expression in Courts of the United States—*e.g. Jones v. Barnes*, 463 US 745, Supreme Court 1983; *Arbaugh v. Y & H Corp.*, 546 US 500, Supreme Court 2006; *Richardson v. United States*, 468 US 317, Supreme Court 1984; and many others. In United Kingdom criminal proceedings, for example, it is equivalent to the "is there a case to answer?" standards. *See Regina v Galbraith* [1981] WLR 1039. *See also* Criminal Procedure (Scotland) Act 1995, s. 97 and the "no case to answer" standard.

e.g. effective occupation,[12] consent by the other agent in the dispute,[13] consent by other states,[14] and/or consent by the international community.[15] That reason should be "colorable" enough to prove that their intended rights are at least sufficiently plausible to be acknowledged, and they can be based on any reasonable circumstances—*e.g.* political, historical, legal, geographical arguments to name a few. For example, in the case of the Falkland/Malvinas Islands dispute it would be unreasonable for Russia to participate in the negotiations in relation to their sovereignty since they do not have any colorable claim over that territory.

To put it in other words, a party will have a colorable claim if *prima facie* they have the right to claim, that is to say they appear to have a probable cause to support their intended right to claim. That is different from saying that they have a right to sovereignty. In the latter case, there is indeed an argument that has weight but that may be later overcome by another more pressing one. So, to have a colorable claim means having at least an argument that offers surface legitimacy—that may or may not translate in the negotiations into granting sovereignty because it only secures the participation in them.

Because a colorable claim recognizes surface legitimacy to claim sovereignty to a party, it does not need to be the case that the sovereign states or the population of the third territory have claims sufficiently equal in strength to give them roughly equal claims in respect of the third territory. In fact, one sovereign state could have a claim that entitled it to double the weight of the other sovereign state or that of the third population. That is because a colorable claim refers only to the right to claim sovereignty, and that is prior to any negotiations. It is indeed in the negotiations when the parties may discuss the weight of their claims.

Each particular ground for a colorable claim needs exploration. In broad terms, a colorable claim can be based on: (1) historical entitlements; (2) the legal status of these claims; and (3) moral considerations. Note that this list is not exhaustive and only includes some of the most common examples in sovereignty conflicts. That is because a colorable claim refers to surface legitimacy and hence can be based on any *prima facie* reasonable circumstance related to the sovereignty over the third territory. Indeed, to have a colorable claim, the claim cannot be an undifferentiated one to the third territory—*i.e.* there must be some connection between the claimant and the third territory other than, for example, the claimant simply having an interest in the third territory.

12 The Island of Palmas Case (or Miangas) *(United States of America v. The Netherlands)*, Permanent Court of Arbitration (1928), and The Legal Status of Eastern Greenland Case *(Denmark v. Norway)*, Permanent Court of International Justice (1933).

13 The Temple of Preah Vihear Case *(Cambodia v Thailand)* (1962).

14 The Legal Status of Eastern Greenland Case *(Denmark v Norway)*, Permanent Court of International Justice (1933).

15 Quincy Wright, "The Goa Incident," *The American Journal of International Law* 56 (1962): 617–32.

First, a colorable claim is based on historical entitlements when any of the claiming parties bases its right to claim on past facts related to the third territory and their intention to be its sovereign. These past facts can be related to actual occupation—for instance, effective occupation. But they do not exclude claiming parties that do not currently occupy the third territory. However, in the event they did not occupy the third territory, their continuous intention to do so would be enough to grant them a colorable claim. That is because they may have been removed or expelled from the third territory. But in one or the other case, effective current occupation or past occupation and continuous intention to occupy the territory, they may have a basis strong enough to have a reasonable chance of being sovereign of that third territory. In other words, the facts they use to support their right to claim sovereignty may be proven in the negotiations. That is different, nevertheless, from saying their claim will actually be granted in the negotiations. Indeed, the historical claim can be controversial and disputed—but it cannot be frivolous. It is the same kind of test used in British law to determine whether there is a possible cause to move forward—*i.e.* if there is a case to answer.

It is important to make clear once again that the colorable claim refers to the right to claim sovereignty—and not to the right to sovereignty itself. Therefore, the historical entitlement is viewed here in order to prove surface or *prima facie* legitimacy. The historical claim will be reviewed in particular and in detail elsewhere in this chapter when discussing the right to sovereignty.

Second, a colorable claim is based on the legal status of these claims when any of the parties use or may use law to support their right to claim sovereignty. In this case, they may use international customary law or treaty law to support their position. For instance, the case of one of the parties that did not have effective current occupation of the third territory but had continuously claimed sovereignty in international forums such as United Nations following international public law regulations.

Third, a colorable claim is based on moral considerations when any of the claiming parties based their right to claim sovereignty on moral grounds—*i.e.* they have moral standing. That is because the claim has to relate to the sovereignty of the third territory and the decision that the parties will arrive at in the negotiations may make a difference, morally, on how that party may be treated.

There is indeed a linked question to the idea of moral standing: Who counts? In general, there can be many answers, from the narrowest by only granting certain populations participation—*e.g.* only human beings that fulfill certain criteria; to the broadest—*e.g.* any human being, and hence any population may potentially have the right to claim sovereignty anywhere. For example, would Zimbabwe have a right to claim sovereignty over the Falkland/Malvinas Islands based on a humanitarian reason such as famine? The answer to this question depends on the frame of reference. This book, although seeking for a just and fair outcome, is not about global justice or morality but about particular sovereignty conflicts—*i.e.* those with two sovereign states claiming sovereignty over a populated third territory. Thereby, the moral considerations will be seen and analyzed within this context in order to decide whether these three parties have a colorable claim, if they *prima facie* have moral standing to a right to claim sovereignty—*i.e.* the claim has to relate to the sovereignty over the third territory and the final decision may make a difference on how the party may be treated.

In this respect, mention should be made of the participation in the negotiations of the inhabitants of the third territory. Some questions may arise and must be answered before any allocation of sovereignty can be proposed: On the one hand, would it be fair for the population in the third territory to share the use and ownership of the territory they are inhabitants of? On the other hand, are there some minimum criteria here to help determine when the residents of the disputed territory get a vote?—*e.g.* what if these residents were brought there by one of the competing parties?

Some difficulties may seem to appear because of the dissimilarities between the cases to which Rawls applies his method and the cases here. One such a difference, the one *sub-examine*, seems to be that the three parties presented in the negotiations appear to be different sorts of party. It may seem as if the kinds of claim that are relevant to the two sovereign states are different from those that are relevant to the third population.

That is not true. Besides, it is an oversimplification. That is because all three parties are somehow claiming sovereignty or at least claiming a legitimate interest in deciding how the bundle of rights and obligations that constitutes sovereignty are distributed. The sovereign states are claiming exclusive sovereignty based on whatever reason. But the third population is claiming sovereignty too. Sovereignty both seen as rights and obligations has an inward and outward facets—as set out in Chapter 2. So, it is oversimplistic to think the third population has different kinds of claims that are relevant for them and hence suggest they are a different sort of party and use that reason not to include them in the negotiations. Their claims have to do with sovereignty too. It may be argued that the sovereign states give relevance to the external sovereignty whereas the third population gives relevance to the internal sovereignty. Yet, they all are claiming different facets of the same group of rights and obligations. Moreover, in all the cases covered by this book—*i.e.* the Falkland/Malvinas Islands, Kashmir, and Gibraltar—the third populations have expressed clearly that they want a measure of self-government and to be able to determine under whose state authority they should fall.

In tune with this, the above questions are indeed interlinked as well as their answers. Although at first glance it may seem unfair for someone to share what is supposed to be his own, the reality is that the sovereignty of exactly that object—in the case under study, the third territory—is the center of the whole dispute among two sovereign states and that nonsovereign territory. The starting point is a piece of land populated by certain people whose sovereignty is being argued over by several parties. These inhabitants do live there, but their right to do so is under discussion. However, it must be highlighted that they are rational beings and human beings and hence they have human rights, even though sovereignty disputes are not an issue of human rights only.

Precisely, there are reasons that support the inclusion of the inhabitants in the negotiation that go beyond that of human rights. Indeed, they have a colorable claim. That is because they either occupy the territory and have been there continuously—historical entitlement, or because they have moral standing—*i.e.* any decision with regard to sovereignty will have a nontrivial impact on their lives since they are there, or a combination of both. They live in the territory and their lives—and that of their future generations—will be affected more than any others by the arrangements that are adopted in the negotiations. In other words, presence gives one a colorable claim. It is true, that it may encourage occupation. But as long as the people have been there long enough to establish roots, whether their occupation is rightful or wrongful, they at least should have the right to participate in the negotiations. How much weight their claim gets is something to be discussed. So it would be unfair to ask them to leave or not to take their claimed rights into consideration.

For example, it is true that Argentina could acknowledge the right of the population currently living in the Falkland/Malvinas Islands to be self-determining but deny their right to be self-determining on Argentinean land—if they want to be self-determining they should go and do it somewhere else, most obviously the United Kingdom. But once again, this would be a practical approach that does not grant a just and fair outcome. The islanders would have their right to self-determination made conditional on being under Argentinean sovereignty—*i.e.* "you can decide your future if and only if it is within my power." Indeed, this would literally imply that they were moved from the British sovereignty umbrella to that of Argentina with consequences for them and their future generations in terms of many aspects directly related to their lives and way of living—*e.g.* law, financial situation, defense, political stability, and so on.

Therefore, to give them participation in the negotiations may have to do with a backward looking justification—*i.e.* colorable claim as historical entitlement—but it is mainly because of the effects any decision in relation to sovereignty will have on their lives, and that gives them moral standing to count—*i.e.* colorable claim based on moral considerations.

With all these elements within the same frame, to ask the population of the third territory to share the sovereignty and consequent benefits and burdens with other populations is fair, provided that their right to own and use the land is welcomed by all the involved agents—*i.e.* they have a colorable claim. The extent of that right is one of the matters under discussion and that will be reviewed in the negotiations when analyzing the different principles involved.

Some may wonder whether fourth parties' humanitarian needs—*e.g.* in cases of disaster, famine, etc.—are sufficient for a colorable claim and whether fourth parties should be distributed some of the burdens and benefits of sharing sovereignty in this context. There are two issues at stake here, both related to the participation or not of a fourth party: (a) if humanitarian reasons can be seen as a base for a colorable claim; and (b) in the case they were considered a colorable claim, if the fourth party should also be distributed contributions and returns.

The answer has to be divided in two parts: (a) humanitarian reasons related to any of the three original claiming agents, that is to say either the two sovereign states or the population of the third territory; and (b) humanitarian reasons only related to a fourth party. In the first case scenario, it has been made clear before that this book assumes a peaceful understanding among the parties. Therefore, secession, self-determination that leads to independence, and so on have been reviewed elsewhere and discarded.[16]

In the second case scenario, there is a misinterpretation of this proposal. For distributive justice principles are brought into this project solely to offer a solution to sovereignty conflicts, and not to put an end to inequalities among the claiming agents' comparative situations or to help them in achieving equal level of welfare. In the examples covered by this book there are sovereign states that already possess wealth and who are likely to hold unequal amounts of wealth. But that is not an issue for this book since it is not asking what constitutes a fair allocation of additional resources among sovereign states that already have unequal holdings. It is only interested in these inequalities in as much as they have consequences for the agreement reached as the following sections of this chapter will show. In consequence, the issue of global justice is set to one side as this book is not concerned with it and therefore the discussion is limited here to the claims of the three major parties—*i.e.* the two sovereign states and the population of the third territory.

The core elements of this book have to do with three international agents that argue in relation to the sovereignty over the same territory. This project is not about offering a solution to humanitarian needs' cases. Therefore, in the event that a fourth party based their claim on humanitarian needs, they would not have a colorable claim. They have in these cases other international remedies—*e.g.* humanitarian intervention, international aid, etc. This is but a tangential argument, that is to say it has only an indirect connection that has nothing to do with the essence and aim of this study. To give an example, it is not discussed here if it would be fair to consider the natural resources in the Falkland/Malvinas Islands as worldly owned or not. This book explores the possibility of solving some international issues related to sovereignty by means of distributive justice principles. And not the other way around—*i.e.* to solve distributive justice issues through sovereignty. This means that the right of a fourth party to take shelter is itself something that may be decided only after the parties with pre-existing claims to the territory have decided how to allocate sovereignty.

A particular mention has to be made in relation to some external populations that might be seen as a fourth party. For instance, Palestinians and Jewish people living abroad. It is true that Jews outside Israel had to be considered in drawing up the institutions and legal code—Israel would not make sense without the Law of Return. But these people were not involved in the actual process of drawing up the code. Interestingly, the same is true of the Palestinians. If there is a peace treaty and the setting up of a Palestinian State, the Palestinians outside the West Bank and Gaza will have to be considered. So, what kind of claim, if any,

16 Refer to Chapter 5.

do these external populations have in this project? They are not a fourth party as that would be a misconception, at least for this model. Rather, they would be considered as part of the third territory and therefore their voice would be part of that of the third party's.

Alternatives for the negotiators: Principles for the allocation of sovereignty

So far there are several international agents—two sovereign states and the population of the third territory—with a colorable claim in regard to their sovereign rights over a territory, who decide to go into negotiations in order to solve in a peaceful manner their differences. Having decided the "who," it is time to define what the competing parties will discuss.

They need to find principles or conceptions, which are general, universal in application, public, and able to put an order on conflicting claims and with finality.[17] They should be general in the sense they can be applicable to every agent claiming rights over the third territory and without distinction; universal in respect to their compliance—*i.e.* every party should be able to comply with them; public as a defining note of any social conception of a just institution that concerns the people as a whole and not in their individuality; they should be able to put an order on conflicting claims as sovereignty disputes are in essence characterized by exclusionary and competing demands; and they should be final because the decision or agreement reached in the negotiation may offer a principle that, if respected, secures a reasonable and conclusive successful solution.

Indeed, one of the first things to decide in order to start the negotiations is which options will be available to the representatives. It would be ideal to present the negotiators with all the possible choices available. However ideal this would be, to do it introduces a series of difficulties.[18] Because of the nature of sovereignty conflicts, the many levels they have and the possible options they may present, the choices the representatives will have will need to be previously delimited. The aim here is, in Rawls's own words, "[n]ot try to say what principles they would think of as possible alternatives. To do so would be a complicated business . . . Rather, simply [to] hand the [representatives] a list of principles, a menu, as it were . . . The [representatives] must agree on one alternative on this menu."[19]

In other words, the representatives in the original position will review a series of principles and see if they are applicable—and how in the case they are—to allocate the sovereignty of the third territory. A first limitation will be given by the principles they will review as they will be offered a list, a menu.[20]

17 For specific details of each feature, *see* Rawls, *A Theory of Justice* (n. 1), pp. 113–117.
18 For specific difficulties related to the original position and the alternatives available to the parties, *see* Rawls, *A Theory of Justice* (n. 1), pp. 105–6.
19 *Ibid.*
20 *Ibid.*

The main reason for this methodological decision is instrumental: To cover every possible principle applicable to distribution would be simply cumbersome and, at the same time unnecessary. Then, the selection will be based on principles that in some instances are self-evident—here in the form of common knowledge or what people with general knowledge would apply in any sovereignty conflict of the kind reviewed in this book—and those used in classic distributive justice scholarly literature and which Rawls has previously reviewed.[21]

It may be questioned why the parties in the original position would not choose other leading alternative ways of distributing burdens and benefits in this context. However, the discussion here is of a global nature and not a domestic one; even more, not just any global nature issue but sovereignty conflicts. What Rawls says in the case of the first original position is fully applicable here. In that respect he maintains that: "[i]mplicit in the contrasts between classical utilitarianism and justice as fairness is a difference in the underlying conception of society."[22] In tune with this, implicit in the selection of the alternatives that will integrate the menu available to the negotiators in the original position as designed in this chapter is the underlying issue they will discuss—*i.e.* to leave aside some alternatives has to do with the nature of this book. Precisely in that respect, as Rawls himself says "[n]o people will be willing to count the losses to itself as outweighed by gains to other peoples; and therefore the principle of utility, and other moral principles discussed in moral philosophy, are not even candidates [here]."[23] Thereby, the negotiators will not consider them as part of the menu listing the alternatives to be reviewed.

The solution that will be achieved then may not be the best one but a reasonable one. That is because the representatives are required to choose one of the available options unanimously. Hence, the decision which they agree upon will be the result of careful reasoning and comparison of the proposed list of available options. Then, the selection of conceptions that the representatives are going to explore is as follows:

(a) The entitlement principle: principle of just acquisition.
(b) The "best interest of the child" principle.
(c) Rawlsian principles of justice:

    (1) the difference principle; and
    (2) the principle of equality.

Two clarifications must be made at this point before advancing with the negotiations. First, although in some cases the principles of justice are designed

21 For Rawls's list of principles and conceptions, refer in particular to *A Theory of Justice* (n. 1), p. 107.

22 *Ibid.*, p. 29. For a more detailed view of the contrasts between utilitarianism and justice and fairness, *see esp.* pp. 24–27.

23 Rawls, *The Law of Peoples* (n. 2), p. 60.

to be applied in the allocation of benefits and burdens related to economy, the following sections will examine if they can be applied here in the allocation in terms of shares of sovereignty over a territory, in particular power and wealth and consequent actual and potential benefits and burdens. Second, two details that are interlinked must be kept present when reviewing each principle: Fairness in distribution should be the end product assuming all the agents want the agreement to be respected by the three populations.

Original position

Introducing the "veil of ignorance"

To recapitulate, it is now clear why the competing parties are going into negotiations—*i.e.* they have a conflict of interests in relation to a nonsovereign territory and want a just and fair way of solving it. Afterwards, the conditions that should be fulfilled to be considered a claiming party and to take part in the negotiations were determined—*i.e.* colorable claim. Then, the list of available options the negotiators will have to discuss was detailed. Now, what principles of distribution would the representatives of the three populations choose in relation to actual and potential rights and burdens over political, economic, legal, social, and cultural aspects of the third territory? Would they opt for equality or for a difference principle for their distribution? Would they choose some other principle? The answer to these questions will depend upon the information the representatives will have, and in fact, they could be misled by such knowledge—hence the importance of defining the characteristics the original position in which the negotiations will be conducted.

The content of the original position is something constructed, and it is constructed it to reflect what it is thought to be morally relevant and morally right—which is precisely what Rawls does. In tune with this, as Rawls does at the individual level, the characteristics of the original position in which the negotiations will happen have to be defined in order to avoid any possible interference from factors that can cause bias and that may lead to a partly unjust or unfair outcome. Hence, a procedure to eliminate the effect of these factors must be used. The "veil of ignorance"[24] that Rawls uses at the level of individuals will be applied in the international scenario, being the populations of the sovereign states and the nonsovereign third territory—all through their respective representatives—the subjects of such a model.

Following Rawls and assuming that the principles agreed on the first level—*i.e.* principles relative to certain institutions within a society—are just and fair does not mean that they will be automatically useful or even applicable in international

24 Rawls mainly develops the veil of ignorance in *A Theory of Justice* but it is also present in his *Justice as Fairness, A Restatement* and *Political Liberalism*.

relations. As Rawls himself points out: "[o]ne should not assume in advance that principles that are reasonable and just for the basic structure are also reasonable and just for institutions, associations, and social practices generally."[25] From there, if it cannot be expected that principles that are considered to be just and fair for some institutions are also applicable to other institutions within the state, to intend to automatically apply the ones decided for societies in relation to their internal institutions into a larger scale such as a sovereign conflict is simply naïve.

At the individual level, Rawls states that "[t]he principles of justice are chosen behind a veil of ignorance. This ensures that no one is advantaged or disadvantaged in the choice of principles by the outcome of natural chance or the contingency of social circumstances."[26] Moreover, he makes it even clearer that "[. . .] the parties are symmetrically situated in the original position."[27] That is to say, they are in equal terms in relation to the knowledge they have about themselves, their circumstances, their societies and any other information. In other words, "[i]t is assumed, then, that the parties do not know certain kinds of particular facts"[28] and they know some others, but in any case, they all know the same circumstances and have access to the same information. But, what are the particular facts the parties do not know in these negotiations? To be more precise, what is the information that is going to be available for the negotiators?—*i.e.* how does the veil of ignorance work in sovereignty disputes?

Finally, it is important to make explicit that any decision made will be taken purely with reference to the rights and obligations in relation to the third territory. The agreement reached will have a target: The third territory and all that it implies in terms of rights and obligations. The principles that will be reviewed are brought in solely to offer a solution to sovereignty conflicts, and not to put an end to inequalities among the claiming agent's comparative situations or to help them in achieving equal level of welfare. In fact, there is no claim here of a completely just society for those in the third territory; the goal is merely to design a solution to the issue of sovereignty. Moreover, because the participants in these negotiations represent parties with colorable claims that are equal in respect to the third territory no party has any obligation to sacrifice its equal claim just because the others are least advantaged.

Adapting the "veil of ignorance" to sovereignty conflicts: Rationality of the parties and their representatives

Before the negotiations take place, it is fundamental to clarify how the methodology on which they are based (Rawls) is applicable here—how the "veil of ignorance"

25 Rawls, *Justice as Fairness* (n. 1), p. 11.
26 Rawls, *A Theory of Justice* (n. 1), p. 11.
27 Rawls, *Justice as Fairness* (n. 4), p. 18.
28 Rawls, *A Theory of Justice* (n. 1), p. 118.

works in sovereignty conflicts. Therefore, the following points have to be addressed:

- Difference between individuals and their representatives.
- How the representatives should be chosen.
- Necessary qualities of the representatives.

From a general point of view, it is assumed the individuals of the three populations in this model are free and rational beings[29] because the objective is to come up with an agreement that free and rational beings could not reasonably reject. Each and every individual has free will "[t]hat is has also the idea of freedom and acts entirely under this idea."[30] In other words, in order to have an individual morally and legally speaking acting in any of these spheres it is a necessary condition that he is a rational being with understanding of his actions and omissions and his will is free from any external constriction. Moreover, they are reasonable beings in the sense that they "[u]nderstand they are to honor [the principles they choose], even at the expense of their own interests as circumstances may require, provided others likewise may be expected to honor them."[31]

A further clarification is in relation to the way they interact with each other. In general individuals may be good intrinsically so they may want to help each other or they may be bad intrinsically so their decisions will be purely self-centered. Nevertheless, it is assumed they are mutually disinterested.[32] Therefore, they intend to accomplish their individual aims but without interfering with those of others. This is particularly important in sovereignty disputes because these are often highly emotional, with the participants taking the view that "victory for us is to see you suffer."[33]

In order to have negotiations the three involved agents will have to select representatives within their communities. Then, each of the three populations would elect their representatives following internal—national and/or local—procedures without any interference from any outside party, involved or not involved in the sovereignty dispute. How the representatives are selected is irrelevant for the purposes of this process. The important point is that as the individuals comprising each of the three populations are rational and free—hence their consent has moral force—their representatives will also be free rational beings. Accordingly, the three populations—and their respective representatives—consist of free and equal rational beings who are mutually disinterested and who

29 *Ibid.*, p. 10.
30 T. Meyer Greene (ed.), *Selections of Immanuel Kant* (London: Charles Scribner's Sons Ltd., 1929), p. 335.
31 Rawls, *Justice as Fairness* (n. 4), p. 7.
32 *Ibid.*, pp. 12 and 131.
33 Philip C. Winslow, *Victory for Us is to See You Suffer: in the West Bank with the Palestinians and the Israelis* (Boston MA: Beacon Press, 2007).

will honor the principles chosen in the negotiations regarding the sovereignty over the third territory, since they stand by their word.

It is also important to neutralize certain elements that may make the negotiators choose options because they are for the advantage of those whom they represent. In tune with this, it is assumed that the representatives do not know certain features. In other words, two limitations in relation to the representatives must be applied in order for the negotiations to start: Firstly, for the negotiations to be just and fair the representatives will not know whom they represent but they know everything else—*i.e.* the information relevant to the sovereignty conflict at hand, everyone's desires, interests and purposes as well as factual and historical data—who the three parties are, the difficulty of resolving sovereignty conflicts, and so on. By acting in this way they ensure that none of the agents is more or less advantaged or disadvantaged when choosing the principles upon how sovereignty will be allocated.

Second, concerning the representatives in their individuality, they are pure rational beings and as such they "are not allowed to know [their own] race and ethnic group, sex, or various native endowments such as strength and intelligence . . ."[34] Ergo, the representatives have to fulfill two necessary conditions—*i.e.* the veil of ignorance applied to sovereignty conflicts means that: (a) they do not know whom they represent; and (b) they do not know a series of characteristics in respect to their own individuality. But they will have information available in respect to the sovereignty conflict, the two sovereign states and the third territory under dispute.

Reasons leading to the principles of justice: The rule of *maximin*

Three populations have selected representatives who will participate in negotiations to allocate the sovereignty over a territory. These representatives do not know which of the three populations they represent and certain characteristics about themselves; they know of the existence of the territory which sovereignty has to be allocated, that the populations they represent have somehow a right to claim it—*i.e.* colorable claim—and the nature of the negotiations they are involved in. Then, in order to allocate the sovereignty of the third territory they know they have to decide which principles are applicable. For that reason, they will analyze the implications certain principles may have in such allocation. However, the first thing the representatives will have to agree upon is the procedure they will follow in the negotiations, the applicable rule.

In terms of the rule the representatives will apply in the negotiations it is highly possible they will choose "the *maximin* rule for choice under uncertainty."[35]

34 Rawls, *Justice as Fairness* (n. 4), p. 15.
35 Rawls, *A Theory of Justice* (n. 1), p. 132.

According to Rawls, it can be defined as follows: "The *maximin* rule tells us to rank alternatives by their worst possible outcomes: we are to adopt the alternative the worst outcome of which is superior to the worst outcome of the others."[36]

Bearing in mind how the original position in which the negotiations will take place has been characterized, it is reasonable that the representatives will have a prudent view making their choice—at least—conservative.[37] They apply *maximin* because it maximizes the position of the worst off party, and since they may represent the worst off party, that is what they would want to do. That is to say, the negotiations present a particular note: Uncertainty—*i.e.* the uncertainty is not only with regard to outcomes but also with regard to who they are. Indeed, sovereignty disputes are under an umbrella of incertitude since all of the agents start with a *status quo* and any decision in the negotiations may imply actions on either side that may result in gains but also losses for any of them. For instance, when the representatives see each of the proposed principles—just-acquisition, the best interest of the child, equality, difference—they know that in any case they will be deciding how to allocate the sovereignty over the third territory. However, they will also consider in their decisions that sovereign rights imply obligations. Thus, the representatives have to bear in mind that, although they may have information about the third territory, they do not know its factual features in the future and that they do not know whom they represent.

Indeed, *maximin* is not a general rule in cases of uncertainty. However, it is the desirable one in situations of high indeterminacy,[38] when the stakes are high and the worst position is tolerable. And the original position applied to sovereignty conflicts has features that translate in such a level of uncertainty that makes the *maximin* rule the option the representatives will choose. In brief, Rawls made clear that the rule of *maximin* is applicable in cases in which uncertainty of choice is present when the following features appear.

First: "[i]t is unreasonable not to be skeptical of probabilistic calculations unless there is no other way out, particularly if the decision is a fundamental one that needs to be justified to others."[39] Second: "It is not worthwhile for him to take a chance for the sake of a further advantage, especially when it may turn out that he loses much that is important to him."[40] Third: "[t]he rejected alternatives have outcomes that one can hardly accept. The situation involves grave risks."[41]

36 *Ibid.*, p. 133.

37 Decision theory principles under conditions of risk: expected value (the individuals discount the maximum payoff of each option depending on its probability and then they choose the highest one); *maximax* or "wishful thinking" (the individuals choose among options depending on which one offers the best of all possible result); *maximin* (the individuals choose under a pessimistic or conservative approach so they opt for the best worst outcome). For a more detailed view about *maximin* and its application in conditions under uncertainty, *see* Rawls, *A Theory of Justice* (n. 1), *esp.* pp. 130 ff.

38 *Ibid.*, p. 133.

39 *Ibid.*, p. 134.

40 *Ibid.*

41 *Ibid.*

By reviewing the original position in which the negotiations will take place in light of the previous mentioned three features it is clear the representatives will be choosing under uncertain conditions that make the rule of *maximin* the option to be taken. That is because firstly, it is reasonable the representatives will be sceptical in relation to probabilistic calculations since their decision may literally imply the populations they represent to be immensely well off or completely disadvantaged. Hence, their decision will have to be justified not only among them in the negotiations but the agreement that is reached also in relation to the represented three populations. Second, although the best possible scenario may see the allocation of only one of the agents with sovereignty as a successful result in many ways—*e.g.* wealth, geostrategic location—it can as well worsen its comparative situation. Third, and in tune with the last idea, an extreme scenario could see the least advantaged of the populations being granted the sovereignty of a useless third territory that may potentially make their comparative situation even worse—*e.g.* more inhabitants for the already deficient health system, larger international debt.

Why then is the *maximin* principle the reasonable rule to be applied in sovereign disputes? Individuals—and hence their representatives—in this model are (as Rawls maintains) mutually disinterested. Each and every agent in a sovereignty dispute intends to maximize their position in regard to the third territory following their respective "state plan of life." At the same time, they all intend to avoid worsening their situation or that of the population they come from. Then, if to allocate sovereignty to only one of them may mean to improve their situation as well as to worsen the reality of either of the populations, the choice implies high risk. Thus, that high risk linked to the uncertainty of the choice will have effects in any case on a whole population. Therefore, in a certain situation in which there is something to be allocated among several claimants and neither the characteristics of the object nor of the claimants are fully known, the same individual granted the allocation may see his position either worsened or bettered, there is a bargaining position. In situations like the ones under analysis, when the full allocation of sovereignty may translate into complete gains as well as total losses, joint ventures may result in bettering off everyone's relative position or—at least—not worsening it, so that the joint venture would be the conservative choice or *maximin*.

In any event, as the representatives would act not knowing whom they represent, even in the worst scenario—if they represented the less advantaged agents in relative terms—they would still obtain a fair share. In tune with this reasoning Gauthier gives an interesting insight of mutual interaction when referring to "Hume's example, of two persons rowing a boat that neither can row alone, is a very simple example of beneficially co-ordinative practice."[42] Sovereignty conflicts are just in the same situation: If none of the agents is willing to cooperate and

42 David Gauthier, *Morals by Agreement* (Oxford: Oxford University Press, 2003), Chapter 1.

start negotiations in order to leave the zero sum game, "the boat may remain static." It is true that if the situation remains a zero sum game it might be better for some parties. But, the main question is whether it would be just.

Whereas the *status quo* or the exclusive ownership of the third territory by one of the agents are valid options, they could literally result in either a loss of claimed rights for one or several claimants or permanent interference when deciding issues with consequences to all of them. If they wanted to have actual use of their claimed rights over the third territory they would have to make mutual concessions; in essence, they would have to "slice" their rights into different portions or shares. It is possible that the agents in the conflict would prefer to be sure of sharing the benefits and burdens in respect to the third territory and the *maximin* rule would be the chosen one for the distribution of benefits and burdens—*i.e.* to share sovereignty. The issue now is to determine the nature and size of each particular share. It is for that reason that in the following it will be reviewed how different principles can be applied to sovereignty disputes.

Finally, for the case of the third population it would be possible to use the reasoning of the original position and *maximin* to derive some conclusions about the kind of provisions that should be made for them. The parties in the original position do not know whom they represent and they have to accept that they might be representing the third population rather than one of the sovereign states. They would have reason to provide some degree of autonomy for the third population since the agreement under which that population lives will affect their lives in a way that it does not affect the lives of the domestic populations of the two sovereign states, as this chapter made clear in the section referred to the colorable claim. So, representatives who are driven by *maximin* would have reason not to subordinate the third population entirely to the decisionmaking of the two sovereign states.

The negotiations: Choosing a principle to allocate sovereignty

The representatives in the original position will review a series of principles in order to allocate the sovereignty of the territory. A first limitation is given by the principles they will review as they will be offered a list or menu.[43] Before examining the principles of just distribution—as proposed by Rawls—the attention will be focused on the principle of "just acquisition." First, because it is usually the one presented by every agent involved in any sovereignty conflict to support its claim; second—as it will be demonstrated, because it is the main reason why this kind of conflict remains in a legal and political limbo. After reviewing "just acquisition," the "best interest of the child" principle will follow. The main reason in proceeding this way has to be with the fact that—at least at first glance—the "best interest of the child" principle offers several elements that are similar to the ones present in sovereignty conflicts.

43 Rawls, *A Theory of Justice* (n. 1), pp. 105–9.

Why "just acquisition" cannot work

Most—if not all—individuals—and any sovereign state—would think it obvious to apply Ulpian's maxim *suum cuique tribuere*[44]—to give to each his due or to distribute to each one his share—in the case of any type of distribution. What can be fairer than to give everyone what is due to them? However, to give to each his due is not a task without difficulties. Thus, it does not necessarily mean that to try to do this automatically produces the most just solution, because it may be hopelessly unclear what each person (or state) is entitled to.

Faced with the idea of applying any kind of principle based on a historical entitlement will confront the representatives with two main problems. First, they would need to agree upon a historical account—*i.e.* what actually happened, who was the first one to discover the territory, or to have a population there, etc. Second, they would need to decide what type of act makes their claimed rights just—*i.e.* the first one setting foot on the territory, the first one to have a permanent settlement, etc. Thus, in relation to the second problem, they would have to choose the theoretical background to decide what is just: *res nullius* or *res communis*—*i.e.* the originally uninhabited territory belonged to no one or everyone had a certain right over it. Besides, if there were conflicts in the past it would need to be decided whether they were just or not and whether the just side won.

In relation to the first issue—the agreement on the historical account—each sovereign state taking part in a sovereignty conflict is certain that it has ultimate and highest right over the disputed territory, and the use and ownership of the third territory is due to them. As a consequence, sovereignty disputes do not move from a zero sum game. That is because, in order to determine the initial acquisition, the agents have to go back and resolve old historical claims only resulting in a practical matter: The competing agents are never going to agree on the "correct" historical version of the events—*i.e.* the historical account is fundamentally controversial.

Thus, it is common to observe in sovereignty differences that the involved agents usually support their claims through historical, legal, political, cultural or geographical arguments—even a combination of many of them. In other words, not only will be the dispute over what the facts are but also what the relative moral significance of those facts is. For example, one party will claim that whoever was the first one in the third territory is its owner and hence, its sovereign, and they were there first. But the opposite party disputes this, supporting their case with historical, legal, political, cultural, and geographical evidence, and arguing either (a) that they were there first, or (b) that being first is not what makes acquisition just, but, *e.g.*, being first to exploit its resources, or establish a community.

Because all the parties argue they were the first to do what gave them a right to the third territory, an approach based on a historical account is futile for providing a solution to sovereignty disputes and the conflicts continue endlessly—*e.g.* arguments about the rightful sovereign of Jerusalem and surrounding areas

44 Ulpian, *Digest*, 1.1.10.

have been present for generations.[45] Should these agents go back to Biblical times in order to prove the current legitimate occupancy of the territory?

In addition to the historical account, even though it was assumed the representatives finally agreed on the facts, it is not easy to see an agreement on how what is due to someone be determined, which way to acquire something is just and fair, and whether a certain way of acquiring the sovereignty over the third territory can be just and fair at the same time for two different agents. For instance, they may apply the just acquisition principle. But even with the application of the just acquisition principle sovereignty disputes produce endless conflict.

The just acquisition principle has been previously related to territorial sovereignty since it has been maintained that: "[a]mongst the objects to which this principle is meant to be capable of applying are portions of the Earth's surface, that is, areas of land."[46] And that is exactly the aim of this project: To find a peaceful way of allocating sovereignty over nonsovereign areas of land. However, the principle of just acquisition is not the answer to resolve these issues. Its main pitfall is that the information required to apply this principle is not epistemically accessible in sovereignty conflicts—*e.g.* how far back would the agents need to investigate so as to determine who the first inhabitants of the Falkland/Malvinas Islands were? What would happen in the case of extinct civilizations? What about cultures that were in Ancient Times nomadic?

To have a better understanding of the principle of just acquisition Nozick comes into play, offering his "entitlement theory." But, although his theory is a more subtle revision of just acquisition theory, examination of it will demonstrate that this principle is not workable in sovereignty disputes.[47] In Nozick's entitlement theory just acquisition becomes the first of three principles (this section is not concerned with the other two):

> An individual A acquires at time t a full property right in an object O which has not previously been the property of any individual if and only if:
>
> (i) A mixes his labour with O at time t; and
> (ii) as a result of O becoming A's private property, no one else is made any worse off than he or she would have been, O having being left unappropriated by anyone and had everyone in consequence been free to use O without appropriating it.[48]

45 *See, e.g.*, Genesis 14:18–20, in which Jerusalem (or Salem) already has enemies. Since Biblical times the region has been the center of disputes in relation to the rightful settlement of different populations.

46 David Conway, "Nozick's Entitlement *Theory of Justice*: Three Critics Answered," *Libertarian Alliance, Philosophical Notes* 15 (1990).

47 Robert Nozick, *Anarchy, State and Utopia* (New York: Basic Books, 1974), in particular Part II, Chapter 7, Section I.

48 *Ibid.*

To establish if any object O has not previously been the property of any individual is one of the main issues in Nozick's model—and that is also the main issue in sovereignty disputes. Although theoretically attractive and practically difficult to demonstrate, in the specific case of sovereignty dilemmas the enigma to be unraveled is precisely to determine which of the involved agents was the first one chronologically—historically—to have something to do with the third territory.[49] Furthermore, even if that was somehow demonstrated, there will also be disputes about the justice of conflicts that result in the seizure of territories by force.

Nozick's model introduces many other issues. Indeed, while Nozick relies on Locke's labor theory of property, his approach raises various questions. For instance, what are the borderlines here? Individuals labor on parts of objects—similarly, the claiming parties only "labor" on parts of the third territory, so why does that give them the right to the whole object? In addition to this, why does mixing one's labor with property cause to own the property rather than lose the labor? Is there some threshold that must be met in order to own the property?—*e.g.* if an individual pours a glass of wine in the ocean does he own the ocean or has he wasted my wine? In tune with this, why would anyone be entitled to more than only the added value his labor has created? And even if the labor theory of property may give an individual ownership of property he has created, why should it give him ownership, for example, of natural resources? Natural resources are not brought into existence by labor, although labor may be necessary before they can be used.

As a result of this, the idea of determining who mixed their labor with the territory first and to a sufficient extent to acquire ownership is always going to be controversial, even if all parties accepted that this was the right test. And even if this works, as pointed out before, there is the issue of whether later seizures of the property from indigenous peoples by force were just.

The principle of just acquisition may work for individuals. For states, it may solve one problem, what one has to do, *i.e.* mix one's labor. But leaves several other issues unresolved—*e.g.* (a) who did it first? (b) how much does each individual own? (new problem, *e.g.* if someone digs, can he claim that plot, the field or the whole island?), and (c) who inherits the property—the inhabitants or their "mother community?"

Any version of just acquisition will have the same problems: People will never agree on the relevant facts and the relevant test, and therefore all this principle would do is guarantee endless conflict. So, the representatives in the original position would reject it. Furthermore, the original position in which the

49 The expression "having something to do" is used here since there are many different theories on how a piece of land can become part of a sovereign state—*e.g.* first inhabited, first seen, etc. In that sense, all the possible variables are included with the use of the previously mentioned expression to avoid tangential arguments. The aim is to discuss how the just acquisition principle implies endless conflict and not the nature of such a concept or the concept itself.

representatives have to decide how to allocate the sovereignty over the third territory neutralizes any argument in that respect—*i.e.* as the representatives do not know which population they are representing they would not be able to use historical entitlement as an argument; then, whether they have access to historical records or not[50] is irrelevant since they would hypothetically not know how to apply them. Therefore, the theoretical device finishes with one of the main issues every sovereignty conflict encounters: Endless discussion concerning historical entitlement that in most—if not all cases—is highly difficult to be demonstrated. Thus, since they would not agree to rely on a principle that guarantees endless conflict, it would be rejected as the principle to resolve these disputes. At the same time, it leaves all the agents with an equal footing to continue the negotiations since none of them can argue a better or more robust right over the claimed territory.

The "best interest of the child" principle[51]

With recognition in international law[52] the "best interest of the child" principle is a particular variant of the "best interest of the third party" principle. Many courts around the world use this principle to decide the fate of children—*e.g.* who will be their legal guardian in the case of divorce, adoption, criminal offences, etc. In order to use the "best interest of the child" principle in sovereignty conflicts, the role usually given to the adults—parents, legal guardian—would be played by the two competing sovereign states and that of the child would be given by the nonsovereign third territory. The idea is that the third territory is like a child, and therefore its interest in ultimate self-determination and self-realization are paramount. So, it is possible—someone may put forward—the claim that whatever custody (sovereignty) arrangements are chosen these should be in the best interest of that territory.

At first glance, the adapted principle would secure the situation of the inhabitants of the third territory. Thus, it would limit the rights of the two sovereign states—the extent of these limits would have to be agreed. Moreover, the two sovereign states would have to fulfill certain obligations towards the third territory so as to secure the inhabitants' wellbeing—*e.g.* as they would be considered in a better situation than that of the third territory, they might provide the means for its defense.

50 Rawls, *A Theory of Justice* (n. 1), p. 160.

51 The expression "child" rather than "third party" is used intentionally. That is because it is usually assumed or thought of sovereignty disputes as having one of the parties—in general, the third territory—in an *immature* state as an international agent and hence, in a weaker position in comparison to sovereign states—*i.e.* very similar to that of a child in relation to his parents. From there, to use an expression such as "third party" defeats the point since it does not offer necessarily the same connotation.

52 UN Convention on the Rights of the Child, art. 3 states: "[t]he best interests of the child shall be a primary consideration."

There are critics of the "best interest of the child" principle,[53] but the main issue in this case is not the principle itself but its application to situations that, although having certain similarities, offer substantial differences that make it inappropriate. For instance, as the negotiators would not know which of the groups are representing, they would not choose a principle that could be translated in the best interest of only one of them—*i.e.* that would go against the *maximin* rule, since they may not be that party. Thereby, there is no reason to give one group priority over another. Moreover, the application of this principle does not always guarantee a just solution for sovereignty conflicts since it can be the case that the least advantaged or most vulnerable agent is one of the claiming sovereign states and not the population of the third territory—*i.e.* in family cases, the child is the most vulnerable subject always dependent on his parents or any other legal guardian.

Finally, the application of the "best interest of the child principle" in sovereignty disputes denies that the rights of the other two parties are of equal importance to the right of the third territory. And unlike the case of parental right, these rights are at least as strong—arguably stronger—than the right of the third territory to self-determination.

In summary, the representatives of the involved agents in the conflict are agreed that the third territory does not belong to its inhabitants (no matter why) and that they will not argue from their supposed historical rights over it. They do not know which group they represent and therefore do not know which set of historical arguments to believe. So they recognize that making the resolution of this kind of dispute central is hopeless. In consequence, they accept that each of them has a right to some sovereignty over the third territory—which is not the same as a right to be the actual and only sovereign. In addition to this, none of the representatives can obtain any special advantage for whoever they represent or can put them in a particular disadvantageous situation.[54]

Consequently, the agreement should offer such a solution that not only is in the "best interest" of just one of the parties but embraces in a way or another those of all the claimants. Therefore, they have realized that to share sovereignty is the best option for all of them (by application of the rule of *maximin*). Similarly, it is also the case that this is just under Rawlsian principles. That is because of the nature of the parties and the fact that each has a colorable claim, which give them some legitimate interest in the sovereignty over the third territory. Then, and as they now need to work out the details of how to share sovereignty, they will explore the possibilities of applying these principles into the negotiations.

53 Lynne Marie Kohm, "Tracing the Foundations of the Best Interest of the Child Standard in American Jurisprudence," *Journal of Law and Family Studies* 10 (2008): 337–76, 370.

54 Cf. Rawls, *A Theory of Justice* (n. 1), p. 130.

The difference principle

At first glance, the difference principle states that whoever is a potential recipient in any distribution will receive an unequal share of whatever will be divided. It applies a prioritarian rule—that inequalities are unjustified unless they work to the advantage of the worst off members of a society. To put it in clearer terms, Rawls states that: "[i]njustice, then, is simply inequalities that are not to the benefit of all."[55]

However appealing, the difference principle presents a main obstacle. It is designed to apply to social and economic inequalities, so it does not lend itself well to sovereignty inequalities because of the particular characteristics of sovereignty conflicts and sovereignty itself. It remains to be seen, though, whether the difference principle has any application in specific cases. The following paragraphs will review some considerations the parties would have with regards the difference principle in the negotiations.

First, as the types of inequalities that can be permitted are not restricted,[56] some of them may go against the interests of the represented populations. To be more precise, the citizens among whom Rawls distributes hold nothing in advance of the distribution and the basic structure that comes out of the original position is meant to distribute all of their wealth and income fairly—the difference principle operates in advance of citizens holding anything. In the case *sub examine*, there are two sovereign states and a third population who already possess wealth and who are likely to hold unequal amounts of wealth. In addition to wealth, all these parties will possess several other elements that are also likely to be unequal among them—*e.g.* power, geographical location, etc. Indeed, sovereignty is not merely a matter of wealth. So, when the representatives think about dividing up whatever the third territory entails, they potentially have to think about what constitutes a fair allocation of additional wealth and any other elements that are attributes of sovereignty among parties who already have unequal holdings.

In that context the difference principle would seem to have a quite different import than it does for Rawls's domestic case. It would seem to require that all of the additional holdings should go to the least advantaged party up to the point at which its situation equals the one of the better off party, whatever the criteria used to judge—*e.g.* judged perhaps in terms of average *per capita* wealth. The difference principle is an offspring of *maximin* and giving everything to the poor party and nothing to the rich party, up to the point of equality, is the way to maximize the minimum.

But the original position in this chapter is slightly different from the one Rawls uses. The original position here is set up in such a way that the agreement reached has a target: The third territory and all that it implies in terms of rights and obligations, benefits and burdens. So, suppose that the two sovereign states are

55 *Ibid.*, p. 54.
56 *Ibid.*, p. 55.

A and B and the third territory is C, and state A is relatively much wealthier than state B and third territory C. Therefore, if A, B, and C are equal joint claimants to the third territory and all that it entails, the fact that B and C are poorer than A is an irrelevant consideration. Why should it be a relevant consideration if it is not relevant independently of the third territory? For example, if Argentina, the United Kingdom, and the Falkland/Malvinas Islands have no responsibility for one another's material wellbeing simply as three international agents, why should they suddenly acquire that responsibility when it comes to their shared sovereignty over the islands? The assumption here is that A, B, and C have equal claims and that A has no obligation to sacrifice its equal claim to B or C just because they happen to be poorer. A simply does not have that sort of special responsibility to either B or C.

Second, Rawls argues the more advantaged will accept the principle because they need the cooperation of the least advantaged. But that is not true here. It fails to explain why the most advantaged population should agree to lower its benefits only because the least advantaged one needs to see its position improved. It may appear that this claim contradicts the veil of ignorance and the *maximin* but it does not. That is because once again it is important to stress that sovereignty conflicts and sovereignty itself are complex. Indeed, the most advantaged would distribute the benefits with the least advantaged. And that seems fair, at least in Rawlsian terms. But what about the burdens? This is a pitfall in the application of the difference principle and not in relation to the veil of ignorance or *maximin*. Since it would imply that the inequalities in the distribution would be fair if they benefited the least advantaged, then the most advantaged party not only would have to share the benefits but also contribute more in terms of the burdens. And that seems unreasonable again.

For example, consider the case of a third territory rich in natural resources but small in population and hence with no defense power and one of the claiming sovereign states with no natural resources, a small territory, large population, wealthy and developed means of defense. By application of the difference principle, that sovereign state would explore and exploit the natural resources in the third territory, would share the resultant benefits and would defend the third territory in case of attack. It is hard to see how or why the sovereign state would accept such an arrangement.

Consider one of the examples Rawls himself provides[57] but adapted to this situation. There are two sovereign states and the population of the third territory at the same level of wealth, with barely the same size population and means of defense. One of the sovereign states and the third territory decide to industrialize, save and invest in defense. The other sovereign state does not. Some decades later both the first sovereign state and the third territory are twice as wealthy as the

57 In *The Law of Peoples* (n. 2), Rawls refers to two examples in which two countries have a similar starting point but, for different reasons, they develop in different ways. See *esp.* pp. 117–18.

second sovereign state. Should then the first sovereign state and the third territory assist the second sovereign state by application of the difference principle?

Third, when the expression "least advantaged" is used in sovereignty conflicts it is not clear in which sense or which criteria should be applied—*e.g.* less economically developed agent, less human rights acknowledged, smaller territory, smaller population, less developed legal system, etc. There are two problems here: (a) which feature or element will be considered to determine the least advantaged; (b) variability.

In the case of the feature or element to be considered in order to determine the least advantaged, sovereignty conflicts and sovereignty itself are indeed complex. It is true that Rawls himself applies the difference principle for material goods but not to rights and freedoms—*i.e.* the claim that different sorts of features are at stake may not be conclusive. However, even in the case these features were considered only as material goods, sovereignty conflicts are still highly complex in the sense most of their features —if not all—imply both benefits and burdens.

Consider, for instance, the previous example of a third territory rich in natural resources with small population and no means for defense and one of the claiming sovereign states with the completely opposite reality. There would be natural resources (and their ownership, exploration and exploitation), consequent benefits, defense (and its means and their maintenance), and consequent burdens. The most advantaged in terms of ownership and/or possession of natural resources seems indeed the third territory in this example, but they cannot explore or exploit them. In addition to this, the most advantaged in terms of exploration and exploitation of natural resources may be any of the other claiming parties. The same could be said about defense.

So, what would be the feature to be counted as relevant to define the least advantaged? If it was natural resources and their ownership and/or use, indeed the third territory would have to share them with the other two parties. Thereby, the one sovereign state in a better position in terms of exploration and exploitation would contribute with a larger share of burdens though—*i.e.* as they would be the most advantaged party in terms of means and wealth for exploration and exploitation of natural resources. This arrangement seems indeed fair. But, what would happen with the defense of the third territory? By understanding the difference principle as applicable to one feature or element, the whole arrangement might be jeopardized. In this case, the third territory would contribute with a larger share of natural resources in what is related to their ownership and/or use. And the better off sovereign state would contribute with a larger share towards their exploration and exploitation and, in addition to this, to the defense of the third territory. Indeed, the same example is analyzed as a whole rather than as particular features or elements only in their individuality, it may result in an unbalanced outcome—*i.e.* benefits distributed evenly but burdens allocated mainly to one of the claiming parties.

Thus, even if the agents agreed on the feature to be considered, to be the least and the most advantaged agent is a factual feature so it can vary in time. Then, the means and outcome would be variable in time too; so a question of amending the distribution would arise once the original position changed. Would that imply a change in the shares of sovereignty too?

To recapitulate, the difference principle does not imply that the worst off must be compensated, but that an unequal distribution is just, if it makes the worst off better off than they would be if no such distribution existed. Thereby, suppose the disputed territory has natural resources, but no means of extracting them. It will be just to allow either or both of the other parties access to those resources provided: (1) the inhabitants of the third territory have a sufficient share of those resources or the profit on them to make it worth their while to allow others to extract them; and (2) the other party(s) retains enough of the resources or the profits to make it worthwhile to extract them. But this is an oversimplistic view. Indeed, the principle can still be applied. This book does not claim that the principle cannot be applied. However, it is unsuited to sovereign inequalities. This book argues that if it is applied it may generate results not in tune with the justice and fairness aimed for.

In that sense, the complications are numerous: (a) it is problematic to determine who the least advantaged is and hence, there will be always two parties who are worst off, in different ways, in relation to the third claiming party; (b) different parties will be the least advantaged with regard to different aspects of sovereignty because sovereignty and sovereignty conflicts are complex and imply both benefits and burdens in many different areas; (c) the least advantaged will vary over time; and (d) why would any of the parties be motivated to let everything work to the advantage of the least advantaged?

The equality or "equal shares" principle

Strictly speaking, the principle of equality would see each individual with an equal share of whatever is to be divided. There is no consideration of their relative situations—*i.e.* it is not taken into account if they are the least or the most advantaged individuals in the society. From there, each and every agent in the dispute would have the right to the same relative portion of sovereignty. Everyone would be benefited equally, as well as having equal burdens, regardless of their state's internal or international situation, the level of effort put in, or the needs they may have. As in the case of the difference principle, the following paragraphs will present some considerations the parties would make in relation to the equality principle.

What appears to be an easy solution—what is fairer than to give to everyone the same share?—offers immediate complications. A problem to be expected is that different goods have to be distributed. For instance, sovereignty covers several different aspects of any territory, population, government and law that imply both rights and obligations. Then, it seems not possible to go with equal shares *sensu stricto*. Moreover, even if that is what the representatives wanted to do, in itself attractive, the term "equal" has hermeneutic problems: What is an equal division? More specific to this project: what is an equal division when dealing with sovereignty issues? There is an extensive literature on the topic. By way of example, the following quotation summarizes some interpretations:

> Some would say that shares are equally good if they are such that none would prefer to trade her bundle of worldly resources with anybody else's [Dworkin's view]. Others would say that shares are equally good if they are such that none would prefer to trade the sum of her bundle of worldly resources and personal resources. And others would say that the shares are equally good if they are such that each is able to attain the same level of welfare . . ."[58]

There is then the first issue of how to interpret what is an equal share. However, that is not the only problem with the principle of equality applied in sovereignty conflicts. Even if the representatives agreed upon criteria on how to define an equal share, sovereignty implies an extensive range of rights and obligations that are difficult to be distributed following the same pattern—*i.e.* defense system and natural resources, financial system against law, civil rights versus political rights, and more basic goods and services. Therefore, the principle of equality *sensu stricto* would not be enough.

A way to solve the difference among criteria to characterize an equal share can be defining them within the negotiation. That is, the representatives in the original position allocate equal shares of sovereignty to each of the three populations determining what they mean by the term "equal." Suppose that the representatives considered sovereignty as constituted by "lumpy goods"—*i.e.* sovereignty would be seen as composed by different "goods" in several different areas such as territory, population, government, and law. Indeed, sovereignty might be also seen as composed by different goods that are qualitatively different in a way that makes some of them incommensurable rather than lumpy—*i.e.* the goods that form sovereignty lack a common quality in order to make a comparison or at least not all of them offer a common element or characteristic so as to be measured or compared. In any case, considering sovereignty as constituted either by lumpy goods or qualitatively different goods, the parties would need to agree on determining what equal division means in this context.

For the purpose of the negotiations suppose they accept that "[n]o division of resources is an equal division if, once the division is complete, any [agent] would prefer someone else's bundle of resources to his own bundle."[59] Indeed, Dworkin proposed this test (the "envy test"[60]) as a criterion for distributive justice. Furthermore, this test could be a solution for the lumpy goods or qualitatively

58 Michael Otsuka, "Self-Ownership and Equality: A Lockean Reconciliation," *Philosophy and Public Affairs* 27 (1998): 65–92.

59 Ronald Dworkin, "What is Equality? Part 2: Equality of Resources," *Philosophy and Public Affairs* 10 (1981): 283–345.

60 *Ibid.*, for the characterization of the envy test, *see esp.* p. 285.

different goods problem. That is because a distribution of resources is not equal if after it an agent envies someone else because of the bundles of resources any of the other agents has received. However, an immediate problem arises: As the representatives would not know which populations they represent, how can they determine their preference? So this solution is inconsistent with the whole procedure being used here, because it requires knowledge of actual preferences and actual preference might even be internally disputed. Moreover, how could each individual know the preferences of those he represents? The Dworkinian system can only work if everyone represents themselves, *i.e.* whose preferences should count? Although they are representatives of the populations, it is oversimplistic to anthropomorphize populations' preferences.

Suppose that the representatives accept each population has defined preferences. Even if they forget they do not know who they represent, how do they deal with the envy test? The pitfall could be resolved by including an auction in which all the participants received the same amount of money—*i.e.* each participant is able to bid for the resources available. But as fair as the auction appears to be, a new problem is introduced as well. The envy test with the addition of the auction would work if there were no great differences among the agents in relation to their particular situations—*i.e.* in an individual, talents and abilities so in a population, for example, level of development, industrialization, and so on. Therefore, a new addition would be needed in order to foresee great differences among the agents only because of their particular situations. But again, they could only bid on packages in the auction if they knew their preferences, and they cannot know this, so the auction does not solve anything.

Evidently, this way of understanding equality is not the most simplistic one and seems to require foreseeing a myriad of difficulties. Thus, they might not prefer anyone else's bundle but might prefer some other arrangement entirely.

There is still a further problem with the principle of equality and it is that of its application—*i.e.* the actual utilization of the share of sovereignty. It is often the case that the veil of ignorance leads to equality, but its application presents several issues—*e.g.* (a) division of economic benefits; (b) fulfillment of obligations; (c) what to do with things or areas that—in principle—may not be shareable—like aspects of the law. In other words, and assuming that the issue of defining what an equal division means was settled, to apply equality *sensu stricto* would mean that unequal parties in many aspects received equal shares of the sovereignty over the third territory and all that it implies in terms of rights and obligations. Therefore, some of these claiming parties would find themselves with a share of sovereignty that did not provide them any benefit—*e.g.* imagine the equal division of the defense of the third territory in the case sovereign state A was able to fulfill its duty but sovereign state B and third territory C had no defense power. Or the case of distribution of natural resources among state A that had the wealth and means for exploration and exploitation and state B and third territory C without even a chance to use their respective shares. Indeed, the application of equality *sensu stricto* is—at least—problematic and may result in an unfair outcome.

Preliminary requirements for a fair distribution

To recapitulate, the representatives rejected just acquisition, the best interest of the child, the difference principle, and equal shares. In one way or another, the difference principle and the principle of equality offer both pros and cons. To be more precise, the principles are rejected not because of the principles themselves but the particular characteristics of sovereign conflicts and sovereignty itself and the way in which the original position has been set up. Indeed, sovereignty implies many aspects of many different levels. Not only is this translated in benefits but also burdens. The previous section showed that a cautious choice would acknowledge both that sovereignty indeed is complex and that it implies benefits as well as burdens in different areas. So, to choose one principle either the difference principle or that of equality across the board would be an oversimplistic decision that may result in grave consequences for the represented populations.

The solution reached must be one that, apart from being intuitively appealing in the negotiations under the veil of ignorance, can be applied when the veil is lifted in such a way that the three populations want to respect the agreement reached. Then, the solution must be somehow beneficial to the three agents, must recognize—to an extent—their claims and the result is not detrimental to any of the agents.

It is usually the case to think and assume that the population in the third territory is the least advantaged or in a more precarious situation in comparison to that of the two sovereign states. But that is not necessarily true in all cases, both theoretically and in reality as some of the examples used in this chapter show and in cases such as Gibraltar or the Falkland/Malvinas Islands in which it is not easy to point out the least advantaged party. Thereby, and in order to succeed in choosing a principle to be applied for the allocation of sovereignty the representatives must bear in mind some circumstances: (a) when the veil of ignorance is lifted it is more possible than not that the claiming parties will be in very different situations in many areas; (b) that the least advantaged party may be but does not need to be the population of the third territory; (c) that sovereignty conflicts and sovereignty itself are complex—*i.e.* they imply both benefits and burdens in many different areas.

In order to address the issue of complexity the representatives must first make clear how the parties will not use any agreement reached for their benefit only—*i.e.* the agreement must not be a subterfuge for any form of domination from one or more claiming parties in relation to the other(s). That is because by application of the *maximin* rule it is plausible to think the representatives will have a cautious view in regards to the outcome. So, it is consistent with the veil of ignorance and the *maximin* that they may want some safeguards in order to secure their respective populations against any form of domination once the veil of ignorance is lifted.

Bearing in mind the previous discussions, it is reasonable for the representatives in the original position to agree on three basic points in order to share sovereignty before deciding how to do it.

First, it is prohibited to interfere with the internal or external affairs of any of the other agents.[61]

Second, each agent will respect the liberties of the three populations; so no agreement reached can be interpreted in a way that curtails the basic nonpolitical liberties[62] of any of these populations. This point means that none of the agents is allowed to interfere in any way with the basic nonpolitical liberties of the inhabitants of any of the other parties.

Third, the agents will conduct their mutual relations in light of the principles recognized by the law of peoples.[63] Following Rawls, it is reasonable to believe that the negotiators will agree on certain familiar principles already recognized by conventional and customary international law.

With these three prerequisites agreed in this hypothetical situation, once the veil of ignorance is lifted the negotiators secure that the agreement is not a subterfuge for domination of any kind, that the individuals of each population safeguard their basic nonpolitical liberties, and that the three agents are free and autonomous from each other—*i.e.* in the case of the third territory that does not mean independence, hence the use of the word "autonomous."

The "egalitarian shared sovereignty"

The question at issue now is to decide, by respecting these three prerequisites, how to share sovereignty. So, the issue is what would constitute a reasonable

61 This first prerequisite—*i.e.* nondomination or noninterference principle—applies in particular to agents that are least advantaged in any area by preventing the most advantaged parties to impose their law, policies, values, or ideals. Hence, although the third prerequisite here will refer to principles recognized by the law of peoples, and therefore include the principles of noninterference and nonintervention according to international law, the one mentioned at this point as first prerequisite is to be understood with a broader meaning—*i.e.* it applies to all aspects of society. Therein, not only does it include law and politics but also culture, tradition, values, ideals, and customs.

62 For a further analysis of basic liberties and its characterization, *see* Rawls, *A Theory of Justice* (n. 1), p. 53. For Rawls the basic liberties of citizens are "[p]olitical liberty (the right to vote and to hold public office) and freedom of speech and assembly; liberty of conscience and freedom of thought; freedom of the person, which includes freedom from psychological oppression and physical assault and dismemberment (integrity of the person); the right to hold personal property and freedom from arbitrary arrest and seizure . . ." Although this section is defined in Rawlsian terms, The reference to basic nonpolitical liberties rather than basic liberties is intentional. To leave aside political liberty has to do with the nature of this project, as sovereignty is indeed a political liberty. That is because, if political liberties were included among the basic liberties in this prerequisite, it would not be possible to construct the model proposed here. It is true that some scholars may see freedom of speech as a political liberty. But Rawls specifically separates political liberty (referred as to vote and run for office) from freedom of speech and other civil liberties. Thereby, the basic nonpolitical liberties mentioned here include all civil liberties, even freedom of speech.

63 As stated in the introduction to this Chapter, it is not that the project embraces Rawls's *The Law of Peoples* fully. In this case, it focuses on his understanding of "familiar and traditional principles of justice among free and democratic peoples." Some of the principles are State equality, right to self-defense, duty of nonintervention, etc. For a more thorough account of the principles of the *Law of Peoples, see* Rawls, *A Theory of Justice* (n. 2), p. 37.

allocation of sovereignty over the third territory among sovereign states A and B and the third territory C as equal claimants, whose equality of claim is in no way affected by whatever other situation they already have; and that allocation has a target: The third territory and all that it implies in terms of rights and obligations. When the representatives applied the difference principle to the issue constructed in that way, the question is whether there could be a division of the third territory among A, B, and C that would be accepted by the three parties. Therein, in the disputed sovereignty case, the difference principle would seem to demand straightforward equality. However, equality *sensu stricto* presented the representatives several problems too.

Instead of the difference principle and the principle of equality, what about working out the solution with all what the representatives have learnt so far? By acknowledging the circumstances in sovereignty conflicts—that is, different agents and an ample concept such as sovereignty—and the way in which the original position has been set up, a revised principle may offer comparable advantages that may make it a reasonable option.

First, the representatives of the three parties are behind the veil of ignorance—as characterized before in this chapter. Hence, they are deprived of knowledge in regard to which party they represent. So, it is reasonable for them and likely to agree that each party has a right to participate in each aspect of sovereignty, regardless of their particular circumstances—*i.e.* their development or ability—because no one would want to be left out. In other words, they would agree that ideally they would have "equal" shares of sovereignty over the third territory, which means that the three claimants would have equal standing or status. Therein, all three parties would have a right to participate and the decisionmaking process in each case would be subject to egalitarian consensus—*i.e.* all the three parties should be granted an equal input into the decisionmaking process. They all have the opportunity to present, and amend proposals in relation to every aspect of the sovereignty of the third territory.

A second point has to do with factual circumstances. The representatives would acknowledge that it would be hard to see how after lifting the veil of ignorance all the three parties had the same relative situations—*e.g.* economic development, defense system, means for exploitation of natural resources, law, and so on. So it is reasonable to think that the representatives would agree that the degree of each party's participation would vary according to each party's ability to contribute. It is also reasonable to suppose that each party would as well have an interest in each aspect of sovereignty. Therefore, and bearing in mind these two circumstances—*i.e.* equal right to participate and different ability to contribute—it is reasonable to maintain that each party would have an interest in each aspect of sovereignty being handled in the most efficient manner.

A third point would be to determine the level of input and output of each party with regard to each objective/area/activity related to the sovereignty over the third territory. In principle, the representatives may think of distributing what benefits or rights each party would enjoy depending on the level of contribution that the party makes. Indeed, they acknowledge that some parties will be able to make a bigger or larger input than others. However, an immediate problem arises. The representatives would realize that by making the output dependant on the level of each party's input this could result in a subterfuge for domination. That is to say, the better off party contributing more towards one or more areas and therefore securing a larger stake while the other two parties were unable to make the same level of contribution that would be translated in an *ad eternum* share of benefits.

But if the representatives added a proviso in order to make sure that the party with greater ability—and therefore greater initial participation rights—would have the obligation to bring the other two parties towards equilibrium, the proposal becomes reasonable. That is because it ensures the most efficient current distribution of rights and obligations but also ensures the party that currently benefits most has an obligation to bring the other two parties up to a position where they can contribute equally—*i.e.* it has the burden to assist the other two parties to acquire the ability to contribute equally to that particular objective/area/activity of sovereignty over the third territory. Therein, the party with the greater ability in whatever area would agree to this because there is no other way of having the cooperation of the other two, and the other two parties would agree because this arrangement requires they receive something immediately and will eventually gain the ability to have an equal share, and they would otherwise get nothing.

It is true that the obligation is potentially onerous: what justifies the ascription of that obligation to the better off party? For example, if A is the stronger, and B and C are the weaker parties, is A obligated to raise the standards of B's and C's economies so that they can afford to invest in the exploitation of natural resources; or is it enough that A gives B and C a specific sum equivalent only to what B and C need to exploit resources on terms equal with A? If A gives that sum to B and C, are they obliged to spend it on exploitation, or can they spend it on something else and so forfeit any future claim to be assisted with the exploitation of natural resources? Why cannot B and C simply issue leases to commercial companies to exploit the resources on their behalf; why do they have to rely on help from A? What does the obligation imply in relation to unalterable inequalities, such as one state's being geographically closer to the third territory than the other?

The way in which the parties fulfill the final agreement or how the parties use the outcomes of the exploitation of their shares have to do with either practical matters that depend on each real scenario or with decisions pertaining internal sovereignty and therefore are out of the scope of this book. Similarly, to think of every possible factual difference among the parties—*e.g.* geographical proximity—would be out of the scope of an academic writing of similar nature, in particular when this is only a theoretical exercise. However, the next chapter will demonstrate—to a degree—how the egalitarian shared sovereignty may be applicable in some circumstances.

In what matters the justification for the obligation owed by the more advantaged claimant, two clarifications must be made. First, there is no claim here that any obligation is *prima facie* owed among the parties and the egalitarian shared sovereignty does not claim that either. The most advantaged party would accept the agreement or—better said, it would be unreasonable for this party to argue it is not fair to accept it. Whether the most advantaged party actually accepts the arrangement or not is a different matter. Second, it is reasonable to believe that if the three parties in the original position agree on: (a) equal standing; (b) making the nature and degree of participation dependent on efficiency; and therefore (c) at first the party with more "input" will receive more "output;" the more advantaged claimant—whoever that turns out to be—will accept to have an obligation to bring about equilibrium in the shares since, in the absence of that equilibrium, the more advantaged claimant would or could dominate the other claimants so there would be hardly a good reason for the other two parties to accept any other arrangement that somehow did not contain a degree of equilibrium. That is because anything less than shares in equilibrium would potentially imply a smaller share in comparison to those of the other parties. Therein, the bigger the share, the riskier the case for any of the parties to have more control on a particular issue pertaining sovereignty or the sovereignty of the third territory as a whole.

This is directly linked to the idea of nondomination presented in Chapter 4, since the possible monopoly of power with regard to particular issue pertaining sovereignty or the sovereignty of the third territory as a whole could degenerate into arbitrary power by the decisions being made mainly—only?—by the strongest party or in benefit only of the strongest party. In consequence, the freedom of the least advantaged parties with regard to the choices they could make with their shares and the originally agreed equal standing could potentially be reduced to the "rubber-stamping" of the decisions made by the strongest claimant. Therein, it is reasonable to believe that the representatives of the parties would find the equilibrium proviso a fair solution to safeguard the interests of the three populations involved.

This way of approaching sovereignty conflicts like the ones discussed in this book is called egalitarian shared sovereignty and can be stated as follows: (Figure 6.1.).

The egalitarian shared sovereignty solves sovereignty conflicts because it simply acknowledges the facts, (a) that sovereignty conflicts and sovereignty are complex

(1) Equal right to participate (egalitarian consensus principle)

(2) Nature and degree of participation depends on efficiency of accomplishing the particular objective/area/activity at issue (principle of efficiency)

(3) Each party receives a benefit (in terms of rights and opportunities) that depends on what that party contributes with (input-to-output ratio principle).

PROVISO:

But the party with greater ability and therefore greater initial participation rights has the obligation to bring the other two parties towards equilibrium (equilibrium proviso)

Figure 6.1

issues; (b) that complexity is given by these issues being constituted by activities and goods that imply both benefits and burdens; and (c) that the claiming agents are—most probably—in very different comparative situations in many senses.

The problem of defining equality is not present because the agreement does not refer to the parties but to the target, the third territory. All the parties receive equal shares of sovereignty since these shares are ideal (they only represent their right to equal benefits and the obligation to equal contributions and only in what is referred to the third territory). Thereby, if they can make equal contributions, they will receive equal benefits. Their relative situations as members of the international society does not count here. They are equal or not in as much as it is referred to the target, the third territory. Coincidentally, if they cannot fulfill their obligations to the same extent, their returns will be affected. It is when the qualitative differences come into play. And they are referred to the situation of each of the parties in relation to a specific good in what matters only to the third territory.

To give an example, if a party A cannot defend the third territory because it does not have any means of defense, then it cannot contribute (so its return will be lessened). As there are three prerequisites and a targeted agreement, the other two parties B and C will have to assist party A in as much as their assistance is needed to let party A have a similar contribution in regard to that specific good or activity (in the example, parties B and C will assist in the development of the means of defense of party A, but only in as much as it is necessary for the defense of the third territory).

Indeed, the egalitarian shared sovereignty provides for the legitimacy of initial differences in the benefits and burdens of the parties in a way that the equality principle does not. So when they reach the ultimate egalitarian shared sovereignty goal of equilibrium among the parties, there will be no problem in knowing what "equal shares" require since these will be similar shares of each of the goods relevant to sovereignty (output) among three agents with similar level of use of their respective shares (input). The term "similar" rather than "identical" is used when referred to the final shares since there will be obviously some elements that because of factual restrictions or limitations cannot be equally or identically used, or at least not to the same extent in the literal meaning of these expression—*e.g.* geographical proximity.

Following the previous paragraphs, a hypothetical situation will be introduced in order to show how the egalitarian shared sovereignty works in the context of a sovereignty dispute. The aim of this example is to demonstrate how by acknowledging certain features and by applying the criteria mentioned before, a shared sovereignty model can work, at least in theory.

Imagine a group of people living on an island named Khemed. The majority of Khemedians are Muslims and there are some other minor religions represented as well. Although the territory is small in size, it is highly rich in a very rare metal only found there. However, they do not possess the means for its exploration and exploitation. Therefore, their main source of income is the exportation of basic products obtained from fishing and farming. They do not have any means to defend the island. Finally, the sovereignty of the island has been continuously claimed by two sovereign states, Syldavia and Borduria.

Syldavia is a medium size sovereign state with a large population, mainly Muslims. This country is situated in another continent and although not having natural resources, it is immensely wealthy, mainly because of its financial services. Syldavians have one of the most developed means of defense in the world.

On the contrary, Borduria is one of the largest sovereign states in the world in terms of territorial size, but not densely populated. Bordurians are mainly Hindus and their economy is based on agriculture. It is a nonwealthy country with heavy international debt, high rates of unemployment, and inflation and governmental corruption. They do not have any means to defend their territory. Geographically, they are located in the continent adjacent to Khemed, so mainland Borduria shares with Khemedians part of the continental shelf.

Table 6.1 gives a more visual account of the example.

Khemed is the most advantaged in natural resources (difference in Khemed's favor), the least advantaged in territorial and population size, and less advantaged than Syldavia in wealth and defense.

Syldavia is the most advantaged in terms of wealth and defense (differences in Syldavia's favor), the least advantaged in terms of natural resources, and less advantaged than Borduria in relation to territorial size and their geographical proximity to Khemed.

Borduria is the most advantaged in terms of geographical proximity to Khemed (difference in Borduria's favor), but the least advantaged in terms of wealth. It is less advantaged than Syldavia in terms of defense.

Before reviewing how the egalitarian shared sovereignty may work in this hypothetical situation, the following paragraphs consider briefly how the principle of equality and the difference principle result when applied *sensu stricto* in this imaginary case.

By applying equality strictly, the agents would all receive equal benefits and contribute equally towards the burdens. How would Borduria fulfill its duty to defend Khemed? How would Khemedians defend themselves? The same could be said about natural resources because although Khemedians, Syldavians, and

Table 6.1

	Khemed	*Syldavia*	*Borduria*
Territory	Island	Mainland	Mainland
Religion	Muslim	Muslim	Hindu
Territorial size	Small	Medium	Large
Population size	Small	Large	Medium
Wealth	Average	Wealthy	nonwealthy (indebted)
Defense	No	Yes	No
Natural resources	Yes	No	Yes
Geographical proximity	Yes	No	Yes

Bordurians would receive the same share in terms of ownership, Khemedians and Bordurians would not have the means to exploit them. Several other implications could be drawn but the point is clear. It is both unreasonable and unfair to expect three parties with different comparative situations in many different areas to contribute in an equal manner or to receive an equal return.

Nevertheless, to apply the difference principle in the same form may have similar consequences. Syldavia is the least advantaged in terms of natural resources, so they will receive a larger share. Khemed is less advantaged than Syldavia in terms of defense, so the latter will provide the means to defend the third territory. But Borduria is the least advantaged in terms of wealth, the natural resources in its territory are not part of the agreement so they are not under discussion, and they do not have any means to defend the third territory (Bordurians cannot even defend themselves). Would they have to receive a larger share of the benefits resultant from the exploitation of natural resources in Khemed with means provided by Syldavia? Indeed, this seems unacceptable.

To recapitulate, there are two sovereign states Syldavia and Borduria claiming sovereignty over Khemed, a third populated insular territory. The three populations through their representatives agreed on sharing sovereignty over Khemed. They understand that they are dealing with many issues—*i.e.* activities or goods, and these many issues imply both benefits and burdens. So, to ask all of them to contribute equally and receive an equal return is not the solution. Neither is it for the better off in any given activity to contribute more and the least advantaged in any other activity to receive a larger benefit. They may either lead to domination or to continuous assistance. And because they do also know that they will maintain the agreement under the three prerequisites, they keep their reciprocal noninterference and consider themselves reciprocally equals. In addition to this, they know it is a targeted agreement only referring to the third territory—*i.e.* this is not an agreement based on humanitarian reasons, domestic or global justice.

Thereby, egalitarian shared sovereignty understood as a balancing principle among Khemedians, Syldavians, and Bordurians bearing in mind their differences implies: Khemedians, Syldavians, and Bordurians have all the same right to participate in every aspect of the sovereignty over Khemed. That is to say, they all have the opportunity to present and amend proposals in relation to every aspect of the sovereignty over Khemed (egalitarian consensus principle). Khemed shares in equal portions natural resources with Syldavians and Bordurians. Syldavia shares in equal portions the means for their exploitation with Khemed and Borduria. And Borduria, because of their geographical location, will grant special privileges for both Khemedian and Bordurian enterprises only related to the exploitation of natural resources in Khemed (or any other activity, but it must be related to Khemed).

Indeed, either Khemed or Borduria may have issues in exploiting at the same level of efficiency as Syldavia their shares of natural resources. Hence, Syldavia must make sure that both the other agents reach the same level of exploitation or divide the benefits resultant among the three parties equally in the meantime—*i.e.* it is a targeted shared model.

The principle can be seen in a larger picture across the board with different activities. At first, the smaller and the larger the contribution, the smaller and the larger the return respectively. But as the agreement aims to avoid domination (secure noninterference) and has a target, it is to be expected a more evenly shared contribution-return relationship among the parties will emerge in the long term. That is to say in the example, at first Khemed would be defended by Syldavia, and the latter would also contribute to the exploitation of the natural resources in the island (principle of efficiency). In principle, Syldavians would receive a larger share of the resultant benefits—*i.e.* the larger the contribution, the larger the return since Syldavia is contributing towards both defense and exploitation of natural resources in a larger manner than the other two agents (input-to-output ratio principle). This covers the burdens–benefits part.

But, because of the targeted agreement, Syldavia must make sure both Khemed and Borduria reach relatively the same level for the defense of the third territory and the exploitation of natural resources (equilibrium proviso). It is then when the contributions among the three will be more even as well as the returns.

Meanwhile, and in order to lessen the gap between contributions and benefits, Bordurians could use the difference they have in their favor—*i.e.* geographical proximity means a more accessible bilateral commerce with Khemed, faster and possibly more effective response in case of international threat or attack, etc., things that Syldavia cannot offer.

Moreover, as the first prerequisite prohibits interferences of any kind, and the second prerequisite specifically protects nonpolitical liberties, different religious beliefs between Khemedians and Bordurians could not be used for the advantage or disadvantage of any of the populations. That is because they are in a certain order of priority. In other words, the principle and the prerequisites are lexically ordered.[64] Therein, no transgression of: (a) the noninterference or nondomination principle; (b) the basic nonpolitical liberties; and (c) the principles recognized by the law of peoples, is allowed under any excuse or reason even if that means not fulfilling the "egalitarian shared sovereignty" principle.

The lexical order dictates the priority among the prerequisites and the principle if there is a conflict in practice. Indeed, the prerequisites and the "egalitarian shared sovereignty" are intended to work together and not individually. However, reality may show instances in which to apply the principle could go against one or more prerequisites. Therefore, the lexicographic or lexical preference ordering applies. That is because the agents will have multiple criteria motivating their choices (discussed in Chapter 7). As they will have a ranking of priorities, the choice among the different alternatives will follow the highest criterion. Inversely, by respecting the egalitarian shared sovereignty the agents will take into account the three prerequisites.

The main reason to proceed this way is to secure a real "equal footing." Indeed, as a result of the lexical order basic rights will only be compared with other basic rights, powers and prerogatives with other powers and prerogatives, and so on.

64 Rawls, *A Theory of Justice* (n. 1), pp. 53 *in fine* and 54 *supra*.

Thereby, arrangements that could imply trading basic nonpolitical liberties for, for example, the exploitation of natural resources, could be avoided. So, none of the agents could use their relative better position at the expense of any of the other parties.

Conclusion

Clearly, this chapter has shown that there are several factors which impact negatively on the resolution of sovereignty conflicts—*i.e.* just acquisition, differences of various kinds among the parties, and so on. In tune with this, it has also shown that by application of the methodology used by John Rawls in *A Theory of Justice* these factors can be eliminated.

In transferring Rawls's methodology to sovereignty conflicts this monograph had to confront several dissimilarities to cases to which Rawls himself applies it—*i.e.* Rawls applies it to a domestic liberal society in which he can take for granted that the citizens among whom he is distributing are free and equal and whose status as citizens and as legitimate claimants is not in question. Rawls also applies his method to international society in *The Law of Peoples* in which he similarly takes for granted that "peoples" (the moral units of international society) have a free and equal status; their standing as peoples is not in doubt. However, in the disputed sovereignty cases, the status of the various parties in relation to the dispute is very much in doubt.

Indeed, these dissimilarities did not foreclose the use of the original position and the veil of ignorance but both had to be adapted accordingly. Thereby, the idea of a colorable claim was introduced in order to define who has the *prima facie* right to claim sovereignty, a list of options in tune with sovereignty conflicts was presented for revision as possible solutions, the necessary conditions for the representatives in the negotiations were listed, and so on.

Specifically, a main outcome emerges from the chapter, that is to say the egalitarian shared sovereignty: (a) this way of understanding shared sovereignty is egalitarian since the three agents start the negotiations on an equal footing and the agreement reached must grant that they remain free and equal autonomous international subjects; (b) sovereignty so defined is shared since the agents agree on distributing the sovereignty of the third territory among them, being all simultaneously supreme authority; and (c) sovereignty in this model has a twofold meaning. First, the three agents will all be seen as sovereign, although not all of them are sovereign states. Hence, the population of the third territory will have the prerogative to decide freely and autonomously in relation to its share of sovereignty. Second, because what is distributed in shares is the sovereignty—*i.e.* supreme authority—over the third territory.

Bibliography

Conway, David. "Nozick's Entitlement Theory of Justice: Three Critics Answered." *Libertarian Alliance, Philosophical Notes* 15 (1990).

Dworkin, Ronald. "What is Equality? Part 2: Equality of Resources." *Philosophy and Public Affairs* 10 (1981): 283–345.

Gauthier, David. *Morals by Agreement*. Oxford: Oxford University Press, 2003.

Kohm, Lynne Marie. "Tracing the Foundations of the Best Interest of the Child Standard in American Jurisprudence." *Journal of Law and Family Studies* 10 (2008): 337–76.

Meyer Greene, T., ed. *Selections of Immanuel Kant*. London: Charles Scribner's Sons Ltd., 1929.

Nozick, Robert. *Anarchy, State and Utopia*. New York: Basic Books, 1974.

Otsuka, Michael. "Self-Ownership and Equality: A Lockean Reconciliation." *Philosophy and Public Affairs* 27 (1998): 65–92.

Rawls, John. *A Theory of Justice*, Revised Edition. Oxford: Oxford University Press, 1999.

Rawls, John. *Justice as Fairness, A Restatement*. Cambridge MA: Harvard University Press, 2003.

Rawls, John. *Political Liberalism*. New York: Columbia University Press, 2005.

Rawls, John. *The Law of Peoples*. Cambridge MA: Harvard University Press, 1999.

Winslow, Philip C. *Victory for Us is to See You Suffer: In the West Bank with the Palestinians and the Israelis*. Boston MA: Beacon Press, 2007.

Wright, Quincy. "The Goa Incident." *The American Journal of International Law* 56 (1962): 617–32.

7 How could shared sovereignty work in practice?

Introduction

The previous chapter showed that egalitarian shared sovereignty is a fair way of dealing with sovereignty conflicts and that it is unreasonable to reject it as a way of solving them. That is because the fairness of the outcomes of the original position was secured by the conditions under which the choice was made. It is now time to evaluate if the general principles of the egalitarian shared sovereignty can be extended to workable institutions that realize these principles. That is the aim of this chapter, to work out what sorts of institutions and arrangements could, and would best, realize the egalitarian shared sovereignty.

In order to work out the institutions some actual sovereignty conflicts will be used. These conflicts will fulfill the criteria defined at the beginning of this book—*i.e.* two sovereign states and a populated third territory. Moreover, the attention will be centered on some of the elements that constitute these particular sovereignty conflicts and that are constitutive of any political society, national, or international—*i.e.* population, territory, government, and law. Indeed, as it would be theoretically impossible and practically cumbersome for a monograph to aim to cover every single aspect of the third territory, criteria will be introduced to select those elements that will be reviewed.

A further point must be made clear before working out what sort of arrangements and institutions may best realize the egalitarian shared sovereignty. Although this chapter will explore the applicability of the egalitarian shared sovereignty in some real cases they are only used as part of a theoretical exercise. Ergo, relevant nonideal issues—*e.g.* lack of compliance—will not be considered. It is assumed that all parties are reasonable and rational and want to resolve their conflict without violence. To put this in another way, this book only claims it would be unreasonable to reject its outcome—*i.e.* the egalitarian shared sovereignty—were all ideal and assumed conditions present.

Delimiting the range of application

Two clarifications have to be made prior the application of the principles reviewed in Chapter 6. First, in order to apply these principles three actual sovereignty conflicts will be used—namely, Kashmir, the Falkland/Malvinas Islands, and

Gibraltar. There are many reasons to proceed in this way, in particular because it is actually possible to see how these principles work in real states of affairs rather than in an only theoretical environment. However, as the selected conflicts have all the elements essential to the model which is the object of this monograph, the conclusions will be fully applicable to similar disputes.

Second, the principles reviewed in Chapter 6 have to be applied in a sovereignty conflict; more specifically, they have to be applied to a populated third territory and all that it involves. However, what does exactly the third territory involve? In order to answer this question, there are some points that must be discussed beforehand: First, to define the constitutive elements of the third territory; and second, to select which of those elements will be analyzed through the proposed principle. The reason to proceed this way is mainly pragmatic. To do an exhaustive analysis of every component of the third territory would be out of the scope of a monograph of this nature. However, to demonstrate how the selected principles work is essential in order to prove the usefulness of this project.

In order to define the third territory and its elements it is convenient to review the definition of a state. A classic view of the sovereign state identifies its constitutive elements, which is ideal for the purpose of the present section. International public law offers a definition in article 1 of the Montevideo Convention of Rights and Duties of States (1933) that declares: "The [S]tate as a person of international law should possess the following qualifications: (a) a permanent population; (b) a defined territory; (c) government; and (d) capacity to enter into relations with the other states." In tune with this definition, the *Oxford Dictionary of Law* says that: "[t]o qualify as a state the entity must have: (1) a permanent population . . .; (2) a defined territory . . .; (3) an effective government."[1] What is clear from these two definitions is that a state consists of at least: Population, territory, and government. By analogy, it can be said that the third territory offers these elements: Population, territory, and government. However, its sovereignty rests in the hands of the two sovereign states.

Although population, territory, and government can be seen as essential elements in order to establish a societal political organization—sovereign or not—they presuppose others that give flesh to them: Currency, market, defense, language, religion, etc. What are the elements or sub-elements to which the agreed principles are going to be applied? To answer this question, different criteria can be followed. Some of these elements are necessary in order for the third territory to exist, some others sufficient and most of them only desirable. Some of them can be divided; some cannot. From this account it can be maintained that the elements that constitute the third territory can be characterized and classified from different angles. However, there is a common feature to all of them and to sovereignty conflicts in general: Controversy—*i.e.* the fact that every involved agent wants a

1 Elizabeth A. Martin and Jonathan Law (eds), *A Dictionary of Law* (Oxford: Oxford University Press, 2006).

larger share, even an exclusive one, over elements or sub-elements considered valuable. Even if some of these elements may be necessary, but not controversial—*i.e.* if the parties are not in dispute about what should be done about them—no negotiation is necessary. However, some others, if they are only desirable, may be matter of controversy. It is to these that the principles reached will be applied.

The "egalitarian shared sovereignty" applied to actual cases

The elements that constitute the third territory and some of their respective sub-elements will be considered, discussing which of these sub-elements are controversial in a chosen actual case. Therein, the principles reached will be applied using the selected cases, specifically the sub-elements which may be the cause of controversy among the involved agents in the dispute.

Population

It is true that issues related to population may seem at first controversial but when looked into detail, sovereignty conflicts are more often than not centered on problems related to territory and government and law. That is not to say, however, that issues related to population are not controversial at all. In fact, they might be controversial but not necessarily to the same extent as territory, government and law ones are. So, to avoid the analysis of population as an element because it might not contribute enough in the discussion is, at this stage, too premature. Indeed, there are cases around the globe in which populations impose upon each other custom, religion, language, and so on resulting in social tension with many negative outcomes—*e.g.* discrimination, human trafficking, precarious employment conditions for those who are not part of the same societal group, etc. How would the egalitarian shared sovereignty deal with the issue of having different populations within the same model?

A dispute that offers several elements attractive for the analysis when reviewing population is the case of Kashmir.[2] The valley of Kashmir has been a center of conflict since ancient times.[3] Some trace the presence of kingdoms in this territory

2 Victoria Schofield, *Kashmir in Conflict, India, Pakistan and the Unfinished War* (London: I.B. Tauris & Co. Ltd., 2000); Sunil Chandra Ray, *Early History and Culture of Kashmir* (New Delhi: Munshiram Manoharlal Oriental Publishers, 1970); H. H. Wilson, *The Hindu History of Kashmir* (Calcutta, India: Susil Gupta Private Ltd., 1960); Mridu Rai, *Hindu Rulers, Muslim Subjects, Islam: Rights and the History of Kashmir* (London: C. Hurst & Co. Ltd., 2004); Balraj Puri, *Kashmir Towards Insurgency,* Revised and updated edition (New Dehli: Orient Longman Ltd., 1995); Prem Shankar Jha, *Kashmir, 1947: Rival Versions of History* (Oxford: Oxford University Press, 1996); Josef Korbel, *Danger in Kashmir* (Princeton NJ: Princeton University Press, 1954); Sumantra Bose, *The Challenge in Kashmir: Democracy, Self-Determination and a Just Peace* (New Delhi: Sage Publications India Pvt. Ltd., 1997).

3 Schofield (n. 2), p. 1.

as early as the times of Herodotus and Alexander.[4] Also, from early periods there have been influences from India and China, and different religions such as Hinduism and Buddhism,[5] whether Kashmir has been part of an Empire or an independent kingdom. For instance, around 1586 the valley was taken by the Mughals, whose center of power was Delhi.[6] In the early 18th century, the Persians invaded Delhi. In 1751 the Afghans took over Kashmir.[7] After that period, the British presence is significant in Asia. In 1809, the British authorities signed a treaty of "Amity and Concord" with Kashmir.[8] The valley was useful for British international agenda because of its geostrategic location against Russia, Afghanistan, and China.[9] In 1846, the British authorities signed the "Treaty of Amritsar" with the Dogra King of Kashmir, transferring authority to the Maharaja in exchange for compensation.[10] But this treaty, which was meant to be "for ever" lasted only about a century until British foreign policy changed and decolonization started;[11] indeed, in 1947 the British left India.

There are often two versions of history.[12] That is mainly because the region presents traces of different and opposed ethnic and religious features.[13] The two main groups are the Hindus and the Muslims. Thus, the Hindus are divided into three main sub-groups—Gors, Karkuns, and Buhers[14]—and the Muslims into others—Saiyids, Mughals, Shias, etc.[15] The differences are notorious not only between Hindus and Muslims but also among the sub-groups.[16]

In this historical context and with this socially divided background, Kashmir was incorporated to the Indian Union in 1947. Tension between the social groups increased and Hindus and Muslims looked to India and Pakistan respectively for help.[17] Since then, the debate as to whether it should belong to one or two nations persists.[18] The region has been divided into two separate administrations, that of India (Jammu and Kashmir) and that of Pakistan (Azad Kashmir).[19]

The Kashmiris are in the theoretical model the people inhabiting the third territory. They will have certain features, like any other group of people that

4 Wilson (n. 2), p. 76.
5 *Ibid.*, p. 77.
6 Schofield (n. 2), p. 3.
7 *Ibid.*, p. 4.
8 *Ibid.*, p. 5.
9 *Ibid.*, p. 10.
10 Bose (n. 2), p. 23.
11 *Ibid.*, p. 24.
12 Jha (n. 2), p. 1.
13 Ray (n. 2), p. 26.
14 Rai (n. 2), p. 37.
15 *Ibid.*, pp. 38–39.
16 *Ibid.*, p. 39.
17 Puri (n. 2), pp. 4–6.
18 Korbel (n. 2), pp. 28 ff.
19 For simplicity in the analysis, the region under Chinese administration is not part of this account.

constitutes a nation. Do any of these features need to be specifically dealt with under the principles reached in the negotiations?

The following paragraphs will focus the attention on some of the sub-elements that constitute the population of the third territory using the example of Kashmir.

Numbers

A large or a small group of people can be consolidated as a state, from China and India with more than one billion inhabitants each to Vatican City with less than one thousand individuals. So, there is no minimum or maximum number of inhabitants to constitute a state. And the same can be said in regard to the third territory. It may seem that numbers matter if there is an argument for people to have a voice they have to have "occupied" the land. For instance, if there were five people living in Antarctica that would not give them a voice. But, if there are five people living on an island that is small in size that may be enough.

Although this argument appears convincing, it is not relevant here for several reasons. First, it may seem like numbers do matter, but not absolutely. Second, this book defined which populations will have a right to sovereignty by characterizing the "colorable claim"—*i.e.* the number of people is irrelevant. Third, it has previously been indicated when a certain group of people had the right to decide upon their political status as a group according to international relations—when self-determination was reviewed. Finally, to use Antarctica as an example is not valid since it has a special international status also previously reviewed here—that makes it impossible for any group of people to become an independent state. Thus, there are other historical cases in which populations obtained independence by settling in large territories although being small in number—*e.g.* the United States, Argentina. Consequently, this element does not generate controversy, *i.e.* there is no need to discuss the size of the population.

But, what about immigration? How many people should be allowed to immigrate to Kashmir and under what conditions? How many people should be allowed to emigrate from Kashmir and under what conditions?

Ethnicity

An ethnic group can be defined as one whose members identify themselves with each other through a common background or heritage (real or assumed) that may involve any or all of the language, culture, religion, race, etc.

Is to be black or white a requisite to be part of a community? Is an African or Asian background necessary? Once again, there are several examples that have a direct answer to the question. In today's world, most (if not all) states have their populations constituted by individuals from various races and many different cultural backgrounds. Although toleration is pushed to its limits under these circumstances, multi-ethnic societies are a reality. It appears that a common ethnicity is not fundamental to constitute a nation. Indeed, multi-ethnic societies are a widespread reality—*i.e.* there is no point in discussing if a mono or multi-ethnic society will be the one living in the third territory. In principle, this element does not imply controversy at theoretical level. However, it is time now to focus the attention on some of the elements that constitute the ethnicity of any nation and, in particular, those that appear controversial in the case of Kashmir: Language and religion.

Language

To have one language, official or not, or to have one or more languages officially recognized, is not an indispensable requisite for a group of people to be a nation. However, languages are directly linked (at least sociologically) with national identity. Is linguistic homogeneity a requirement for a unified population? If so, is that a necessary or a sufficient condition?

The answer to the previous questions is both simple and complex. Language as a tool to enable inter-subjective relation is necessary. However, the use of the same language is not. On the one hand, there are states around the world that show linguistic diversity, for example, by having two or more official languages (*e.g.* South Africa, Montenegro, Israel, and Switzerland). On the other hand, to have one common linguistic element as a way of interacting evidences a desirable option (at least from a theoretical point of view). It would help in the cohesion of any group of people (hence, nation); it could be seen as a common bond (as part of their culture or ethnicity); it is a very easy aspect to identify.

Indeed, it may be even possible to argue that language is indispensable for any individual living as a member of a group so as to be able to communicate with the others. However, caution must be applied since although having a language as a tool for communication is an essential requisite for an organized population, to have only one is not. From there, linguistic homogeneity could be considered as a desirable element but neither is it necessary nor sufficient. Hence, if to have a language is by default a requisite in any societal organization but homogeneity is not, there is no point in including in the negotiations this sub-element. The population of the third territory will have a language which can be either of the sovereign states' languages or a third one, or they may use all three. In theory, this element does not generate controversy.

According to the art. 343 of the Constitution of India Hindi in Devanagari script is the official language, and according to its art. 345 each state can adopt any one or more languages. According to art. 66 of the Constitution of Jammu and Kashmir, Urdu is the official language of the state. Thus, the official language of Azad Kashmir is also Urdu. However, an interesting element is given by the fact that the Kashmiri language is different from Hindi or Urdu.[20] Is the *status quo* to remain, or is a language to be added?

20 Schofield (n. 2), p. 1; Puri (n. 2), p. 9.

Religion

There are states with official religions (*e.g.* Argentina, Monaco, and Vatican City). There are several that are considered secular states or—in other words—without any official state religion (*e.g.* Bolivia, France, the United States). Moreover, those states that do have an official religion usually recognize in their constitutions freedom of conscience; so, although there is an official religion, inhabitants of these states are able to profess the religion of their choice. From there, a particular religion—or even to uphold one—cannot be seen as any kind of condition for a group of people to be recognized as a nation. Thus, the particularities of the original position and the prerequisites secure equal liberty of conscience.[21]

This element cannot imply controversy per se. Nevertheless, religious tension has been often the cause of social struggle in Kashmir when one dominant group has oppressed the minorities. In actual percentages, the Muslims represent 96.40 percent of the population whereas the Hindus represent 2.45 percent in the area of Kashmir only.[22] The combined figures including the whole state of Jammu and Kashmir showed that from a total of 12,541,302 people 68.31 percent are Muslim and 23.43 percent are Hindu.[23]

The above paragraphs show that the sub-elements that constitute the population of a state are not, in principle, controversial per se. However, all these can in fact be controversial if one party, or more, may wish to impose language, religion or cultural domination—the case of Kashmir. So, it is not that there is no controversy, but that: (a) this form of imposition is not necessary; (b) a just approach must resist and exclude it.

Several solutions have been proposed in order to untangle the dispute in Kashmir.[24] However, in all cases at least one of the parties is left outside the picture. To grant the sovereignty to Pakistan would be opposed by some minorities—Hindus and Buddhists. The opposite solution, sovereignty handed over to India would have the opposition of most of the Muslim population. Then, neither of these two solutions is welcomed by the Jammu and Kashmir or by Azad Kashmir inhabitants.[25] But, even though independence is what the majority of the inhabitants of both Kashmirs want,[26] it is threatened by both India and Pakistan

21 John Rawls, *A Theory of Justice*, Revised edition (Oxford: Oxford University Press, 1999), pp. 180–85.

22 Percentages referred only to Kashmir (Census India 2011).

23 Figure and percentages referred to the state of Jammu and Kashmir that includes Kashmir, Jammu, and Ladakh (Census India 2011).

24 For an insight, *see* BBC News, "The Future of Kashmir?" http://news.bbc.co.uk/1/shared/spl/hi/south_asia/03/kashmir_future/html/default.stm (last accessed December 30, 2016).

25 Robert W. Bradnock, *Kashmir: Paths to Peace* (London: Chatham House, 2010), pp. 15–17.

26 *Ibid.*, pp. 15–16.

because it would imply losing claimed territories, consequent rights over them and could result in a possible improvement of their peers' situation.

Indeed, the inhabitants of Jammu and Kashmir and Azad Kashmir seem opposed to joint sovereignty.[27] However, the model proposed here introduces features that make it a more attractive option also for them. That is because, if Kashmir, India, and Pakistan decided to share their sovereignty over the territory under dispute, by applying the egalitarian shared sovereignty, none of the involved parties would interfere with the internal affairs of any of the other parties—first prerequisite—and they all would respect the basic nonpolitical liberties of the three populations—Kashmir, India, and Pakistan—by fulfilling the second prerequisite. Thus, they would conduct their mutual relations according to the principles recognized by the law of peoples—the third prerequisite.

The allocation of sovereignty will be given by: (a) equal right to participate (egalitarian consensus principle); (b) the nature and degree of participation depends on efficiency of accomplishing the particular objective/area/activity at issue (principle of efficiency); (c) each party receives a benefit (in terms of rights and opportunities) that depends on what that party cooperates with (input-to-output ratio principle); and (d) provided the party with greater ability and therefore greater initial participation rights has the obligation to bring the other two parties towards equilibrium (equilibrium proviso). How is that translated into Kashmir's reality and its population? The answer has two parts: (a) the qualitative differences among the parties; (b) the real concerns of the inhabitants of Kashmir.

There are several agents in this particular dispute with various features in terms of population and therefore, there are undoubtedly several differences among them. In what follows, some of these differences will be used to show how the egalitarian shared sovereignty works. For example, India presents the largest of the three populations with 1,210,854,977 people[28] and the biggest economy with a nominal GDP *per capita* of 1,617.[29] Meanwhile, Pakistan has a population of 132,352,279 people[30] with a nominal GDP *per capita* of 1,450[31] and Jammu and Kashmir showed a total of 12,541,302 people[32] with no official figures with regard to their GDP *per capita*.[33]

By combining these figures, it is easy to see that India is both larger in terms of population and nominal GDP *per capita* in comparison with Pakistan, and this

27 *Ibid.*, p. 18. The study in question does not define "joint sovereignty" so its content and what has been explained to the people participating in the study remains unclear.

28 Census India 2011.

29 International Monetary Fund estimates for 2015—in US dollars.

30 Census Pakistan 1998 (the only official figure so far). For more details, *see* www.pbs.gov.pk/sites/default/files/other/pocket_book2006/2.pdf (last accessed on January 5, 2017).

31 International Monetary Fund estimates for 2015—in US dollars.

32 Figure and percentages referred to the state of Jammu and Kashmir that includes Kashmir, Jammu, and Ladakh (Census India 2011).

33 There is no International Monetary Fund estimate for Jammu and Kashmir.

offers a difference in this conflict that can help to achieve a solution. That is because in relation to the inhabitants of both parts of Kashmir (under Indian and Pakistani administration), although they do think the dispute is important for them personally, for a very large majority the main concerns are other issues. Unemployment, government corruption, poor economic development, human rights abuses are what the Kashmiris are really interested in.[34]

In general, by applying the egalitarian shared sovereignty, as Kashmiris would be citizens of both sovereign states, they would have a common passport—a Kashmiri passport—valid in both Pakistan and India. In relation to their language, it is a fact the three main spoken ones are Kashmiri, Urdu, and Hindi; so they all can be made official. In religion, as the second prerequisite recognizes basic nonpolitical liberties, freedom of belief would be adopted at a constitutional level, so that no one may be discriminated based on religion. All this is controlled by the lexically prior prerequisite of nonpolitical liberties.

In particular, as the difference in this example is given by the larger society and stronger economy in India, this state would have a stronger constraint in being a welcoming party for the Kashmiris (input-to-output ratio principle). In that sense, the main concern for them—unemployment—would be acknowledged (principle of efficiency). That is because, although Pakistan would also have the obligation to welcome Kashmiris as its citizens in its territory, the Kashmiris would have the right to opt to be nationals of both states—*i.e.* they have the right to relocate to either state. Thus, even though it is a fact that both populations, that of Pakistan and that of India are large in comparison to Kashmir, they would not be a threat to local employees since in order to work in Kashmir restrictions on nationals of either states would apply—because they would be nationals of either India or Pakistan, but not Kashmiris.

In regard to governmental corruption and threats to human rights, reciprocal control among the three parties (egalitarian consensus principle) could secure an improvement in the present situation—a point to be discussed when dealing with government in this chapter. In particular, employment opportunities generated within the boundaries of both Kashmir because of the exploitation of natural resources, could be the result of a joint enterprise, details of which will be discussed when considering territory.

To recapitulate, shared sovereignty would involve recognizing the sovereignty over Kashmir of both India and Pakistan. In terms of population, the only ones affected would be the Kashmiris, who would be nationals of both states. Moreover, their basic nonpolitical liberties must be respected by both India and Pakistan. Hence, they would have rights in both states, as nationals. They would be equal before the law with any Pakistani or Indian citizen and no discrimination on any grounds would be permitted. As a direct consequence, they would have the right to freely move and reside in any of the three territories—respecting local

34 Bradnock (n. 25), p. 5.

regulations. The status of Kashmiri national, its acquisition and retention would have to be agreed among the parties. Finally, there would be immigration controls to prevent people from moving to Kashmir in order to obtain rights in India or Pakistan that they could not obtain directly. The particulars in relation to law will be reviewed later in this chapter when dealing with government.

This example shows that divisions of religion, language and ethnicity are not obstacles to shared sovereignty, provided that India, Kashmir and Pakistan respect the prerequisites: (a) noninterference or nondomination; (b) nonpolitical liberties; and (c) principles of the law of peoples. Furthermore, shared sovereignty offers a viable way to do it when these three parties acknowledge their qualitative differences—*e.g.* larger population, stronger economy, to name only a few. Moreover, it secures a permanent feature because of the mutual controls and reciprocal concessions, both things that aim for equilibrium among all the parties.

Territory

The Falkland/Malvinas Islands international dispute has all the elements for the type of conflict this monograph discusses, namely two sovereign states (Argentina and the United Kingdom) and a nonsovereign third territory (Falkland/Malvinas Islands). Indeed, it has features that are often the main cause of controversy in sovereignty conflicts. A very brief historical account[35] will put this into context. There is doubt about who first sighted the islands and about the first landing (Ferdinand Magellan and/or Amerigo Vespucci or the English sea captain John Davis) in the 1500s. British and Spanish settlements appear afterwards. Argentina declared its independence from Spain (1816) and then claimed rights over the islands as they were part of the region previously under Spanish dominion (1829). The United Kingdom and Argentina have had continuous presence and/or claimed exclusive sovereign rights over the islands since then, both bilaterally and internationally with a climax in 1982 with a war between the two.

According to the 2012 census[36] the islands had 2841 inhabitants.[37] Most of them (59 percent) considered themselves “Falkland Islanders” and a large percentage identified themselves as British (29 percent).[38] Bilateral relations have been reestablished after the war. However, the sovereignty dispute over the islands continues nowadays. Commerce and trade between the islands and Argentina have been an issue. Because of the lack of negotiations, Argentina has threatened

35 For a more detailed historical account, *see* http://www.falklands.gov.fk/our-people/our-history/ (UK) (last accessed December 30, 2016) and http://www.mrecic.gov.ar/es/la-cuestión-de-las-islas-malvinas/antecedentes (Argentina) (last accessed December 30, 2016).

36 Falkland/Malvinas Islands Census Statistics 2012 http://www.falklands.gov.fk/headline-results-of-2012-falkland-islands-census-released/ (last accessed December 30, 2016).

37 As nonresidents, military personnel were not included in the census. Excluding contractors at Mount Pleasant Airfield (MPA), the population figure of the Falkland Islands is 2,563.

38 Falkland/Malvinas Islands Census Statistics 2012 (n. 36).

an economic blockade,[39] an idea supported by other Latin-American states[40] with visible immediate negative results for the islanders.[41] In March 2013 the Falkland/Malvinas Islanders voted in a referendum whether they wanted (or not) to remain as British Overseas Territory. By a large majority (99.8 percent) they made clear their wishes to remain British.[42]

It is true that the islanders are predominantly British because the United Kingdom has controlled the islands for years—does this weaken the residents' claims? The answer is negative for various reasons—at least in this model. First, they have a "colorable claim." Second, the model neutralized the historical arguments—in Chapter 6. Third, this is a hypothetical analysis to see the feasibility of a joint solution so it is assumed they will have right to self-determination. And because of the hypothetical negotiations, they have realized that self-determination will lead to shared sovereignty because it settles the conflict—by application of the rule of *maximin*.

The Falkland/Malvinas Islands are the third territory in the model. Territory, in principle, can be defined as an area owned and possessed by the population (in land, water, space and, perhaps, cyberspace).[43] Like population, it is a necessary but not sufficient condition of a state. Like population, it may have features that could cause controversy. Some of the features that constitute territory will be reviewed using the Falkland/Malvinas Islands conflict as an example. Those that introduce controversy will be analyzed using the model proposed here.

Extension

From Vatican City or Montenegro to Australia or Russia, the worldwide context has an ample spectrum of states in terms of their territory size. No particular size is necessary, sufficient or even desirable to produce a state. Most third territories are in fact small pieces of land highly rich in natural resources or geographically

39 *The Guardian* (February 1, 2012) https://www.theguardian.com/uk/2012/feb/01/argentina-falklands-economic-blockade (last accessed December 30, 2016); *The Telegraph* (February 2, 2012) http://www.telegraph.co.uk/news/worldnews/southamerica/falklandislands/9055913/Argentina-planning-economic-blockade-of-the-Falkland-diplomats-warn.html (last accessed December 30, 2016).

40 *The Guardian* 06/02/12 https://www.theguardian.com/uk/2012/feb/06/falklands-argentina-britain-blockade (last accessed December 30, 2016).

41 *La Nación* (February 7, 2012) http://www.lanacion.com.ar/1446528-ya-se-sufreen-malvinas-el-bloqueo-comercial (last accessed December 30, 2016); and *Clarín* (February 7, 2012) http://www.clarin.com/politica/Malvinas-aseguran-bloqueo-afecta-pesca_0_rJSgVsP3PQx.html (last accessed January 5, 2017).

42 Official Press Release (March 12, 2013) http://www.falklands.gov.fk/results-of-the-referendum-on-the-political-status-of-the-falkland-islands/ (last accessed December 30, 2016).

43 It will not be discussed here whether cyberspace should or not be considered as part of the sovereignty of a state—as it is out of the scope of this book. However, for a further insight on this topic, *see* Patrick W. Franzese, "Sovereignty in Cyberspace: Can It Exist?" *Air Force Law Review* 64 (2009): 1–42.

strategic—*e.g.* the Falkland/Malvinas Islands, Gibraltar. But their size is not in any way a matter of controversy among the parties in this kind of conflict.

Borders

This could be a matter of controversy. For instance, if Jerusalem came under shared sovereignty, boundaries between Palestine, the joint territory and Israel would have to be determined (perhaps similarly with Kashmir). In the particular case of the Falkland/Malvinas Islands, although it may seem that borders are not an issue—as they are islands—the exclusive economic zone often creates tension between Argentina and the United Kingdom. For instance, who has the right to explore that exclusive sea-zone? What happens in the zone in which Argentina and the Falkland/Malvinas Islands overlap? As this point is intrinsically linked to natural resources, it will be examined after introducing the latter.

Defense

National defense will be seen here as the protection of each and every interest a state has—*e.g.* possessions, territory, and population—through different means—*e.g.* military, economic, and diplomatic. The international scenario offers very diverse realities, from large states in terms of territorial size, with formidable military power—*e.g.* the United States—or almost none—*e.g.* Argentina—to small or medium size ones with a well-equipped and trained army and navy—*e.g.* the United Kingdom—or with none—*e.g.* Costa Rica, Andorra, or Vatican City. Although it may seem desirable for a state to have its own means of defense reality shows it is not a necessary requisite. There are several states in which the army and navy are not big, well equipped or trained enough in order to defend their territory or population but they are still respected as states. There are others that in fact do not have military defense at all, their defense being the responsibility of another country or an international organization—*e.g.* NATO.

There seems to be no problem with defense. The territory being defended is obviously desirable although the task is one which can be shared. However, what would happen if another party—*i.e.* a sovereign state with no part in the conflict—decided to invade the third territory? In the hypothetical scenario that Chile decided to invade the Falkland/Malvinas Islands, who would defend them? The ways in which the situation may develop are as follows: (a) both sovereign states may remain neutral; consequently, the new agent would take over the third territory if the inhabitants were unable to defend themselves; (b) one of the sovereign states may respond to the invasion and defend the third territory; (c) both sovereign states may respond to the invasion and defend jointly or independently the third territory.

Is defense a right or an obligation? International public law assumes self-defense as a right against attack.[44] At the same time, states have the right and are obliged

44 *See* UN Charter, art. 51: "Nothing in the present Charter shall impair the inherent right of individual or collective self-defense if an armed attack occurs against a Member of the United Nations . . ." *See also* UN General Assembly Res. 3314 for a definition of aggression.

to defend their own interests and their population. Consequently, any act of defense is fair and just as long as it is a result of an illegitimate threat or attack. However, in a sovereignty conflict, it seems difficult to determine the one who could/should be defending the third territory in the event of an attack on what appears to be a common interest for all the involved parties: The third territory. In theory, both sovereign states are free international agents able to determine their actions independently. Moreover, they can decide their action plan without having their peers in the conflict in mind. Nevertheless, in terms of their interests it is desirable that they defend (jointly or independently) the third territory; if they did not do so, the invader could gain a better position in terms of sovereign rights over the disputed territory (at least at the factual level).

In addition to the way in which the parties would defend the third territory, there are two other crucial elements that need to be agreed—even if joint defense was the case: (a) the extent to which the burden can be made proportionate, with those with more of the appropriate resources taking the larger share—if they can be trusted not to turn their forces against the other two parties, which is a serious consideration; (b) and the extent to which one considers what combination of contributions will be the most efficient, using, *e.g.*, both the local knowledge of the people in the territory, and the equipment best adapted to defending it. Indeed, if they take on sovereignty, they must take on the obligation to defend. However, how would Argentina, the Falkland/Malvinas Islands, and the United Kingdom share the defense?

The egalitarian shared sovereignty addresses the three elements that seem to be crucial in order to have shared defense: (a) resources; (b) training and opportunities; (c) safety of the other two parties—how to avoid misuse of power. By respecting the prerequisites (noninterference or nondomination, basic nonpolitical liberties, and principles of the law of peoples), the fulfillment of the requirements that constitute the egalitarian shared sovereignty will secure the distribution in terms of the defense of the third territory. Then, the permanent character of the agreement is granted through the involvement of all the agents, since none of them will be in a better position with respect to the others. Thus, all of them are interested in protecting the third territory that is shared among them.

The egalitarian shared sovereignty states that the allocation of sovereignty is given by: (a) equal right to participate (egalitarian consensus principle); (b) the nature and degree of participation depends on efficiency of accomplishing the particular objective/area/activity at issue (principle of efficiency); (c) each party receives a benefit (in terms of rights and opportunities) that depends on what that party cooperates with (input-to-output ratio principle); and (d) provided the party with greater ability and therefore greater initial participation rights has the obligation to bring the other two parties towards equilibrium (equilibrium proviso). In what is specific to its defense, this means all the agents will have an equal responsibility to defend the third territory (egalitarian consensus principle). But how is this translated into terms of means of defense if the agents have different levels of development?

The differences in the case of defense are numerous—*e.g.* geostrategic location; economic resources; level of military development; training and facilities; number of troops; etc. But a combination of contributions can make these differences work together in an efficient form, taking into account that these may be things which one agent can provide but which cannot be provided by any other agent.

As in the Falkland/Malvinas Islands' case, it will be highly probable that the parties have a different level of development in terms of their respective defense systems (input-to-output ratio principle). Then, the egalitarian shared sovereignty can be fulfilled in two ways: (a) following the most efficient combination in terms of contribution (principle of efficiency)—*e.g.* using both the local knowledge of the people in the territory (Falkland/Malvinas Islands), the geostrategic location (Argentina), and the equipment, resources and any means best adapted to defending it (the United Kingdom); (b) the agent with the better comparative situation—in whatever aspect—may contribute in developing the other parties or granting them exclusive privileges (equilibrium proviso)—*e.g.* the United Kingdom could train Argentinean and Falkland/Malvinas troops in exchange for the use of locations in any of them.

It is clear that the egalitarian shared sovereignty aims only to achieve the same level of opportunity and development for all the involved parties so they are able to defend the third territory (not the territory that is already part of the sovereign states). Thus, even if there were variations in the future in terms of wealth status and defense development among the involved participants, the reciprocal obligation would always be the same for all the agents, *i.e.* to combine to produce the most efficient result.

It is important to say that all the agents would participate in the decision process and in the administration of means for the defense of the third territory in the event of an attack. As a consequence, the agents would have reciprocal checks so none of them could become "too powerful" and threaten an otherwise peaceful understanding. The details of the joint administration of the forces involved in the defense would be reached in a new agreement that does not contradict in any sense the principles agreed in the original position.

Natural resources

Natural resources are any material in raw condition present in the territory, organic or mineral, that is not initially a product of any kind of human activity. Some states are rich in natural resources; others are not. No particular amount of natural resources defines a state. But the distribution of natural resources is usually one of the main problems when dealing with sovereignty disputes even though the involved sovereign states may already be wealthy ones; it is a feature that always presents controversy.

Leaving the discussion about natural resources in already sovereign states aside—as it is outside the scope of this book—the focus is on the ones that are part of the third territory. Following the model, it is assumed the parties decided to distribute them. But this does not solve the controversy either. That is because, even though the parties agreed to distribute natural resources, other highly controversial issues remain. This is not only a matter of distribution because the resources have to be farmed, or mined, or piped, and someone has to do the work, and someone, whether a private individual or the state, has to own the farms, mines, pipes, etc.

The egalitarian shared sovereignty may rule out extreme situations, that ownership, public or private, should be totally in the hands of the territory where the mines, etc., are situated, without regard to the needs of the two sovereign states, or that it should be totally in the hands of the sovereign states. It would also rule out the idea that existing ownership should automatically continue, or that everything should be left to the market. In brief, in order to acknowledge the controversial features that natural resources present and still apply the egalitarian shared sovereignty solution and hence distribute them, the following points have to be addressed: (a) just distribution as the aimed outcome; (b) the ownership system of natural resources; (c) the exploitation system; (d) the gains and losses of the agents involved; and (e) the needs and capabilities of all three parties.

Equality *stricto sensu* and the difference principle do not work in relation to the distribution of natural resources because the question here is not just of a distributive nature. Natural resources have to be owned, explored and then exploited. But that exploitation must also be efficient if a solution is going to be reached and respected. The egalitarian shared sovereignty offers a reasonable result. The second prerequisite secures the respect of the individual ownership rights which the inhabitants of the third territory may have at the time of the original agreement. Then, whatever they owned at the onset will still belong to them (as private owners). Respecting the third prerequisite, the fulfillment of the requirements that constitute the principle will secure a fair allocation of natural resources and all that this implies.

The egalitarian shared sovereignty says that the allocation of sovereignty is given by: (a) equal right to participate (egalitarian consensus principle); (b) the nature and degree of participation depends on efficiency of accomplishing the particular objective/area/activity at issue (principle of efficiency); (c) each party receives a benefit (in terms of rights and opportunities) that depends on what that party cooperates with (input-to-output ratio principle); and (d) provided the party with greater ability and therefore greater initial participation rights has the obligation to bring the other two parties towards equilibrium (equilibrium proviso). The differences in relation to natural resources imply several different aspects—*e.g.* means for the exploration and exploitation, geographical location, relevant knowledge, etc.

It is for that reason that the shares will be represented as bundles of rights and obligations, benefits and burdens. However, in terms of property rights, all the agents will have the co-ownership of the natural resources (minus the ones originally owned by the inhabitants of the third territory, as per the second prerequisite), and this will involve both rights and obligations—*i.e.* egalitarian consensus principle. A combination of elements may fit in the aim of the egalitarian shared sovereignty if and only if the combined elements or resources that an agent may exploit could not be exploited to the same efficient extent in any other way (principle of efficiency)—*e.g.* joint ventures. However, two points must be made clear: Because the model aims to safeguard the interests of all the parties, the different combinations of natural resources in the bundle is in terms of their exploration and exploitation—not their ownership or the distribution of consequent benefits; and as this requirement is defined by bundles, each bundle may be constituted of diverse elements that taken together offer the same outcome: An efficient exploitation. Therefore, this implies a solution by means of an efficient model with safeguards for all the participants.

The egalitarian shared sovereignty has a twofold application. First, the most efficient combination of exploration and exploitation of natural resources bearing in mind the differences among the parties. Second, an agent better off in relation to a given difference will make sure the other parties are able to exploit their respective share of natural resources to the same extent—when possible—or compensate the inequality. Then, even if variations appeared in the future in terms of either natural resources—*e.g.* drought, scarcity, lack of trading value—or the level of development or wealth of any of the agents, their ownership rights would still be the same for all of them as well as their rights and obligations in terms of exploitation and the way benefits were allocated (equilibrium proviso).

From the previous paragraphs it is clear that by agreeing on various sorts of divisions of labor among the parties, the resources are exploited to full advantage. But, it may be not that clear what the differences are and how the principle may work. Thereby, consider the idea to the conflict *sub-examine*. In the case of the Falkland/Malvinas Islands, the three parties could be considered as co-owners of the natural resources located in the territorial sea and the exclusive economic zone. Undoubtedly, there are several differences among Argentina, the United Kingdom, and the Falkland/Malvinas Islands in relation to natural resources that have to do with these islands. Therein, some of these differences will be used to show how the egalitarian shared sovereignty could be realized.

The first difference is given by the fact the islanders possess the total of natural resources at stake (100 percent).[45] By applying the egalitarian shared sovereignty, each party receives the rights to the same ideal portion—*i.e.* 33 percent of the ownership of natural resources, minus original ownership of the inhabitants of the third territory. As set out in the previous chapter, it would be either oversimplistic or naïve to imagine Argentineans or Falkland/Malvinas Islanders to be able to explore and exploit to the same level their shares of natural resources in comparison to the United Kingdom (second difference). However, both Argentineans and Falkland/Malvinas Islanders have some elements that put them in a better position in relation to that of the United Kingdom—*e.g.* local work force, geographical proximity (third difference).

With all these differences in mind, and with regard to the exploration and exploitation of the natural resources in these areas—*e.g.* hydrocarbons, it could be completed by the United Kingdom (as they are the party most developed

45 The figures and percentages used are assumed and for illustrative purposes only.

technically and economically to do it), and both the islanders and Argentina could offer the work force for the joint venture and grant privileges in terms of location to British companies. Thus, Argentina could also offer the United Kingdom certain exclusive rights in the sea-zone that overlaps with the Falklands/Malvinas.

In order to avoid continuous assistance from the United Kingdom to Argentina and the Falkland/Malvinas Islands that may be translated in a permanent feature—*i.e.* it may lead to domination or an unbalanced relationship, the United Kingdom would have to help Argentina and the Falkland/Malvinas Islands in developing their means of exploration and exploitation to relatively the same level they have. From there, at the beginning of the agreement the United Kingdom indeed would be contributing more towards the exploration and exploitation and hence have a larger return. However, these uneven distributions of burdens and benefits among the parties would only be in the short term. Natural resources and all that they imply in terms of rights and obligations are part of a wider agreement that has a target: The third territory as a whole. Thus, it respects noninterference or nondomination—first prerequisite, nonpolitical liberties—second prerequisite—and principles of the law of peoples—third prerequisite. Hence, no unbalanced relation or continuous assistance leading to domination is permitted.

Finally, the way in which each party redistributes the benefits of this shared model within each population is entirely a matter of national or local distribution and hence may have various forms. That is to say, the egalitarian shared sovereignty gives the basic structure of the solution; the details are subject to actual rather than hypothetical negotiation. As an example only—without claiming it is the way they will choose, the resultant revenues of some or all the joint activities could be destined to a distribution fund.[46] For instance, at first, the larger the contribution towards the exploration and exploitation, the larger the return. From there, the United Kingdom could receive a larger percentage, Argentina and Falkland/Malvinas Islanders proportionally smaller ones, and leave part of the total for securing the development of the means for exploration and exploitation for both Argentina and the Falklands/Malvinas.

To put it in simple terms, and assuming the larger and smaller contributions, 40 percent of the revenues for the United Kingdom, 25 percent for Argentina, 15 percent for the Falkland/Malvinas Islanders, and 20 percent to be invested only in Argentina and the Falkland/Malvinas islands and only for the development of means for exploration and exploitation of natural resources. Note the different percentages between Argentina and the Falkland/Malvinas Islands because of another difference—*i.e.* population size.

The final outcome, the revenues obtained from the exploitation of natural resources could indeed be destined to a distribution fund. That is to say, each party would take a certain part of the revenues for reinvestments—*e.g.* 5 percent

46 Actual examples of this proposal are the Oil Revenue Distribution Funds (ORDFs) in Alaska (oil-royalty investment account) and Norway.

of their shares in terms of revenues, and the rest would be distributed among the inhabitants of each of the claiming parties. In the example, the United Kingdom received 40 percent of the total revenues and hence 5 percent of this 40 percent would be reinvested by the British government in exploration and exploitation of natural resources; the rest would be destined to a distribution fund for British nationals. With Argentina and the Falkland/Malvinas Islands the same procedure would be applied, but with their respective percentages. And 20 percent of the total would have to be invested in both Argentina and the Falkland/Malvinas Islands for the development of their means for exploration and exploitation of natural resources in the third territory. It is important to make clear again this is but one way in which the parties may distribute the benefits within each of their respective populations.

Two clarifications: First, and ideally, both Argentina and the Falkland/Malvinas Islands would reach a point in which their means for exploration and exploitation of natural resources in the third territory were similar to that of the United Kingdom. So, the 20 percent destined to develop them would be lowered until it was not necessary at all. From there, that 20 percent would integrate the total to be distributed among the parties—*i.e.* now they would be able to offer similar contributions so they would roughly have similar returns. Second, this example deals with just a few differences in relation only to natural resources for simplicity in the demonstration. But taking into consideration sovereignty and all that it implies, Argentina, the United Kingdom, and the Falkland/Malvinas Islands would have to take into account all the various contributions—*e.g.* defense, geographical location, financial system, and so on; and the differences in each case in order to determine the qualitative content of the shares. As stated before, the egalitarian shared sovereignty gives the parties the basic structure of the solution; the details are subject to actual rather than hypothetical negotiation.

The details of any joint enterprise as well as the ones referred to the joint administration of the exploration and exploitation and compensation procedures (in case they were necessary) would be reached in a new agreement that cannot contradict in any sense the one reached in the original position.

Government

The last case of sovereignty conflicts is Gibraltar. The focus is now government, and Gibraltar has already taken the first steps for what may be a future joint solution. Gibraltar prior to modernity was occupied by the Spaniards, Arab and Muslim kingdoms, and some other cultures.[47] It was in 1713, after a war between

47 George Hills, *Rock of Contention, a History of Gibraltar* (London: Robert Hale & Company, 1974). For more details about the early history of Gibraltar (official version), *see* https://www.gibraltar.gov.gi/history (last accessed December 30, 2016) and for a contemporary account, *see* in particular http://www.gibraltar.gov.gi/political-development (last accessed December 30, 2016).

Britain and Spain, that Spain ceded Gibraltar in perpetuity to the United Kingdom under the Treaty of Utrecht. However, after this agreement the dispute in regard to the peninsula has continued, with Spain claiming sovereign rights. The Gibraltarians rejected Spanish sovereignty in referendums twice (1967 and 2002). In the last referendum, the Gibraltarians rejected shared sovereignty between the United Kingdom and Spain.[48]

However, shared sovereignty in this case did not consider the Gibraltarians in the negotiations. Currently, and under the Gibraltar Constitution Order (2006), Gibraltar remains part of the United Kingdom's dominions. But, the British government cannot enter into arrangements with other states in relation to the sovereignty of Gibraltar against the Gibraltarians' wishes. The Constitution recognizes the right to self-determination. Although Gibraltar is in charge of its internal affairs, the United Kingdom deals with foreign affairs and defense. In relation to Spain, a trilateral process of dialogue started in 2004 allowing finally the principle of "two flags, three voices."[49]

Government can be defined as a person, group of people or body that create and apply the law for the population in a given territory. Together with population and territory, it completes the necessary elements that constitute a minimal political and societal organization. Government offers also some controversial features that will be reviewed in the following paragraphs using the case of Gibraltar to show their implications.

The focus will be first on the financial system and later on specificities about power share. The main reason to proceed this way is because power sharing has many different implications, and among other sub-elements law. Thereby, and in order to have a clear picture it is advisable to deal with one issue at a time, review it, see how egalitarian shared sovereignty could be best realized and only then move on to another sub-element as with others in this chapter. But, as the case of government will be centered on two main areas—*i.e.* wealth and power, they will be reviewed as follows: An account of wealth through autarchy and financial system first; and only after, how it may be possible to share power and the many implications that egalitarian shared sovereignty may have.

Autarchy and financial system

Finance in the context of a sovereign conflict means the monetary policy, market system, taxation system and way of dealing with debts (internal or international) of a given state. Autarchy is the economic independence a state—in this case the third territory—must have in relation to other states; the ability a state has to balance its gains and losses without external aid.

48 *The Guardian* (July 26, 2002) http://www.guardian.co.uk/politics/2002/jul/26/foreignpolicy.uk (last accessed December 30, 2016).

49 Peter Gold, "The Tripartite Forum of Dialogue: Is this the Solution to the 'Problem' of Gibraltar?" *Mediterranean Politics* 14 (2009): 79–97.

The fact that a population is not able to meet its needs and has to appeal to its peers to achieve a certain balance in its account may militate against its sovereignty. It is not that autarchy is a necessary condition for a state to be sovereign. However, it can be seen as a desirable feature in order to avoid any possible interference in internal affairs. In the particular case of sovereignty disputes, as in any conflict in which there are two sovereign states, it is more than possible that they do not have the same strengths in terms of their financial system. It is often the case that third world countries or—more modern—emerging economies borrow large amounts of money. Even developed states do so for very different reasons—*e.g.* to cover overdrafts in their expenses, to stimulate international trade, to soften bilateral relations. Therefore, the result is usually an unbalanced relationship that may be translated into different relative positions in any bargaining situation. Indeed, this presents consequences to the least advantaged populations that are far from being just, fair, or even desirable—*e.g.* special priority in the exploitation of natural resources, local corruption, human trafficking, arms trafficking, etc.

The third territory is open to the same problems and may have either a solid or a weak economy which may have an impact on its bargaining power and international standing. In the particular case of Gibraltar, it is easy to identify three parties with different levels of welfare. Although all of them have been affected by the recent worldwide financial crisis, the Spanish economy has evidently deteriorated. The financial system is a feature giving rise to much controversy, and so it will be analyzed through the proposed model. Therein, what financial system should be used in Gibraltar?

The possible choices that could be taken in relation to the third territory and its financial system are many: A financial system anchored to one of the sovereign states, an independent financial system or one linked flexibly to both sovereign states. As it is highly improbable that any of the sovereign states would agree to the third territory having its financial system anchored or linked flexibly to only one of them, these options would be discarded for instrumental reasons—ruling out extreme options. However, it is possible that they would accept a more conservative scenario in which the third territory could either have an independent financial system or one linked flexibly at the same time to both sovereign states.

The egalitarian shared sovereignty states that the allocation of sovereignty is given by: (a) the equal right to participate (egalitarian consensus principle); (b) the nature and degree of participation depends on efficiency of accomplishing the particular objective/area/activity at issue (principle of efficiency); (c) each party receives a benefit (in terms of rights and opportunities) that depends on what that party cooperates with (input-to-output ratio principle); and (d) provided the party with greater ability and therefore greater initial participation rights has the obligation to bring the other two parties towards equilibrium (equilibrium proviso). In the case of Gibraltar, there are several differences in relation to the financial system of the parties—*e.g.* strength of the currency, international credit rating, international debt, etc. As in all the previous elements and sub-elements, the shares will be represented as bundles of rights and obligations, benefits and burdens. Therefore, all the parties have both the right and the obligation to participate and support the financial system of the third territory (egalitarian consensus principle).

The egalitarian shared sovereignty will work in two ways: First, following the most efficient combination in regard to contribution (principle of efficiency): *e.g.*, the currency of the third territory could either be anchored to the one currency that was stronger (input-to-output ratio principle) or anchored to a basket of other currencies. Second, as the application of the principle does not imply any investment from the two sovereign states in the third territory, the latter has no obligation to divide with them any internal or international revenues—unless a form of compensation was agreed, *e.g.* investments, exclusive privileges. So, there is efficiency in the financial system but without allowing any form of domination (equilibrium proviso).

What is specific to regulating the financial institutions will be dealt when law as an element is analyzed. It may imply either the creation of a higher financial institution that regulates the third territory with equal representation granted to the three agents; or a procedure in which the financial institutions of the three agents will have the opportunity to be equally involved in the creation, amendment, or cancelation of financial policy.

Government: To "share in" and to "share out" sovereignty

Following the classical tradition of classifying according to the number of representatives (one, a few or all) the basic forms of government are monarchy, oligarchy, and democracy. Without entering into an analysis of "forms of government" (not the object of this project) it is possible to highlight the existence of actual states fulfilling different models, from states that claim to have absolute monarchies (*e.g.* Brunei, Oman, Qatar), through constitutional ones (*e.g.* the United Kingdom, Denmark, Spain) to representative democracies (most cases). The globe offers a wide spectrum of examples in which, although the form of government differs, in all cases they are still states. There is no controversial feature at this point.

In the particular context of this book, this sub-element does not offer controversy either. However, there are other sub-elements that constitute any government which may not be so straight-forward. If sovereignty is not shared, then it is clear who elects representatives and chooses them—the inhabitants if the territory is independent or the inhabitants as part of a sovereign state. But what happens when sovereignty is shared? Then, there are two different issues: (a) representatives and administration; and (b) law. It follows from this that the two most challenging practical issues raised by shared sovereignty in relation to government seem to be:

(i) what sort of governmental arrangements shared sovereignty requires; and
(ii) how governmental authority can be shared and yet be workable.

In general terms and at first glance, the third territory will have certain authorities and institutions to govern its population. In order to work out the principles of egalitarian shared sovereignty through these authorities and institutions—*i.e.* the government of the third territory, it seems reasonable to think of either granting participation in all the institutions to every claiming party or to divide the institutions among them. In other words, the two ways in which sovereignty may be shared, in principle, are as follows.

First, the relevant parties are all members of an institution that possesses some form of sovereignty, *e.g.* legislative sovereignty. They "share in" sovereignty by participating in its exercise. For example, they are all members of the legislature. This form of shared sovereignty does not divide sovereignty itself—*i.e.* the sovereignty of the institution remains undivided. The "sharing" is a sharing in the exercise of the institution's sovereignty.

Second, the relevant parties divide sovereignty among them; *i.e.* they "share out" sovereignty. They might do so by each having sovereignty over a different sphere. Or they might have overlapping authorities or identical authorities.

The following sub-sections will review these two options to consider their respective viability, take note of any conflicts and either accept or reject them. The argument will be in defense of the "sharing in" option and against the option of "sharing out" sovereignty. Only after this careful consideration, the egalitarian shared sovereignty will be applied.

Division of powers: To "share in" sovereignty

There are states around the world with different degrees of separation of powers. Consequently, to have only one central power or to have it divided into branches does not alter the existence of a state; and cannot condition the third territory either. This feature does not offer controversy. Yet, division of powers is a way to embrace the egalitarian shared sovereignty paradigm and may secure the success of the model by recognizing the participation of all three parties. So, in the following, the model will be applied in order to give shape to a possible organization of the government of the third territory.[50]

In choosing the way in which power will be divided in the third territory, the possibilities are various. In this section the representatives of the population are divided into a political trinity: Executive, legislative, and judicial power. Then, this choice offers an ample spectrum. Thus, it assumes the third territory would have representatives divided in different functions and levels to create, execute, and apply law.

The territory in which both sovereign states will have equal sovereignty will already have its own government and administrative organization (as in the case of Gibraltar). Depending on the size of the territory and the population it may administer a few basic functions or a whole range of them. The choices in relation to a government and authorities in the third territory are either to create a whole

50 Based on the Constitution of the Principality of Andorra.

new administrative organization; or to leave the administrative organization as it is at that point in time. The main problem for a shared sovereignty paradigm to be developed and accepted by all the involved agents and, at the same time, to avoid conflicts of law, is to grant all of them a certain level of participation in the law making process (in particular for Gibraltar, the principle of "two flags, three voices").

In that sense, the model here opts for an eclectic vision by combining elements of the classical legal systems and the fact that the source of law is multiple rather than singular—*i.e.* the ultimate authority in terms of the creation, execution, and application of law will be plural. In any case, the legal system for the third territory would be autonomous in relation to those of the sovereign states part in the original dispute. They would only participate through representatives in certain areas to grant them equal presence and control over the issues pertaining the third territory.

There could be many models that may respect the principles reached—*i.e.* there may be many ways in order to realize the egalitarian shared sovereignty in what has to do with government. The one offered below is only an example of its application. Therefore, the agreement will have the face of a constitution, and it will be alterable only with the consent of all the three parties—only this meets the egalitarian shared sovereignty requirements. From there, and following a classical division in regards to how the law is created, executed, and applied in a given territory, an option to develop a feasible model in respect to sovereignty disputes is a compound executive power constituted by several representatives designated in equal number by each sovereign state, and at the same time a government elected by the population of the third territory. In other words, two—or more—co-governors—to give them a name—would be head of the third territory and would have joint and indivisible authority with equal powers.

On the one hand, and out of theoretical interest only, they would symbolically represent the shared values of the enterprise. On the other hand, and in more practical terms, they would secure an actual balance in the relationship between the sovereign states. Together with the co-governors there could be a governmental body of authorities that would secure a fair and just representation for the population of the third territory. They would be in charge of the third territory administration.

A legislative power or council, that would be responsible for the creation of applicable law, could either be elected by only the population of the third territory or have also representatives from the two states. In the former case, this body would have representatives elected directly by the population of the third territory by universal, free, and equal vote. To that extent, the population would have their interests protected and the two sovereign states would be equally situated, since neither of them would have any participation in the legislative process. In the latter case, the population of the third territory would still elect their representatives but the two sovereign states would designate also delegates to participate in the legislature.

In any of the previous cases—with or without participation of the states in the legislative power, their rights and obligations over the third territory accepted in the original agreement could not be altered or lessened in any way—by granting benefits and burdens the agreement offers stability to the two sovereign states. Any norm against the agreement reached in the original position would be completely invalid to secure the superiority of the shared value of the model, the individual and collective interests. In order to secure this feature, a ratification process by all the three parties could be put as a requirement for the validity of any norm that may be related to the interests of any of the parties or may go against the original agreement.

A judicial power elected as per internal procedures with lower and upper magistrates and a Higher—and multi-competent—Court of several members, being designated in equal number by each sovereign state and the third territory. As the ultimate authority within the legal hierarchy in the third territory, the Higher Court would secure the representation of all the involved agents—namely, the two sovereign states and the population of the third territory. Nevertheless, all the judges, lower and upper ones—including those in the Higher Court—would be independent in the sense they would not represent any specific interests that the agents in the original conflict could have.

With this model the equal participation of the two sovereign states and the protection of the interests of the population in the third territory are granted. Administratively, the third territory would be fully autonomous. However, the sovereignty would remain with the two sovereign states who, by participating at the same time and with equal prerogatives and representation in the legal system of the third territory, would have an equal status.

A general question (or concern) may arise and has to do with how the three parties would make decisions within the institutions. That is because simple majority voting raises the prospect of two of the parties joining forces to outvote the third. In consequence, it would seem that the model proposed here would be acceptable to them only if it included some kind of safeguards. As a general rule, none of the norms, at any stage—creation, execution, or application—could be or could be intended to be against the content of the agreement reached in the original position. In the event there was a contradiction between a norm of the third territory and the original agreement, derogation would be applied resulting in the invalidation of such a norm. A further and complementary safeguard would be given by the veto power granted to the three parties (or their representatives in each institution) when their wishes were being systematically overridden in the decisionmaking process used in the institution.

From the above paragraphs, it is clear that the egalitarian shared sovereignty is fully operating with the prerequisites. In what matters the principle itself, all the parties receive an equal share in the sense they all participate in each and every governmental power and hence each and every instance in the creation and the application of the law of the third territory.

Two legal systems and one territory: To "share out" sovereignty

Consider now a different arrangement to share sovereignty. So, instead of having institutions in the third territory in which all the parties "share in" sovereignty by participating in them, this time they decide to divide sovereignty among them. To put a specific example, suppose the United Kingdom was in charge of the judiciary, Spain was in charge of the executive power and Gibraltar elected its own Parliament or Congress. Is this a viable option? What conflicts can arise, in particular in terms of law? If there were conflicts, what would be the way to deal with them?

Clearly, there would be not one but at least two legal systems with this way of institutionalizing the egalitarian shared sovereignty—in the example, the legal system of Spain and that of the United Kingdom. To have two legal systems devised from two different and sovereign states operating in the same territory will involve conflicts of law. Indeed, this is the crucial problem with shared sovereignty—arguably, a fatal one. What legal system will be valid in the third territory? To what extent is it possible that two legal systems are valid at the same time over the same territory and in regard to the same population? And what about the existence of a new set of norms specially created for the third territory? Should Gibraltar have a legal system that combined British and Spanish law? Should it only follow British tradition? Controversy is clearly present here.

Although a conflict between two norms within the same legal system can be avoided, by having rules of precedence—*e.g.* the later law overrules the earlier one, or statute overrules precedent, conflicts between norms of different and independent legal systems appear to be normal. In relation to conflicts of law, Kelsen states:

> [a] conflict exists between two norms when that which one of them decrees to be obligatory is incompatible with that which the other decrees to be obligatory, so that the observance or application of one norm necessarily or possibly involves the violation of the other. The conflict can be bilateral or unilateral. . . . The conflict can be total or only partial . . .[51]

Following this quotation, the simplest option to avoid any potential conflict of law in the model proposed here appears to be a separate administration of each other's interests in the third territory. Another option could be given by the establishment of a common center to take decisions that concern vital or important issues related to the third territory—safeguarding the interests of all the parties. Then, the agents may choose one of several possibilities: An independent legal system (Gibraltarian law), a legal system anchored to one of the sovereign states (British law for Gibraltar), one anchored to both of them (British–Spanish law), or to a third state not involved in the conflict.

In addition to the choice of the legal system that has to be valid in the third territory, it will be necessary to define the procedure to follow in the event that a specific case has to be revised by a superior authority—*e.g.* extraordinary appeal.

51 Hans Kelsen, *General Theory of Norms* (Oxford: Oxford University Press, 1991), p. 123.

Which of the two sovereign states' body of authorities—*e.g.* Supreme Court, Higher Court, etc.—would be the competent one to revise such a case? Once again, there is a possible conflict of law.

So, there are two major issues to decide when dealing with law in a sovereignty conflict of the kind analyzed in this book: (a) what legal system is to be valid; (b) who are to be the superior authorities in the event of further revision in a particular case. In the following, classical solutions for conflicts of law will be considered. The aim here is to review if any of these classical solutions for conflicts of law can help in making two different legal systems work together in the third territory. That is because if the parties decided to "share out" the sovereignty of the third territory, assuming each party had sovereignty over a different sphere—executive, legislative, and judicial powers—there would be more than one legal system with consequences to the same population—in the example, the Gibraltarians. So, conflicts of law can be expected. It is then that by reviewing classical ways of dealing with conflicts of law a solution may be found. From there, the one that best responds to the interests of all the agents will be selected. Then, the egalitarian shared sovereignty will be applied.

Derogation

If a conflict between two norms arises in a particular legal system, derogation is usually the remedy—*e.g. lex superior* and *lex inferior*, *lex posteriori* and *lex anteriori*, etc. However, it does not need to be the solution to every conflict of norms and it only happens when a given norm determines it.[52] More particularly, it does not work when the conflict is between two systems of law, in that no rule (or no obvious rule) can be given. That is to say, even if derogation was the rule in solving conflicts of law, it cannot be the solution in the context of this book. Although it may seem obvious that derogation can only be used within a single normative system[53] when comparing the relationship between legal and moral normative orders, the same principle is applicable if a conflict between two norms of two different and independent legal systems arises. Letting one of the norms of one of the legal systems override another norm of another independent legal system would simply mean that the second legal system would be inferior in respect to the first one and hence nonsovereign. In the case of the model developed here, the solution must guarantee the equal sovereign level of both legal systems even in the case in which one of the conflicting norms belonged to one of the sovereign legal systems and the other one, to its peers. Derogation, however simple and straight forward, is not a solution for conflicts of law in sovereignty disputes.

In the example, consider that the United Kingdom was in charge of the judiciary, Spain of the executive, and Gibraltarians of the legislative power. Then,

52 *Ibid.*, p. 125.
53 *Ibid.*, p. 126.

in the event a judge from the United Kingdom had to apply the law in a case in Gibraltar, would he apply the British legal system? Or that of Spain? It is assumed here that Spanish law was more benign and hypothesized that for a murder British law still considered death penalty as a possible sanction while Spanish law did not. In addition to this, the British judge understanding in the case in which someone murdered another individual in Gibraltar, after considering the facts, found the accused was guilty. Should the judge sentence the criminal to death? Or should he consider the British law overridden by the Spanish law in this case? But, he would know that if he did so it would mean recognizing the supremacy of Spanish criminal law over British law. And that is unreasonable. As stated before, derogation may be simple but it is not the solution here.

Coordination

Kelsen may give a hint towards the solution of the dilemma when incorporating the international legal system in the context of his analysis about norms. The following quotation makes the point clear:

> Let us assume [Kelsen says] that there is not just one state legal system, but that many state legal systems are valid, and that they are coordinated, and thus, legally separated from each other in their spheres of validity. If one recognises . . . that it is positive international law that accomplishes this coordination of state legal systems and the reciprocal separation of their spheres of validity, then one must conceive of international law as a legal system above the state legal systems, bringing them together in an universal legal community . . .[54]

Why would coordination between two legal systems imply that the selected system of coordination had to be above the sovereign states? How could both legal systems be coordinated so as to be applied to legal issues within the third territory and still be seen as hierarchically equal and sovereign, without recognizing, implicitly or explicitly, an order superior to them?

In the example, the United Kingdom, Spain, and Gibraltar have indeed what may be seen as a third coordinating legal system, European Union law. But, although promising, it is not the solution either. That is because both the United Kingdom and Spain delegate to a certain degree their sovereignty on the European Union (vertically) but they do not do so reciprocally (horizontally). Therefore, even though the legal system may act as coordinator between the two in the example, it does not do so to the extent needed to make the law in Gibraltar

54 Hans Kelsen, *Introduction to the Problems of Legal Theory* (Oxford: Oxford University Press, 1992), p. 71.

workable—at least if they "share out" sovereignty and have two independent legal orders to be coordinated.

Principles to solve conflicts of law applicable in coordination of legal systems

Admittedly, coordination of two sovereign legal systems is a nonsatisfactory way to proceed. For the time being, however, consider this option for further analysis. By going back and forth the solution may still be found. Although there are differences between conflicts of law happening within the same legal system or between two legal systems of states belonging to Federal nations (*e.g.* United States), the approach taken in both cases could be applied to conflicts of the kind analyzed here, bearing in mind its particular characteristics. So, a series of general concerns when in presence of conflicts of law will be explored. That is because conflicts of law in Federal nations are resolved by means of coordination. Thereby, this path will be followed here. It will be considered if some of the general concerns could be used as criteria from which to select a way to avoid conflicts of law but specifically in sovereignty disputes. The main concerns when dealing with any conflict of law seem to be:

> (1) The needs of the interstate and international system; (2) The state's interest in having its courts apply its own local law unless there is good reason for not doing so; (3) The state's interest in having its courts effectuate the purpose of its relevant local law rule in determining a question of choice of law; (4) Certainty, predictability, and uniformity of results; (5) Protection of justified expectations; (6) Application of the law of the state of dominant interest; (7) Ease in determination of applicable law, convenience of the court; (8) The fundamental policy underlying the broad local law field involved; (9) Justice in the individual case [. . .][55]

In the following, each individual concern and its implications will be reviewed in the context of sovereignty conflicts so as to draw some preliminary conclusions:

"(1) The needs of the interstate and international system"

The states involved in the conflict and the population of the third territory will have different interests and a different experience of a legal system. The model needs a system that protects the interests of the population in the third territory—since the legal system in question will apply to them—and, at the same time, a system that does not lessen the sovereign states' respective positions in relation to that third territory, their actual and potential benefits and burdens. To opt simply for one of the three existing systems does not seem advisable. In fact, it

55 Robert A. Leflar, "The Nature of Conflicts Law," *Columbia Law Review* 81 (1981): 1080–95.

seems reasonable to opt—among many other choices—for an independent legal system with independent or shared superior authorities—*i.e.* an independent legal system with parties that "share in" or "share out" their sovereignty.

"(2) The state's interest in having its courts apply its own local law unless there is good reason for not doing so"

The parties will have to decide between the two sovereign states legal systems, a combination of both, a coordination of both or the creation of a third new legal system only applicable in the third territory and for its population. Although this particular point refers to courts that already have a given legal system to interpret, it highlights the importance of its determination: Once chosen, the judges must use only that legal system for the third territory. This implies a third system, however based.

"(3) The state's interest in having its courts effectuate the purpose of its relevant local law rule in determining a question of choice of law"

In this case, the concern is related to conflicts of law within the same legal system and does not have much to do with this project. Only once the legal system was determined for the third territory, would this concern have relevance in the event that there was a conflict between its norms.

"(4) Certainty, predictability,[56] and uniformity of results"

This is a common goal in any conflict of law, internal or international. It is of ultimate importance to decide the legal system with its principles, rules and procedures that will be applied in legal issues within the third territory so as to let its population—and foreign individuals, states, and the international community—have a sense of legal security. In other words, anyone wishing to invest, exploit, work, or simply live in the third territory will want to know what is permitted, prohibited, and obligatory within its boundaries and the consequences of the violation of those permissions, prohibitions, and obligations. Moreover, once the norms were acknowledged and the judges had applied them, it would be possible to reach a certain level of predictability in decisions when similar cases arose. And this is expected of any legal system. This implies one system, whatever it is.

"(5) Protection of justified expectations"

With regard to the previous points, any individual—or group of individuals—has expectations. A legal system does not escape people's expectations. They expect the rules or norms and decisions to be certain, predictable and uniform, if that legal system is to be fair and just. It is for that reason that the selection of a legal system must fulfill people's expectations—those who are the inhabitants of the third territory and whoever wants to deal with them.

"(6) Application of the law of the state of dominant interest."

56 The word "predictable" is used here according to the notion developed by Oliver Wendell Holmes in *The Path of Law*.

Which state has the dominant interest in the case of sovereignty conflicts? The concern mentioned above refers to the usual case of conflicts of law between states who are part of a federation (*e.g.* when someone from one state commits a criminal offence in another state part of a federation). However, there will be here a sovereign state more powerful and with probably more interest in the third territory—hence, dominant—that will prefer its law to be the law valid also in the third territory. Yet, the interests of any of the sovereign states must be left aside—apart from those rights and burdens actual and potential settled in the original agreement. In addition to regular conflicts of law when dealing with foreign individuals in a foreign territory, alien companies, multinationals, etc., in the particular case of sovereignty conflicts the main interest is given by the population of the third territory who will in any event be the one that actually experience fully the chosen legal system.

"(7) Ease in determination of applicable law, convenience of the court"

The fact that the applicable law is easy to be determined within the third territory not only is convenient for the local courts but also for its population. Not agreeing on the law to be valid in the third territory and, at the same time, granting shared sovereignty to both sovereign states, would undoubtedly result in conflicts. The selection of a legal system or—at least—principles or procedures to achieve that goal is imperative to avoid endless argumentation.

"(8) The fundamental policy underlying the broad local law field involved"

There is the matter of the broad nature of law to be determined. In any territory there will be the necessity of acknowledging the existence of public and private law—in general terms. In both cases there will be special principles and procedures, different set of concepts and ways of addressing cases. However, the common fact in all these instances will be given by the unique characteristic of having two sets of sovereign authorities.

"(9) Justice in the individual case"

The ultimate goal in any legal conflict is to arrive at a just and fair decision. Although an interesting matter, the main object of this project—hence, of the negotiations—is to reach agreement in determining a valid legal system for the third territory. Ultimately, justice in the individual case will depend upon that legal system and its interpretation by the respective judges.

Approaches in conflicts of law within a sovereign dispute

A few partial conclusions can already be drawn from the previous paragraphs: (a) There has to be one system of law; (b) It cannot simply be one of the existing three systems; (c) To construct such a system of the existing three ones is like dealing with a conflict. What is the best and fair way of dealing with conflicts of law in sovereignty disputes if a shared sovereignty model is applied? However, before going into this analysis, there is a prior question that has to be answered: Is this to be settled by legislation or by the judges?

To recapitulate, the aim here is to work out how governmental authority can be shared. This subsection assumes that the claiming agents would try to "share out" their sovereignty over the third territory in terms of government. From there, one claiming party would create the law—Gibraltar would have the legislative power; another party would execute the law—Spain would have the executive power; and one party would apply the law—the United Kingdom would have the judiciary.

Coincidentally, these parties would have to decide a linked issue: The law applicable in the third territory. In tune with this, if they decided to work with two legal systems—the United Kingdom and Spain, they would reject derogation and coordination as solutions.

Nevertheless, by revising how federal states deal with a similar issue at national level—*i.e.* coordination of overlapping legal systems—it has been concluded that one system is advisable.

Yet, even if one legal system for Gibraltar was accepted, a further decision would still be needed. Indeed, there are different ways to apply and create the law—*i.e.* in the particular case of Gibraltar, there are two main ones, "common law" system based mainly on judges' decisions and "Roman law" system based on legislative creation. As a result, it is crucial to decide who will settle the one legal system: Judges or legislators.

In order to decide whether judges or legislators are the answer, and as guidance for those drawing up the new system, five major approaches when dealing with conflicts of law will be reviewed.[57]

SINGLE CONCEPTS OR PRINCIPLES

This option gives the judges—or those who interpret and apply law—a set of concepts and general principles to be used in the event that a conflict of law arises. The reasons detailed later with regard to each of the other possible solutions show this one is the most practical. To mention a few basic principles[58] the following are good examples: "Legal rules of a jurisdiction have effect only within that jurisdiction's territorial limits; or apply only to citizens of that jurisdiction."

In other words, once the law for the third territory is determined, that will be the law to be applied. Even in the case that the third territory's law is similar to—if not the same as—one of the sovereign state's legal systems, a coordination of both or a third legal system, in actual terms the third territory will have an autonomous and independent set of norms and jurisdiction with its own judges to interpret and apply it.

57 For the idea of approaches to the conflicts of law, see William Tetley, "A Canadian Looks at American Conflict of Law Theory and Practice, Especially in the Light of the American Legal and Social Systems (Corrective vs. Distributive Justice)," *Col. J. Transnat'l L.* 38 (1999): 299–373.

58 Quotations from Tetley (n. 58).

"All nations . . . are equal and independent. Each of them may therefore legislate freely as sovereign entities." This is the characteristic that defines the central problem when dealing with conflicts of law in sovereignty disputes. The model has two equal and independent states and each of them legislates freely as sovereign entities in respect to their own territory. However, in the case of the third territory they will have to share that sovereignty; thus, they will have to share the right to create, execute, and apply law in regards to its population. To determine in which way and to what extent they will share that right becomes both desirable and necessary.

"The laws of each nation exclusively govern all conduct within that nation's territory." In the context of this project, many of the issues will be decided among the representatives of the three populations. In reference to the law, that system of norms that will govern the conduct of the population of the third territory, is one of the many issues to be determined by them. However, once determined, it will only govern the conduct of the individuals of that population and that population will only be governed by that system of norms.

"Each state possesses exclusive jurisdiction over its territory, so that no state can bind persons or property located outside that territory." This point has been treated before when discussing all nations are equal and independent. The legal system may be a compound one with elements from both involved sovereign states, a third different one or similar to only one of the sovereign states but in effect it will have its own jurisdiction. In practice, it would and should be compound.

The previous paragraphs settle the question—by the legislator, not the judges. That is because the concepts and principles applicable in the third territory must be general, applicable only within its boundaries but to all the citizens in that jurisdiction.

MULTIPLY NUMBERED RULES

This particular option tries to give the judges choices for every possible—or imaginable—case. Although some general rules could be accepted, this solution does not depend on principles or general conceptualizations—as the one reviewed before. Different possible solutions are to be presented to the judges in order for them to interpret the law and apply it to the particular case. Despite the fact that in theory this is an attractive idea, to anticipate every possible—or imaginable—conflict of law case would be both intolerably cumbrous and in every way not feasible.

GENERAL TEXTS, COMMENTARIES AND ESSAYS

This option seems helpful in order to ease the interpretation of the law in any given case—with or without conflict of law. It would not be obligatory to research into the opinion of specialists in the subject matter, but it would be advisable in general terms to do so in any given conflict of law, since scholarly doctrine could be observed as another interpretative tool the judges will have in order to apply the law.

INTERNATIONAL CONVENTIONS AND NATIONAL LEGISLATION

It is exactly this case that may be the object of this project in regards to conflict of law, its outcome. Once the representatives have decided how to resolve conflicts of law, the law that will be valid within the boundaries of the third territory and the legal authorities that will revise the case in the event of extraordinary revisions, they will have to accept these terms through an agreement, a convention.

A METHODOLOGY

Since the law to be applied and the legal authorities that will understand in the event of extraordinary revisions have to be determined, the question of methodology seems appropriate at this stage of the negotiations. The representatives will have to agree on substantive law and once these questions are settled, let the designated authorities develop their own methodology.

In brief, the legislators are indeed the ones that will settle the question. Nevertheless, it is also clear that they could act in several ways. However, what is best way to choose the best laws? That is to say, it may be agreed that the legislator will create one legal system for the third territory. But in "sharing out" sovereignty that would mean that one party would create the law for the third territory and another party would apply it—*e.g.* Gibraltarian Parliament would create the law and British judges would apply that law to particular cases. And it is here when a wall has to be faced again. How do they coordinate the creation of law in Gibraltar with its application by British judges to Gibraltarians? It does seem unreasonable.

However unreasonable, it does not mean that there is no lesson here. First, it is clear now that the advisable way to proceed would be one legal system however created. Second, that it cannot be just one of the existing ones. Third, that conflicts of law between sovereign legal systems can be avoided by adopting a third and different legal system for the third territory. Fourth, that the legislator will settle the legal system. And fifth, that to "share out" sovereignty does generate problems.

The egalitarian shared sovereignty could be realized because it does embrace the previously mentioned five outcomes. But before doing that, the following section will briefly consider some minimum standards the law in the third territory should follow in order to offer the population law that would best fulfill the egalitarian shared sovereignty goals.

Better and best law

What is the difference between a better law and the best law? In what way any of them is possible? How can the best law be defined? When is a given law better than another one? How is it possible to determine the best legal system for the third territory? Among the options of coordination, selection of only one of the sovereign legal systems or the creation of a new legal system only valid for the third territory, which one is the best choice—if any?

To develop a broad comprehensive response to the previous questions in relation to the value of a whole legal system does not appear realistic. The immediate answer points to the particular case that is being analyzed. In other words, for a given case there are a limited number of possible solutions depending on the norm to be applied. For one line of interpretation, among these solutions there will be one better than all the others: The best solution for that particular case. However, to choose the best legal system for a whole population is a matter of different nature. Then, the same question arises again: How can the best law—or the best legal system—be determined?

The best law for the third territory—as in any other case—will be the one that follows the procedures to be created by the competent authorities—formal validity—in consonance with any superior law—material validity—and that is respected by the community is intended to be addressed to—effectiveness. Although this formulation may be correct, a critical eye would point out that only once the law was applied to the case and the consequent conduct of the community was observed, it would be possible to describe that law as just or unjust, the best one or not for the matter in question—and in large, the best legal system or not for the third territory. Indeed, the analysis and the determination of the best law would be then *a posteriori*, once the case was decided, once the discussion was settled, once the legal system was already valid in the third territory—and this seems futile. The key here—as in all the previous sections—not only is to choose the abstractly best law for the third territory but also a reasonable legal system that can actually be put in place. But this cannot be just any legal system. It needs to be a legal system in tune with the content of the original agreement.

As there are three parties that have—at least—two different legal systems, it is assumed first that these legal systems are of a different nature—*e.g.* in the case of Gibraltar, common law of the United Kingdom, and Roman based law in Spain. Hence, they follow different substantial and procedural norms. Second, it is presupposed that the parties have decided to have one legal system for the third territory—for the reasons previously reviewed in this chapter. The task now is to "make" these two legal systems work as one, the best one for the third territory.

What appears to be the main problem—various legal systems to choose from—is not. That is because there are some minimum principles of law recognized by all nations—either implicitly or explicitly by customary international law and/or international agreements—that may be called "general principles of law" and they can be used as the minimum requirements for the determination of the best law for the third territory. In consequence, bearing in mind "general principles of law" and justice and fairness as the main aim, any solution in terms of law should—at least—consider acceptability (by the three parties), humanity (respect of the basic rights of the inhabitants of the third territory), effectiveness (actual respect of the legal system by the inhabitants of the third territory), simplicity, and justice.

Besides, that is in tune with this book. So, the best legal system for the third territory will be that one with the best elements from any of the legal systems of the sovereign states, provided they respect "general principles of law" and the conditions agreed in the original position.

The egalitarian shared sovereignty applied to government and law

This section started with the aim of proposing a way in which governmental authority could realize the egalitarian shared sovereignty. It reviewed two ways in which sovereignty may be shared: (a) the claiming agents "share in" sovereignty by each of them participating in all the institutions in the third territory—*i.e.* executive, legislative, and judicial powers; and (b) the claiming agents "share out" sovereignty by each party having sovereignty over a different sphere.

Indeed, it discarded the latter but draw some positive conclusions along the analysis: (1) the third territory will have one legal system; (2) this legal system will not be one of the existing ones; (3) it will be created by the legislator; (4) the agents will "share in" sovereignty; (5) the legal system will have certain notes—*i.e.* acceptability, humanity, effectiveness, simplicity, and justice.

What is clear is that the question related to law is a matter not of equality but of acceptability to all parties by applying the egalitarian shared sovereignty. As in the previous cases, the egalitarian shared sovereignty addresses the controversies introduced when selecting the applicable law. It must be highlighted once again compliance with the prerequisites is understood in order to deal with the requirements of the egalitarian shared sovereignty. So, the allocation of sovereignty is given by: (a) equal right to participate (egalitarian consensus principle); (b) the nature and degree of participation depends on efficiency of accomplishing the particular objective/area/activity at issue (principle of efficiency); (c) each party receives a benefit (in terms of rights and opportunities) that depends on what that party cooperates with (input-to-output ratio principle); and (d) provided the party with greater ability and therefore greater initial participation rights has the obligation to bring the other two parties towards equilibrium (equilibrium proviso). In what is specific to government and law it means, first of all, the third territory—Gibraltar—will have an independent legal order based on all three systems, in the sense it uses what is best—so defined by its acceptability, humanity, effectiveness, simplicity, and justice, provided it coheres with the rest of the system (egalitarian consensus principle and principle of efficiency).

Second, it means that all parties are involved in the administration—*i.e.* they "share in" sovereignty. Therefore, the shares will be represented as bundles of rights and obligations. In this case, the three agents have equal rights and obligations to participate in every step in the creation, execution, and application of the law—*i.e.* what Kelsen calls formal validity. Thus, as the second prerequisite must be respected, the liberties of the inhabitants of the third territory are protected—*i.e.* what Kelsen calls material validity. Following the general aim of the model proposed here, the legal order would be divided into three branches—one for each step in relation to the creation, execution, and application of the law.

Thus, each branch should secure the representation of the three agents. Besides, in case of conflicts of law there would be a Superior Tribunal or Higher Court with representatives of the three agents. The details in respect of the election of the authorities and their internal procedures would be reached in a new agreement that cannot contradict in any sense the principles agreed in the original position. They may also agree on keeping the current institutional organization of the third territory with the addition of representatives of the two sovereign states—as long as the original agreement is complied with.

Third, the rights of all the parties must be respected. Then, as all the agents will participate in the making and decision process—*i.e.* what Hart called rule of adjudication and rule of change, the elected authorities of the third territory would create, execute, and apply law with the only limit being the principles agreed in the original position. Therefore, in any instance in which there was a contradiction between a norm and the agreement reached in the original position, the contradictory norm would be automatically invalid—safeguarding the interests of all the parties. For instance, in the case of the Gibraltar Constitution Order, the first paragraphs would be immediately affected as they refer to Gibraltar as a dominion of the United Kingdom. And, as has already been pointed out, the agents (through their representatives in the institutions of the third territory) would have a further safeguard given by the veto power should their wishes were being systematically overridden in the decisionmaking process used in the institution.

In summation, the previous paragraphs demonstrate how it is both possible and advisable to deal with conflicts of law in a sovereignty dispute as a way of solving the difference. By recognition of equal actual and potential rights and burdens over the third territory (egalitarian consensus principle), each agent would be in a relative similar situation—including the inhabitants of the third territory. In particular, in regards to the law, among several options, the establishment of an independent legal system appears as a reasonable choice since it would secure the interests of the population of the third territory and, at the same time, the presence and equal relative position of both sovereign states (in Gibraltar, the principle of "two flags, three voices"). Although it would be an independent legal system, it would be recommendable that the authorities in charge of the creation, execution, and application of law had representatives of the three involved agents—namely, both sovereign states and the population of the third territory. By doing so, there is a shift from equality to acceptability.

Therefore, it would give the legal system a permanent feature that would support its predictability and would result in the stability of the model as a whole since it would embrace the interests of all the parties and would not leave any of them in a comparable disadvantageous situation (equilibrium proviso). Indeed, the combined working of the legal system, and in some ways the political one, seem to require less use of the egalitarian shared sovereignty than other areas and more use of choosing and combining elements from existing systems in order to maximize and have a more efficient running of the system. But, these are still parts of the solution proposed here, the egalitarian shared sovereignty in the form of (a) egalitarian consensus; and (b) principle of efficiency that result in (c) equilibrium among the parties.

Conclusion

This chapter has focused on showing how the egalitarian shared sovereignty could be extended from general principles to workable institutions and how these institutions may realize these principles. In order to do that this chapter considered three sovereignty conflicts—*i.e.* Kashmir, the Falkland/Malvinas Islands, and Gibraltar, because they offer all the elements required by the model; that is to say, two sovereign states and a populated third territory.

Each of the three sovereignty conflicts has been reviewed individually through one of the elements that constitute the third territory. Thereby, the chapter discussed population using the example of Kashmir; territory with the Falklands/Malvinas' case; and government with Gibraltar. In all instances, despite the fact of having a myriad of sub-elements, the attention was centered on those that are controversial in sovereignty disputes.

In each case it has been considered how the egalitarian shared sovereignty could be realized. The chapter has then addressed a number of significant issues in sovereignty disputes—*e.g.* immigration, natural resources, law, defense, and so on. All these controversial sub-elements in sovereignty disputes show that all the parties' good reasons to accept egalitarian shared sovereignty and its implications can be extended from general principles to workable institutions.

Bibliography

Bose, Sumantra. *The Challenge in Kashmir: Democracy, Self-Determination and a Just Peace*. New Delhi: Sage Publications India Pvt. Ltd., 1997.

Bradnock, Robert W. *Kashmir: Paths to Peace*. London: Chatham House, 2010.

Franzese, Patrick W. "Sovereignty in Cyberspace: Can It Exist?" *Air Force Law Review* 64 (2009): 1–42.

Gold, Peter. "The Tripartite Forum of Dialogue: Is this the Solution to the 'Problem' of Gibraltar?" *Mediterranean Politics* 14 (2009): 79–97.

Hills, George. *Rock of Contention: A History of Gibraltar*. London: Robert Hale & Company, 1974.

Jha, Prem Shankar. *Kashmir, 1947: Rival Versions of History*. Oxford: Oxford University Press, 1996.

Kelsen, Hans. *General Theory of Norms*. Oxford: Oxford University Press, 1991.

Kelsen, Hans. *Introduction to the Problems of Legal Theory*. Oxford: Oxford University Press, 1992.

Korbel, Josef. *Danger in Kashmir*. Princeton NJ: Princeton University Press, 1954.

Leflar, Robert A. "The Nature of Conflicts Law." *Columbia Law Review* 81 (1981): 1080–95.

Martin, Elizabeth A. and Law, Jonathan, eds. *A Dictionary of Law*. Oxford: Oxford University Press, 2006.

Puri, Balraj. *Kashmir Towards Insurgency*, revised and updated edition. New Delhi: Orient Longman Ltd., 1995.

Rai, Mridu. *Hindu Rulers, Muslim Subjects, Islam: Rights and the History of Kashmir*. London: C. Hurst & Co. Ltd., 2004.

Rawls, John. *A Theory of Justice*, Revised Edition. Oxford: Oxford University Press, 1999.

Ray, Sunil Chandra. *Early History and Culture of Kashmir.* New Delhi: Munshiram Manoharlal Oriental Publishers, 1970.

Schofield, Victoria. *Kashmir in Conflict, India, Pakistan and the Unfinished War.* London: I.B. Tauris & Co. Ltd., 2000.

Tetley, William. "A Canadian Looks at American Conflict of Law Theory and Practice, Especially in the Light of the American Legal and Social Systems (Corrective vs. Distributive Justice)." *Col. J. Transnat'l L.* 38 (1999): 299–373.

Wilson, H. H. *The Hindu History of Kashmir.* Calcutta: Susil Gupta Private Ltd., 1960.

8 Conclusive remarks, implications, and limitations

It is time to bring together these pages so as to assess if they fulfill their aim—*i.e.* if the model is just and viable, what has been learnt, and to point out any possible limitations either theoretical or in what relates to its application.

This book aimed to achieve a peaceful solution to sovereignty conflicts by the application of principles of distributive justice through the use of Rawlsian methodology. In order to do that, a series of problems were evaluated and possible ways of addressing them were examined. For instance, what at first glance seemed to be the main obstacle for the shared sovereignty model, that is to say, that sovereignty appeared to be absolute—hence, unlimited, not shareable—is in fact a wrong belief. Chapter 2 demonstrated that sovereignty, still being defined as supreme authority, is a limited concept. So, as limitations can be applied to sovereignty, all sovereignty is—to an extent—shared. Chapter 3 compared other ways of conceptualizing shared sovereignty—and similar expressions—and made clear why they fall short in solving sovereignty conflicts of the kind approached in this book.

Chapter 4 then showed how these limitations work by applying the method of analogy and illustrating how a similar concept such as self-ownership was in tune with limitations. In addition to the conceptual analysis, Chapter 5 showed why in realpolitik other international remedies are not reasonable either in these cases—or at least, that they are solutions that often present controversy. At this stage, Chapter 6 introduced a theoretical exercise to evaluate if it is possible to apply distributive justice as developed by Rawls in sovereignty disputes. By comparing different principles under particular circumstances, that secured a just and fair outcome—one that cannot be reasonably rejected—*i.e.* the "egalitarian shared sovereignty." Even though it was just and fair in theory, its viability had to be assessed. Therefore, Chapter 7 applied the egalitarian shared sovereignty principle to different real cases. By doing this, the egalitarian shared sovereignty principle proved to be potentially useful in order to offer a solution to sovereignty disputes, provided that all ideal and assumed conditions were present.

However, promising though it is, there are some limitations regarding this project that must be mentioned. First, although it has been shown that the model can work in the real world, the "real world" cases used to assess the institutions that may realize the egalitarian shared sovereignty principle were reviewed, but with the application of certain assumptions. Thereby, this work has not explored nonideal issues that may undermine its actual applicability. For instance, it still needs to be considered whether the three populations would actually accept such an agreement. In order to do that, a referendum or a similar procedure has to be followed. But that is an issue to be carried out in the future should any of the parties in these conflicts agree upon it. In fact, very recently one of the cases used in Chapter 7 was the object of a referendum—*i.e.* the Falkland/Malvinas Islands.[1] Therefore, it would be interesting in the future to have the opportunity to do both: (a) to give voice to the inhabitants of the third territory through a referendum; and (b) to make clear what shared sovereignty could embrace.

Second, there is the question whether the model may be extended to other situations. Indeed, sovereignty disputes are on a very extensive spectrum. The book focused on some of them, *i.e.* the ones that fulfilled certain criteria. Nevertheless, there remains the possibility of applying the procedure designed here to disputes that present a different scenario.

Third, even if the model of "egalitarian shared sovereignty" was accepted by referendum by the three populations, and consequently applied, its continuity in time may still be somewhat weak. As the only definitive constraint the agents would have to respect their agreements would be their goodwill, the model assumes features that are ideal. Nonetheless, this work was mainly a theoretical exercise to show that it would be unreasonable not to respect the model of "egalitarian shared sovereignty." To that extent, it showed that its aim is feasible. Either to put it into practice or to grant its actual continuity once accepted are some of the many implications the model presents.

The monograph proved that different states—hence different populations—can work together towards common goals, even in a conflict of interest such as a sovereign dispute. Thus, by working together and—at first glance—limiting reciprocally their spheres of sovereignty, they can do things that before were impossible, more difficult, or disadvantageous in many ways—*e.g.* defense, finance, etc. Then, their actual range of possibilities is extended.

Another implication is toleration. The case of sovereignty conflicts does not necessarily imply either resignation, indifference, curiosity, or enthusiasm but a different form of toleration.[2] All the agents have the power to act upon the third territory, the knowledge of the existence of that third territory and their opponents and they refrain from fully exercising their claimed rights. Without entering into a discussion about the reasons why they omit fully to exercise their respective argued sovereignty over the third territory (*e.g.* avoiding a military conflict, lack of resources, economic implications, etc.), they simply omit to act fully. In consequence, in every actual case of sovereignty conflicts there is a certain level of toleration among the agents.

1 For details about the Falkland/Malvinas Islands' referendum, dates, and questions, refer to http://www.falklands.gov.fk/dates-and-question-set-for-the-referendum-on-falkland-islands-political-status-2013/ (last accessed December 30, 2016).

2 Different forms of toleration as proposed by Michael Walzer, "The Politics of Difference: Statehood and Toleration in a Multicultural World," *Ratio Juris* 10 (1997): 165–76.

What kind of form or level of toleration is then needed to move from the zero sum game and start negotiations in relation to sovereignty? One of the outcomes of the "egalitarian shared sovereignty" proviso is indeed toleration. That is because toleration would include not only the *status quo* cases but also those in which the agents involved in sovereignty issues were willing to negotiate their differences. A first step in solving sovereignty conflicts is to acknowledge each other's presence within the dispute; from there, to accept the fact that each and every agent has certain claims over the third territory; and finally, to start negotiations in regard to those claims with the aim of reaching a solution—all three steps covered in order to achieve "egalitarian shared sovereignty." Similarly, these steps are also covered by the umbrella of toleration both in a negative and a positive way: negative, since the non-interference principle is still part of the agents' interrelation; positive, since these same agents accept and recognize other participants in the dispute and are willing to start negotiations and respect the outcome.[3]

This book started with a disagreement or a conflict of interest among three agents—two sovereign states and the population of the disputed territory—and offered a way to resolve the difference. The "egalitarian shared sovereignty" model is useful in solving sovereignty conflicts because it provides the parties with a reasonable agreement that secures their individual interests, letting them put into practice their claimed rights and offering a range of possibilities that would otherwise be—at least—difficult to achieve, fostering a peaceful international approach that other international remedies cannot duplicate. Although idealistic, these conflicts will remain—at best—stagnant in a *status quo* should no action be taken. But that action cannot be just "any" action. It must be appealing for all the parties and make them realize that not only is it feasible but also that it is the most reasonable for their respective populations. The "egalitarian shared sovereignty" model offers an answer to these disputes that is just, fair, reasonable, and beneficial to all, and one which no one could reasonably reject. It rests on the decision of the representatives of each claiming party—in large, each population—to leave aside egoistical, self-centered, or personal reasons and work collaboratively towards—what may be—the beginning of a universally peaceful and tolerant *civitas maxima*.

Bibliography

Galeotti, Anna Elisabetta. "Contemporary Pluralism and Toleration." *Ratio Juris* 10 (1997): 223–35.

Walzer, Michael. "The Politics of Difference: Statehood and Toleration in a Multicultural World." *Ratio Juris* 10 (1997): 165–76.

3 For a view of toleration in a positive and negative sense, *see* Anna Elisabetta Galeotti, "Contemporary Pluralism and Toleration," *Ratio Juris* 10 (1997): 223–35.

Index

For Product Safety Concerns and Information please contact our EU representative GPSR@taylorandfrancis.com
Taylor & Francis Verlag GmbH, Kaufingerstraße 24, 80331 München, Germany

www.ingramcontent.com/pod-product-compliance
Ingram Content Group UK Ltd.
Pitfield, Milton Keynes, MK11 3LW, UK
UKHW011013180926
475701UK00004B/725
9780367193485